More Praise for *World Christianity*

"Kima Pachuau's book is marked by wide res[...]
It is a tour de force of missiological scholarship. One can only hope that the [...]
logical academy will read this book and take it seriously. It could change the way they do
theology and think about the church."
—**Stephen Bevans**, SVD, Louis J. Luzbetak, SVD Professor of Mission and Culture,
Emeritus, Catholic Theological Union, Chicago, IL

"This may well be the best introduction on the emergence of world Christianity in the
majority world. The analysis of its continuities and discontinuities with western Christianity is particularly helpful. I recommend it wholeheartedly."
—**Hwa Yung**, Bishop Emeritus, The Methodist Church in Malaysia

"Kima Pachuau's personal journey from Mizoram [India] to Kentucky informs this important work on the reshaping of world Christianity. He deftly ties together the rational North
and dynamic South insisting that despite profound differences these two are inextricably
bound in theological terms as a truly global Christianity. How the faith navigates this tension
will help shape its thousands of local expressions as well as its ongoing global mission."
—**Todd M. Johnson**, Director of the Center for the Study of Global Christianity,
Gordon-Conwell Theological Seminary, Boston, MA

"This book marks a new milestone in the rising discipline of world Christianity by taking
the intentional perspective of the global South and firmly establishing theology as the
foundational component of the book."
—**Wonsuk Ma**, Dean and Distinguished Professor of Global Christianity, Graduate
School of Theology and Ministry, Oral Roberts University, Tulsa, OK

"Kima Pachuau gives here a new and challenging perspective on the changing nature of
world Christianity. The focus on the majority world, the 'global South,' is a particular
strength that this work achieves, coming as it does from a leading Asian Christian scholar."
—**Allan H. Anderson**, Professor of Mission and Pentecostal Studies, Department of
Theology and Religion, University of Birmingham, Birmingham, UK

"This is a carefully researched and documented work on arguably the most important
Christian discipline of our time, world Christianity. It builds on the foundations already
laid by such familiar names as Andrew F. Walls, the doyen of the field, and compatriots
Lamin Sanneh and Philip Jenkins and several others in between. In this new addition,
Lalsangkima Pachuau welds together fresh historical and theological insights into world
Christianity. It is a volume that will serve both the academy and practitioners seeking a
twenty-first-century understanding of what has been described as the shift of the major
heartlands of the Christian faith from the northern to the southern continents of Africa,
Asia, and Latin America."
—**J. Kwabena Asamoah-Gyadu**, Director of Graduate Studies and Professor of Contem-
porary African Christianity and Pentecostal/Charismatic Theology, Trinity Theological
Seminary, Legon, Accra, Ghana

WORLD CHRISTIANITY

A Historical and
Theological Introduction

Lalsangkima Pachuau

Abingdon Press
Nashville

WORLD CHRISTIANITY:
A HISTORICAL AND THEOLOGICAL INTRODUCTION
Copyright© 2018 by Abingdon Press

All rights reserved.

This book is printed on acid-free paper.

Library of Congress Cataloging-in-Publication Data has been requested.

ISBN 978-1-4267-5318-3

18 19 20 21 22 23 24 25 26 27—10 9 8 7 6 5 4 3 2 1
MANUFACTURED IN THE UNITED STATES OF AMERICA

Dedicated to the memory of my father,
Laldailova Pachuau of Aizawl, Mizoram, India

CONTENTS

CHAPTER 4

CHAPTER 5

CHAPTER 6

CHAPTER 7

Contents

ACKNOWLEDGMENTS

I sincerely thank Asbury Theological Seminary for a generous sabbatical program that provided me the time and the means to complete this work. I owe a debt of gratitude to my students at Asbury in Wilmore, Kentucky, and at the United Theological College in Bangalore, India, together with others in institutions I have served in Nigeria, the Philippines, and northeast India during the writing of this book. They provided good listening ears and inquisitive classroom interactions, which stimulated and shaped the thoughts and observations presented here. If it were not for the many conversations and dialogues with colleagues and friends in different institutions, academic guilds, and churches, I may not have had the courage and motivation to undertake this project. The editorial team of Abingdon Press under the able leadership of David Teel, Senior Editor for Academic Books, did a wonderful job to make the writing much easier to read and understand. Despite all the motivation, assistance, and cooperation I have received from all these friends and colleagues, there will be deficiencies and shortcomings in this work. Such flaws and limitations are certainly mine alone.

PREFACE

The year was 1985 and I was asked to spend time in two churches in the village of Keitum, located in Mizoram, my home state in northeast India. Most people would not expect this small village to have two mainline ("mission") congregations. During my time there, I was asked to preach every evening and twice on Sundays in each church. Upon learning how the village came to have two Presbyterian congregations, I realized the challenges I was facing.

The larger congregation was known for singing translated Western hymns, and the smaller church dedicated itself to sing only the "new" (revival) songs in the indigenous tunes. This was the reason for the split into two congregations, I was told. Because Western hymns are higher in tone and the pace of the drumbeat is slower, the villagers often referred to the larger congregation as "slow drum," and the smaller one as "fast drum" for the quicker pace of the drumbeat required of native hymns. Behind the two competing styles of singing hymns is a deep tension that has caused divisions and angst in the churches—especially the mainline or mission churches. As I have shown in an earlier book,[1] Christianity in Mizoram is largely a product of charismatic revival movements. These revival movements that have made the Mizo people Christian have also made Christianity Mizo in a good sense of the term. From its origin in the Welsh Revival of 1904, revivals began in the first decade of the twentieth century in Mizoram and recurred each decade, successively becoming more and more indigenized. Mizo Christianity came to be shaped by the dynamic yet uncomfortable tension between what the people consider "foreign" systems and their own "indigenous" practice of faith. The general Christian populace does not seem to give any preference to either one above the other in subconsciously embracing both.

What I have observed in the Mizo Christian story is a mere shred of the Christian experience in the larger Christian world of the global South and East. The deep tension between the desire for innovation associated with the new religion and the embedded indigeneity in the way they embrace and express the newfound faith is a common experience of most "new Christians" of the majority world. Scholars who have made close social and historical observations of Christianity in Africa[2] or elsewhere in Asia have shown such tensions in different ways. In embracing Christianity newly, communities often go through different phases. Those who embraced the new religion en masse tend to indigenize the religion quicker and sometimes in messy ways. In other instances, the new religion is embraced for want of something new and different. Yet, a religion owned always become a religion indigenized.

Christianity exists between the universal claim of its message and the particular way of practicing the faith. As Andrew Walls convincingly argues, Christianity in history has always been seized by "two opposing tendencies," both of which have their origins in the gospel.[3] The first is the tendency to identify with the world as it is and the second is the insistence on transforming the world. By identifying with the world, the gospel indigenized itself to the cultural practices and social milieu of the people. By seeking to transform the world, the gospel also presents itself as an alien rule and entity. The tension between the particular and the universal, the native and the pilgrim characters, governs the enterprise of theology. Be it a theology of liberation, an "inculturation"[4] theology, or a theology that relates with other religions, all forms of contextual theology are molded out of this tension.

I locate contemporary world Christianity at the intersection of three major bodies of Christian faith: the influential and domineering Western Christianity, the complex and enduring Eastern Christianity, and the diverse and animated newer Christianity of the majority world. What earned the qualifying designation "the world" to be called "world Christianity" or "global Christianity" is the rising new Christianity of the majority world, and thus, our stress in this work. The modern missionary movement of the West birthed the new Christianity of the majority world, leaving its indelible impression on the latter. Thus the interaction between Western Christianity and the majority world Christianity colors much of the discussion on world Christianity.

INTRODUCTION: WORLD CHRISTIANITY AND ITS STUDIES

World Christianity as a Phenomenon

If the world as a whole manifested itself chiefly in terms of conflicting patriotism and nationalities in the first half of the twentieth century, and if conflicting "superpowers" largely defined the second half, the closing decade of the twentieth century and the early twenty-first century saw an intensified consciousness of global oneness. This global consciousness is accompanied by the rising awareness of the need for partnership among nations, and with other living beings as the world leapt to the age of unprecedented technological advancement in global communications. The phenomenon is named "globalization," which is defined appropriately by one scholar as "the compression of the world" characterized by a new and intensified "consciousness of the world as a whole."[1] For better or for worse, both advocates and critics of globalization agree on the power of this global consciousness. To some, the new consciousness is about interdependency for the good of all. Others see global systems as created and driven by profit-seeking capitalists who exploit the phenomenon for

1

selfish gains, and relate the phenomenon to injustice on the global scale. There are winners and losers with globalism; But all exist under its spell. The Christian missionary movement is one of the most important catalysts of the emerging global consciousness.

Christianity both enhanced and challenged the historical phenomenon of globalization. While the Christian practice of foreign mission reinforced globalization, its theology could not be identified with all aspects of globalization. As the socioeconomic and political globalization conspicuously triumphed by the first decade of the twenty-first century, Christianity had also reached global status in terms of reach and character. At the most basic level, world Christianity refers to the worldwide reach of Christian faith. Historians in the past have used terms like "expansion" or "spread" of the Christian faith. Yet, what world Christianity has marked in history is more than a *spreading* of the faith. World Christianity expresses the worldwide *character* of Christianity as it came to be owned at heart by people of diverse cultures and societies from every region and every continent, and portrayed in the multiplicity of church traditions, cultural expressions of faith-practices, and doctrinal voices. This worldwide, diverse, and multifaceted character of Christianity as a (single) religion is what we have come to call "world Christianity." While most scholars have treated it mainly, and rightly so, as a historical development in the late twentieth century, world Christianity has also lent itself as a particular perspective on contemporary Christianity. Therefore, it has important theological implications both as a perspective and a method of understanding Christianity as a whole. To emphasize the diverse nature and characters, some have used the plural "World Christianities,"[2] affirming multiplicity of Christian identities, confessions, and traditions.[3] The term "global Christianity" has also been popularly used interchangeably with "world Christianity." Because the term "global" can be closely associated with a more controversial socioeconomic and political phenomenon of globalization, some are reluctant to use the term "global Christianity." While we generally see the more neutral term "world Christianity" in use today, we, however, do not differentiate between the two. We treat *global Christianity* and *world Christianity* as synonyms and use them interchangeably.

The terms "world Christianity" and "global Christianity" first came to missiological parlance as a result of the worldwide demographic changes of Christianity. The extent and means by which Christianity reached some parts of the world may be controversial. Most studies of world Christianity in recent years centered on dramatic demographic changes. *World Christian Encyclopedia*,[4] is the most popular statistical source from which narratives of global demographic changes have been drawn. As some have rightly raised doubts on the possibility of obtaining accurate global statistics, it is reasonable to suspect the reliability of this data. Even so, most scholars accept the overall picture of the demographic shift this encyclopedia presents. Even if we doubt the details of the numbers, the trends are credible. By the beginning of the twenty-first century, Christianity emerges as the largest religion in the world, and also has the largest presence on all continents except Asia. Michael Jaffarian, a researcher for the *World Christian Encyclopedia* said: "By continent, relative to population growth, in the twentieth century, Christianity saw amazing growth in Africa, strong growth in Asia, slight decline in North America, even slighter decline in Latin America, but more serious decline in Europe."[5] At the beginning of the twentieth century, 80 percent of the world's Christians lived in Europe and North America, but by 2010, more than half of those who identify as Christian—60 percent—were from Africa, Asia, and Latin America.[6] Numerically, the majority of the world's Christians are now living on continents that were considered to be essentially non-Christian throughout most of the nineteenth century.

An important mark of world Christianity is the multiplicity of the religion's self-expressions in different contexts, traditions, and practices. Christianity's essential nature is to be able to incarnate itself in any context to transform such contexts for the knowledge and likeness of God in Christ. What antagonizes world Christianity is not the diverse local and indigenous expressions of Christianity, but the failure to recognize these as meaningful and to impose the older Western form on others as if it represented a universal form. The focus of those who study world Christianity today is on indigenous expressions. While Christians in the non-Western world are at ease to recognize and affirm their form of Christianity as a piece of a larger pie, the older forms of Christianity in the West found it harder to accept the concept of world Christianity. Do Western Christians understand the implications of world Christianity and their place in it? This is a lingering question as historic churches are still striving to recognize the global character of the Christian faith. Because the term "Christianity" by itself commonly refers to the dominant Western form of Christianity,[7] the term "world" becomes necessary to express what Christianity should truly mean.

World Christianity has unity and diversity. Christianity is multifarious, and consists of traditions with different confessions and doctrines, some of which are quite distinct. Because Christianity by nature does not have a particular culture or civilization (though it emerges from one) and is essentially dynamic to adapt and transform, Christian diversity follows human social and cultural diversities. On the unity side, there are theological or doctrinal constants that unify the differing denominational bodies and confessional claims.[8] As we will note throughout, the current discussion on world Christianity follows a historical tension between the West and the non-West. Because Western nations have dominated the rest of the world for the past few centuries, sociocultural and political tensions between the West and the rest continue even in the postcolonial period. Furthermore, since the diffusion of Christianity followed the path of Western domination, the development of world Christianity follows the same line of tension between the West and the rest. Not only is the West and the non-West tension unavoidable, it is a pertinent point of departure to discuss world Christianity today. Until the closing decades of the twentieth century, most studies of Christianity focused on Western Christianity. The rise of world Christianity challenged Western domination by bringing into focus the non-Western world. Scholarship on world Christianity, therefore, engages the emerging newer Christianity, that is, Christianity beyond the West. In recent years, a more positive term for "non-Western world" has been in vogue, that is, the "majority world." With the understanding that world Christianity has to necessarily engage the newer non-Western Christianity in order to balance (perhaps subvert?) Western dominance, the present study focuses on *majority world* Christianity.

The Discovery and the Study of World Christianity

Although the phenomenon we are treating here centers around historical occurrences in the late twentieth and early twenty-first centuries, the idea has been in vogue in some circles much longer. The ecumenical movement in the twentieth century dealt with what we may call world Christianity as a form of conciliar cooperation among churches in mission around the world. Beginning with the World Missionary Conference held in Edinburgh in 1910, Christian churches around the world have sought unity in diversity resulting in the formation of the World Council of Churches and its regional and national affiliate councils. As a description for the ecumenical endeavor surrounding the World Council of Churches, Henry P. Van Dusen had invoked "world Christianity" in the 1940s. Although there were others who had used the term "world Christianity,"[9] Van Dusen's treatment was perhaps the earliest academic work to give specific meaning of the term. Van Dusen described "world Christianity" in reference to the ongoing movement of world mission and churches' unity that has already impacted the world and has the potential to influence much more. With Christians averaging "less than 3 per cent" of the population "in all 'mission lands'" at the time, he affirmed "the enormous numbers of mankind as yet untouched by Christianity."[10] Yet, the worldwide character and impact of Christianity through the missionary movement is incomparable with any movement or entity, he argued. Van Dusen's comparative words may sound triumphalist to some ears, and perhaps insensitive for some readers today, but he clearly expressed the global characteristics of Christianity:

There is no other force spread widely through our contemporary world and disseminating through the whole body of humanity influences of the righting of its wrongs, the healing of its deepest maladies, the bridging of its division, possibly even the halting of its fatalistic descent toward conflict and chaos. There is no other agency reaching out toward every corner of the earth, toward every people and every aspect of human life—for health and enlightenment, for reconciliation and redemption. There is no other institution or movement that still holds together the shattered fragments of humanity, as an earnest example to all men of what God intended the life of mankind to be and what someday the family of nations may become.[11]

Although the ecumenical movement as represented by the World Council of Churches may have failed to become a home to world Christianity, van Dusen's ecumenical vision anticipated what we are now calling world Christianity. By the closing years of the twentieth century, it became clear that the ecumenical movement, as organizationally represented by the World Council of Churches, had turned itself into a particular confessional body representing one theological tradition among others. The loss of an ecumenical vision for the church from within the council itself and the domestication of this vision by its own members[12] led to the eclipse of ecumenicity in the World Council. By narrowing itself to a confessional tradition, the World Council of Churches fails to characterize "world Christianity." The Council's positioning has become rather passive on missionary expansion and practically discarded the importance of numerical growth of the church, especially since the 1960s. This apparent lack of missionary zeal dissociated the council from the major growth of Christianity in the Southern hemispheres. Yet, the ecumenical movement played a significant role in other aspects of world Christianity. Although it failed to hold together confessional diversity to the extent that a large number of growing churches in the twentieth century existed outside the movement, the ecumenical movement itself surrounding the World Council of Churches has done more than any other to promote relationships among churches, denominations, and confessional bodies around the world in the twentieth century.

In the 1970s and the 1980s, a few watchful scholars began to depict a worldwide changing demography of Christianity as they saw what Andrew Walls calls "the massive movement towards the Christian faith in all the southern continents."[13] Two scholars in particular, Walbert Bühlmann

(Catholic) and Andrew F. Walls (Protestant), brought the phenomenon to attention as they uncovered and analyzed the development and forecasted the implications. Bühlmann dubbed this rising church in the southern continents the "Third Church," and he announced its arrival as an "epoch-making event" in his 1974 book *The Coming of the Third Church*.[14] The Third Church or "the Southern Church," he said, is the "church of the Third World" as well as "church of the third millennium" from which "the most important drives and inspirations for the whole church in the future will come."[15] The first millennium belonged to "the First Church, the Eastern Church" when all the first eight councils were held under its tutelage.[16] The Second Church, the Western Church, dominated the second millennium, "shaped the Middle Ages and, from the time of the 'discovery' of the New World, undertook all missionary initiatives."[17] The turning of the tide from a Western church to the world church and to the Third Church, he said, had happened among Catholics in 1970 when "51 percent of all Catholics were living in the southern continents: Latin America, Africa, Asia-Oceania."[18] With this, he wrote, "the centre of gravity of Christianity in the West has shifted more and more… [toward] southern continents."[19] Bühlmann equates the rise of "third Church" with the advent of the "world church" but sees the latter as a part of a changing phase of the Western church. He said, "We are therefore, almost without noticing it, witnesses of a dramatic change in the Christian church; the predominance of the Western church has been radically altered. From being the church of the West it has become a world church with an evident presence in all six continents."[20] This point is reaffirmed in his other book published almost ten years later where he writes, "A Western church, with its world hegemony, has become a world church, comprised of six continental churches…, all endowed with equal rights."[21] Bühlmann's point may be understandable when placed within the Catholic Church's concept of the church's organic oneness. This does not deter him from forecasting a world church that is decentralized, intercontinental, intercultural, and consequently "pluriform"[22] in nature.

Others have written more than Andrew Walls on the subject of "world Christianity," but we can hardly identify anyone who has done more to elevate the topic of world Christianity. Walls has been contributing to an expanding notion of world Christianity in at least three major ways: First, together with Bühlmann, he pioneered the study by identifying the movement and its major characteristics, sketching its fundamental features. Second, through his collegial and solicitous mentoring of thinkers and institutions, Walls has significantly heightened the knowledge of, and helped to establish, world Christianity as a major subject of inquiry. His leadership and founding of the Centre for the Study of Christianity in the Non-Western World (later renamed Centre for the Study of World Christianity), first at the University of Aberdeen and later when it moved to the University of Edinburgh, became foundational to the study and development of discourse on world Christianity around the world. Third, Walls models and promotes intercultural learning through his tireless studies and travels as he enriches and disseminates knowledge of various aspects of world Christianity to the ministerial and academic guilds around the world.

Walls first studied southern Christianity in Africa, and over the past four decades expanded his study to Asia, Latin America, and Oceania. Through his method of comparative historical research, he demonstrates the authenticity and validity of southern Christianity and places it on par with Northern forms of Christianity. His thoughts revolve around the transmission of Christian faith across times, cultures, and social locations. Through his historical analyses of the transmission of faith, he formulates important historical wellsprings and viewpoints, and expresses theological principles rooted in important missiological themes.

One aspect of Walls's genius is his natural combination of in-depth knowledge with an authentic spirit of humility and collegiality.[23] Since the 1970s, he drew together scholars of repute and left indelible marks on some who became significant figures in the study of world Christianity. As his former colleague Harold Turner once expressed, "If the sign of an educated man is that he can do things he has never done before, Andrew exhibits the sign and had contributed to my own education at every turn."[24] His strong influence on colleagues and students sometimes makes it hard for later observers to distinguish his contributions from theirs, especially in identifying the origin of some important viewpoint. Alongside Lamin Sanneh's significant contributions on mission and Christian translatability, we see Walls's voice on the same topic in different analytical frames. Following and mirroring his comparison between the early Christian church and the new southern churches, his former student, colleague, and friend Kwame Bediako made a profound study of Christian identity and culture by comparing Hellenistic theologians of the second and third centuries with contemporary African theologians.[25]

The first few years of the twenty-first century saw the publication of several important works on world Christianity. Perhaps the most significant is the massive data-rich, two-volume encyclopedia previously referenced. The first edition, edited by David Barrett, published in 1982, was already a major achievement and had already become the standard reference. The new edition—obviously intended to present the demographic picture of world Christianity at the turn of the century—is significantly expanded in size and breadth, and quickly became an indispensable and popular research tool on world Christianity.[26] It clearly confirmed that Christianity is a worldwide religion with adherents in every nation of the world. With the exception of Asia, Christianity is the largest religion on all the continents. As Michael Jaffarian, an associate editor of the *Encyclopedia* testified, "No other religion on earth is spread as widely as Christianity among the diversity of the human community. Only Christianity has adherents among every one of the world's 238 countries."[27] Despite its bias for, and unclear categorization of, nondenominational (or post-denominational) "independent" churches, and some questionable church statistics in some countries,[28] *World Christian Encyclopedia* remains a stunning achievement. As Gerald Anderson rightly states, "There is nothing comparable" in the field of empirical research on world Christianity and other religions.[29] Two of its three editors, David Barrett and Todd Johnson, have co-authored a follow-up volume that interprets the findings separately.[30] Today, Todd Johnson is carrying this torch at The Center for the Study of Global Christianity at Gordon-Conwell Theological Seminary. As a part of the centennial celebration of the World Missionary Conference in Edinburgh in 2010, Johnson, Kenneth Ross, and Sandra Lee, together with a team of international scholars, produced what may be billed as the most comprehensive volume on the state of global Christianity.[31]

Two influential authors publishing works on world Christianity in the early years of the twenty-first century draw our attention for their broad influence and contrasting viewpoints. In 2002, Philip Jenkins's book *The Next Christendom* appeared to become one of the most influential volumes—if not the most influential volume—among Western readers. A year later, Lamin Sanneh's *Whose Religion Is Christianity?*—written in a style accessible to a wide readership—was published. Because Sanneh's book represents an ongoing work built upon his earlier publications, we begin with him.

Sanneh's major contribution in the study of world Christianity is located in the thesis of a book published a decade earlier, namely *Translating the Message*.[32] At the heart of Sanneh's works is the idea that Christianity, by nature, is a translated and a translating religion. By translating out of the linguistic and cultural world of its origin (Judaism) into other cultures represented at first by Gentile culture, Christianity relativizes its culture and community of origin and destigmatizes other cultures, thereby adopting and adapting all cultures.[33] As a scholar of comparative religion, Sanneh came to realize that the modern missionary movement's emphasis on Bible translation has far-reaching consequences for inculturating the gospel in indigenous cultures. In his autobiography, Sanneh said Christianity is "a form of indigenous empowerment by virtue of vernacular translation."[34] This translatability is the root of Christian universality through which it developed itself as a worldwide religion. "By translation, the faith acquired its universal ethos, and entered into each cultural idiom fully enough to commence a challenging and enduring engagement."[35] Although Christian missionary movements tend to transmit the faith through "cultural diffusion," Christians owned the faith through cultural appropriation.

The translatability of the Christian faith formed the foundation of Sanneh's understanding of world Christianity. In his studies on the modern missionary movement, Sanneh saw tension between cultural diffusion via Westernization and the appropriation of the indigenous culture through translation. He opposes the former and advocates the latter as Christianity's key and essential feature. In defining world Christianity, Sanneh tries to disconnect Christianity from its Western form of domination:

> World Christianity is the movement of Christianity as it takes form and shape in societies that previously were not Christian, societies that had no bureaucratic tradition with which to domesticate the gospel....World Christianity is...a variety of indigenous responses through more or less effective local idioms...without necessarily European Enlightenment frame.[36]

Here Sanneh limits "world Christianity" to an indigenized form of Christian faith as he dissociates it from broad Western culture and Western Christianity. To Sanneh and many other non-Western scholars, Christianity has to shake off its Western-dominated identity and character to birth an authentic world Christianity. Sanneh dealt with this issue fervently in his book *Encountering the West: Christianity and the Global Cultural Process.*[37] In his effort to identify world Christianity as distinct from domineering Western forms of Christian faith, he even distinguished "world Christianity" from "global Christianity." In contrast to his definition of world Christianity as above, he depicts "global Christianity" as "the faithful replication of Christian forms and patterns developed in Europe" and links it closely to "Christendom." Sanneh's differentiation of global Christianity and world Christianity does not persuade most scholars. But the distinction he shows between "a variety of indigenous responses" and a "replication" of western Christianity needs to be taken seriously in any discussion of world Christianity.[38] Sanneh's opposition to link world Christianity with globalization especially in its economic and political forms is shared by critiques of globalization especially from the majority world.[39]

In *Disciples of All Nations: Pillars of World Christianity,*[40] Sanneh identified major "pillars" in the building of world Christianity. In the history of Western Christianity, such pillars are located in historical processes such as the breaking out of Christianity from Judaism to the Gentile world through the apostles, in Christianity's encounter with Islam in the medieval period, and in the trans-Atlantic interactions and subsequent encounter of the Christian missionary movement with European colonialism.

Among the pillars of post-Western Christianity the *charismatic* and *primal* pillars are particularly significant for Christian movements in Africa. In both, Sanneh highlighted the contributions of indigenous Africans and African Americans in the nineteenth and early twentieth centuries, which set in motion the movement toward African Christianity. Here, reaction to the Western control and independent indigenous spiritual ministries of African prophets such as William Wade Harris signify the character of world Christianity. As a scholar, Sanneh's strength and emphasis are on Africa and his book concludes with a brief highlight of the post-Western resurgent Christianity of the late twentieth and early twenty-first centuries. Quite similar to Walbert Bühlmann's "Third Church," Sanneh calls this period of resurging Christianity "the Third Awakening" and describes it as "the post-Western awakening" where charismatic Christianity is taking the lead.[41] The growth of Christianity in Africa and fervent Christian movements in China are key highlights of this current awakening. On the movement in China, he comments, "It is clear that in the religion's eastward shift what happens to the church in China will have incalculable consequences for the rest of the world generally, and for the post-Christian West in particular. China could correct the one-sidedness of Western Christianity."[42]

Again, Sanneh plainly contrasts "world Christianity" with "global Christianity" by relating the former to indigenous responses to Christianity in the majority world and the latter with Western Christendom. This use of Christendom directly contradicts the use of the same term in the now-famous book by Philip Jenkins. The very title of Jenkins's main work on world Christianity, *The Next Christendom*, designates the emerging Christianity of the majority world "Christendom." He predicts that such a new Christendom will arise from southern Christianity, especially Africa and Latin America—the two new centers of Christianity. When Christianity in these two regions "launch a revolutionary new era in world religion" through their mutual interaction and mutual discovery, he writes, "we really would be speaking of a new Christendom, based in the Southern Hemisphere."[43] It is interesting to note that Jenkins's book *The*

Next Christendom was published the year before Sanneh's *Whose Religion Is Christianity?*

Jenkins does not claim to bring anything new to the discussion.[44] As one knowledgeable reviewer of *The Next Christendom* rightly pointed out, he "assembles much of the familiar documentation, ranging from Walbert Bühlmann to David Barrett to Andrew Walls, to demonstrate the southward shift of the center of gravity in global Christianity."[45] The main thesis of the book is that Christianity is not dying, it is moving south; the southern Christians, deeply conservative in their theology, will soon outnumber the northern Christians. As we have already shown in the last few pages, this is not a new thesis; Walbert Bühlmann and Andrew Walls have been saying these things since the 1970s and 1980s, and David Barrett's first edition of *World Christian Encyclopedia* demonstrated it clearly in 1982. The strength of Jenkins's book lies in his skillful narration for the nonspecialists. Written in a style both accessible and thought-provoking for general readers, the book succeeds in bringing the topic of world Christianity to the North American reading public. If it alarms liberal Christians, it delights conservative Christians. While most scholars from the majority world did not give it much attention, it became the most popular book on world Christianity in North America.[46] Named as Top Religion Book of 2002 by *USA Today*, its reviews appeared in *The New York Times*, *The Wall Street Journal*, *The Christian Century*, and other national magazines where reviewers greatly sensationalized the thesis as fresh and original.[47] From these popular reviews, what seems to have drawn the readers' interest is the optimistic presentation of Christianity, especially Jenkins's confident prediction that in fifty years (2050), the non-Latino white will be a minority and the Christian world will be dominated by people from the Southern Hemisphere. It provoked reactions and affirmations and led to the production of other books.[48] The catchy phrase that summarized his thesis, "the center of gravity of the Christian world has shifted...southward,"[49] as we have seen, is originally coined by Walbert Bühlmann, and was already a popular point among missiologists. But many readers now associate this phrase (as well as knowledge of global Christianity) with Jenkins's work.

Key for Jenkins is the emerging conservative theological stance of the southern Christians. He extends this thesis in his *New Faces of Christianity: Believing the Bible in the Global South*. While giving important caution not to use the American liberal-conservative divide as a norm to view these southern Christians, he could not free himself from that dichotomy. Like *The Next Christendom*, this book is descriptive in nature and clearly written. But it does not add much to his previous work. In its effort to demonstrate in simple terms that in the growing southern churches "the Bible speaks to everyday, real-world issues of poverty and debt, famine and urban crisis, racial and gender oppression, state brutality and persecution,"[50] the book fails to show the complex nature and inner theological tensions in southern Christianity. Jenkins's failure to consider networks of influences and their patterns in the majority-world Christianity gravely weakens his argument in this book.

Reading Jenkins from the majority world viewpoint,[51] there are several issues. First, his use of "Christendom" to depict Christianity in the non-Western world is problematic.[52] In an article published first in 1995, Walls contrasted Northern Christendom with the new southern Christianity and described the latter as "Christianity without Christendom."[53] Second, while Jenkins is quite sensitive to the dignity of people from the southern hemispheres, his branding of all pre-Christian traditions of Africa derogatorily as "pagan"[54] shows some theological and intercultural limitations. His lack of interest in the pre-Christian worldview of the people impedes him from understanding the intricate indigenization of Christianity.[55] Third, while Jenkins debunked much of the Western ignorance and failure to recognize the significance of southern Christianity, his attempt to explain away the rise of southern Christianity sociologically comes off as offensive and is likely objectionable to Christians in the global South. His analysis explains the success of Christianity in the South as "a by-product of modernization and urbanization" where social vacuums created by these developments were met by "the most devoted and fundamentalist-oriented religious communities."[56] Statements like, "The new churches are succeeding because they fulfill social needs"[57] and, "The chief centers of Southern Christianity are also the regions hit hardest by

AIDS"[58] are reasonable social explanations. But offered as an explanation of the people's spiritual experience, they disregard the people's own spiritual self-understanding and claims. For those African, Asian, and Latin American Christians whom he described, it is God's Spirit that led them to Christianity. His objective description of the people's spiritual claims is noble. But his offering of an alternative social explanation other than the people's own spiritual explanation would be objectionable to them and becomes another form of cultural domination.

A number of books have followed these trailblazing works on the historical emergence of world Christianity. Some are multi-authored, bringing a rich mix of perspectives and themes while others expand the range of world Christianity. From this host of volumes, we select a few for the distinct elements they added. One lingering question about world Christianity from the presentations of Sanneh and Jenkins is just what world Christianity includes. Following their predecessors Walbert Bühlmann and Andrew Walls, both of them use the terms "world Christianity" and "global Christianity" to describe the rising southern and/or non-Western Christianity. In its simplest form, world Christianity is about the worldwide presence of Christians. Some of the newer books deal specifically with Christians and Christianity in the different continents of the world. Douglas Jacobsen's straightforward description of the contemporary Christians around the world is helpful.[59] Methodologically, the volume by the husband-and-wife duo Kirsteen Kim and Sebastian Kim, *Christianity as a World Religion*,[60] provides one of the most comprehensive treatments of world Christianity. To make their case that Christianity by its nature and its current form of existence is a world religion in the true sense of the term, they describe Christianity in six continents, each from six different angles. The six lenses they use are topography, theology, geography, society and politics, history, and structure. The strength of the book lies in giving an independent outlook to Christianity in each of their selected continents, and the balanced treatment of each using the six-pronged approach. Understandably, they cannot go beyond providing general pictures of each. Focusing attention on how theology may be done in the new global context, *Theology in the Context of World Christianity* by Timothy

Tennent engages traditional Western systematic theological themes in dialogue with contextual issues in the non-Western world. Dealing with key ideas like God, revelation, Christology, ecclesiology, and others, Tennent provides a model of theologizing that engages the world context and is grounded in theological orthodoxy.[61]

The British scholar-leader duo Noel Davis and Martin Conway wrote *World Christianity in the Twentieth Century*[62] and published it with a companion reader.[63] Both volumes are organized into three separate sections: The first section discusses the development in four Christian traditions, which is followed, second, by studies on seven selected regions. The concluding section is on major themes occupying twentieth-century Christians. The companion reader brings together a rich collection of writings from around the world and from different ecclesiastical and confessional bodies together with some historic ecumenical texts of the twentieth century. Calling the twentieth century "the century of the ecumenical movement"[64] the set presents this movement and its quest for unity as the centerpiece of world Christianity. True to the tradition of the ecumenical movement, the authors are critical of "quantitative" measures of world Christianity, seeking "quality measures." They identify three main quality measures equal to those used by the United Nations as its focus: peace, human rights, and the concern for the poorer peoples.[65]

The *World* of World Christianity

Robert Wuthnow remarked that "the concept of 'global Christianity' is…a fairly recently invention."[66] Although I disagree with Wuthnow that the concept itself is a recent "invention" (it is theologically founded in the doctrine of the universal church), my brief narration of the historical emergence of the phenomenon supports the claim that Christianity as a truly world religion is a somewhat recent development. Despite the fact that demographers have rightly observed that "only Christianity has adherents among every one of the world's 238 countries,"[67] other Christian groups also strongly emphasize that there are many "unreached people groups" in the world.[68] Against the background of such seemingly contrasting Christian demography is the lingering question of what we mean

16

by "world" in the discussion of world Christianity. It is clear that "world Christianity" does not mean that the whole world is Christian. What world does world Christianity then claim?

First, at the conceptual level, the "world" indicates that the Christian message of the gospel is meant for, or directed to, the world. It belongs to every part, every people, and every creature of the world. Christianity is about God's work in and for the world in Christ; it belongs to the world, and to every cultural group of the world. At the heart of the Christian message is its universal invitation and applicability contained in the very pronouncement of the meaning of Jesus at his birth, "good news of great joy for all the people" (Luke 2:10). In Christian doctrinal terms, catholicity (or universality) is an essential mark of a true church. By pointing out the worldwide extent of the Christian message in a sweeping manner like this, we do not disregard the difficulty of coming to terms with the global or universal nature of Christianity. Christians of every age encountered this challenge as a stumbling block. Because religious faith is first and foremost a local practice, and that faith can succeed only in its rootedness to the culture and life context of the people, to uphold the validity of one's faith in a different form by others is never easy. To balance the global and the local is a challenge faced by Christians in different periods of history. It seems relatively harder for those who held their forms of practices with longer and more established history.

The history of the global spread of Christianity is a tale of both beautiful redemption and genocidal terror; it is a story both good and bad. Christians cannot deny some of the devastating ways numerous Christians have attempted (and succeeded) to spread the faith. In affirming the expansion of Christian faith, we do not condone unscrupulous modes and practices linking cross, sword, and colonization. Yet the core of Christian faith is God's good news, which calls for communication and dissemination since it is good news for all.

Pioneering scholars and others who have studied the historical growth of Christianity in the "global South" emphasize the distinct charismatic-Pentecostal flavor of the religious experience within the region. Walbert Bühlmann, Andrew Walls, Lamin Sanneh, and Philip Jenkins are

representatives of this group. Some of these scholars give more importance to numerical changes while others emphasize the changing character
or expression of Christianity. Jenkins stresses the dramatic demographic
change and its social factors while Sanneh focuses on the indigenous factors to account for the growth. Except for comparative reason, scholars in
this category do not make an effort to study older Northern or Western
Christianity independently. The second-generation studies we have outlined broadened the subject to include all or most of the inhabited continents including those associated with "older" Christianity. The changed
emphasis shifted the direction and approach. Whereas the first group used
Christianity's "shifting center of gravity" as the hallmark of the phenomenon and how the new centers distinctly absorbed the faith, the second
generation relativized Christian traditions and emphasized Christianity's
multiple confessions, theologies, and identities. Here, early ecumenical
proponents' emphasis on a multiplicity of confessions and regional diversity is brought back into the mix along with the new phenomenon of
global South's charismatic and numerical growth.

In the present study, due in part to our interest in capturing the new
characters of global Christianity, we continue the emphasis of the pioneers
by focusing on the newer Christians in the South and the East with a full
awareness of the works of the second generation scholars. We locate the
hub of world Christianity in the relation between the older Christianity
of the West, or more accurately the North and West, and the newer Christianity of the so-called global South, or more accurately global South and
East. Instead of older terms such as "developing nations," "Third World,"
or "non-Western countries," we use the term "majority world." These
other terms either came to be used in pejorative senses or describe the
regions in question based on what these geographies/peoples lack. "Majority world," on the other hand, is qualitatively neutral and states the
quantitative fact. As we have said before, world Christianity relativizes
Christianity in the world, and pushes everyone to conform to Christianity's core teaching that each is a part of the larger whole, and that none
can claim to be superior (Acts 10:34-35). Whereas the newer Christians
of the majority world naturally accept such a condition, it is harder for the

older forms of Christian faith to surrender and conform to this new condition of world Christianity. To highlight the contributions of the newer Christians and what they bring to the whole, we focus our attention on the majority world. Thus, by showing what the majority-world Christians bring to the table of world Christianity in relation to the nature of older Christianity, we intend to offer a more balanced and holistic picture of world Christianity. This study largely presumes basic knowledge of the better-known—some would say, dominant—Western Christianity, and focuses on Christian faith in the majority world to present a new portrait of world Christianity.

Although world Christianity has become a popular topic in some Christian circles, the larger body of Christian academia and churches is not aware of or meaningfully engaged with this reality. World Christianity (its reality and studies devoted to it) is rapidly becoming a game changer in Christian ministries and theological reflections. Full of potential, it provides an opportunity for Christian ministers and theologians. For churches and ministries, ignoring this historical phenomenon is not only a missed opportunity for wider ministries, it also diminishes the effect and impact of Christian ministries in today's world.

Linked with technological advancement, global consciousness is also bound up with another phenomenon, namely migration. Through migration, global social media, and communication superhighways, the world is interconnected economically, politically, and culturally. Neighborhood landscapes are changing rapidly and local communities are increasingly finding themselves in close proximity with new migrant Christian communities. Partnerships with these communities are not optional. If we do not partner with them, they become our religious and spiritual competitors! Not only are mission fields arriving in the backyards, but many are potential threats if unattended. What some call "homegrown terrorism" grew out of ignored migrant communities in the West.

This book is a modest attempt to characterize world Christianity from historical and theological viewpoints. As vast a topic and as broad a subject as world Christianity is, the book necessarily charts a particular pathway in the maze following a phenomenological approach. We begin this first chapter by discussing the phenomenon of world Christianity and how it has been treated as a field of study. In chapter two, we deal with the Western precedence of world Christianity. This explains the point of departure we are taking in our interpretation of the phenomenon. The Western Enlightenment distinguishes the West from the majority world in contrast to the Christianity of the majority world. Yet, there is that strong continuity between modern missionary movements and world Christianity. The following two chapters, three and four, describe new Christian movements of what we may broadly call the post-colonial period. In chapter three, we deal with the rejuvenating forms of Christianity in Latin America even as demographic analysis reveals a decrease in the percentage of Christians in these countries. In the same chapter, we offer an account of the rising African Christianity that is recasting the entire face of global Christian faith during the past few decades. In chapter four, we deal with the complex and immense story of Christianity in select regions of Asia and the Pacific Islands.

Chapters five and six deal with theology, especially contextual theology that reshapes the entire theological discipline in global perspective. While chapter five focuses on the concept and origins of contextual theology, chapter six looks at the three major southern continents and the core theological works in each of those contexts. One cannot miss the missiological orientation of the entire development of world Christianity both historically and theologically. Yet, the missionary dimension has its limit by design as the intent is a passing/handing over of the core Christian message to be owned by new Christians. The tension between the missionary contextualization and the new Christian theologizing in context is part of the larger challenge we see in these zones of growth. For many analysts, my dealing with the charismatic[-Pentecostal] movement as a part of contextual theologies in the majority world may be surprising, if not unacceptable. But charismatic Christianity expresses new Christian characters from which contextual theologies of renewal are emerging. The missionary contributions of Christians in the majority world are significant. In the context of a worldwide reconceptualization of Christian mission, Christians in the majority world revive and reconfigure missional practices. As an introductory text, we can only show some of the pathways of Christian missions from the majority world in chapter seven.

While my engagement is unabashedly academic in its path, it is also my desire to bring the discussion to the wider church. Within the broad and general topic of world Christianity, I try to chart useful and meaningful pathways to capture the big picture in broad strokes without losing the thematic foci. One's worldview determines what is presumed to be known or understood. I must admit that I operate with the presumption that readers know and understand basic Christian history and general theological principles. Recognizing the fact that every description represents a viewpoint, I do not shy away from owning the descriptions and interpretations as well as the selections of materials and resources.

I am an academician from the majority world trained in the Western educational system. If my academic interlocutors are Western in viewpoints, my experience of majority-world Christianity and my Asian cultural upbringing also shape my perspective. In my professional career, I consciously live and work in three different worlds simultaneously.[69] I try to bring my worlds and those outside into creative interaction. Thus, the principles by which I gather and integrate stories, ideas, and thoughts are necessarily influenced by these multiple worlds and the tensions among them. I have my biases and limitations. I am conscious of some, and others I cannot name. I recognize the Protestant bias of the work. Although I try to incorporate relevant material and issues from other confessional bodies, readers may still find my selection of materials and argument lacking in some parts of the book. Despite these limitations, it is my desire that this book helps readers to gain a deeper understanding and fresh perspective on Christianity worldwide as we embark on a new world of twenty-first-century Christian faith.

Chapter 2

MODERNIZATION, MODERN MISSIONS, AND WORLD CHRISTIANITY

Western Enlightenment, Modernization, and the Making of World Christianity

In his provocative work, *The Clash of Civilizations*, Samuel P. Huntington has a chapter on "the West and the Rest," which obviously places the West at the center of the geopolitical universe. Yet, he identified Islamic and Chinese civilizations among "the Rest" as posing major challenges with "the declining relative power of the West."[1] The West and the Rest, or the West versus the Rest, received a wider and more controversial treatment in Niall Ferguson's book *Civilization: The West and the Rest*.[2] Ferguson traces six ways the West exceeded and dominated the rest of the world and calls them the "killer apps": competition, science, property, medicine, consumption, and work. If Huntington's work is predictive by nature—forecasting civilizational wars to be fought along new fault lines of religious and cultural identities—Ferguson's is a historical work that somewhat advocates for Western superiority and its continuation.

23

In a climate of human rights and equity where anything imperialistic is seen as immoral, the "West versus the Rest" as a conception has been contested (and detested). As Donald Kagan wrote in *The New York Times Review* of Ferguson's *Civilization*, many of his observations "will not win Ferguson friends among the fashionable in today's academy."[3] Ferguson's work received some furious criticisms charging him to be a right-wing pro-colonialist scholar.[4] Much of the criticisms against the "West versus the Rest" concept are based on the moral indignation against what is considered unfair domination in imperialism and/or colonialism. Ironic is the fact that fairness as a moral basis for judging the ideologies and world order of the West is itself largely a product of the dominant Western enlightenment tradition. As much as the concept is detested for its imperialistic connection, it is also a historical reality one cannot ignore.

Our discussion on the emerging forms of world Christianity is also done largely within this framework of "West and the Rest." In this work, we locate the emerging world Christianity between Western Christianity that has dominated the Christian world throughout the modern period and the multifarious versions of Christianity developing in the majority world since the third quarter of the twentieth century. The tension between the two groups largely defines this new face of Christianity we call world Christianity. We acknowledge that the tension may be temporary and could fade away in time, yet today's Christianity in the world exists between Western Christianity and the emerging majority world Christianity. Our focus in this work is on the latter as it defines itself largely in its interaction with the former.

To help us understand one dominant influence within Western society that characterize its inner nature, we turn to a brief discussion of the Enlightenment. Our purpose is to identify what distinguishes Western worldviews from the majority (non-Western) world, and also to see how these differences define Christianity as we know it today.

The Enlightenment

A major component that changed the West and essentially distinguished it from the "rest" was the philosophical and social revolution called the Enlightenment. The age produced successful applications of human reasoning power in experimental science, mathematics, and philosophy. By the middle of the eighteenth century, the "thinking people" among Europeans, in Lesslie Newbigin's words, had a profound feeling of the new age of the Enlightenment (Aufklärung, Lumières, Illuminismo) as they came to "a conviction that Europeans now knew the secret of knowledge and therefore the secret of the mastery of the world."[5] The Enlightenment is a period in history that witnessed a shift from human confidence in authority (royal, ecclesial) to faith in the human reasoning power. It is a celebration of human reason, a recognition of its power, and a revolt against any authority that impedes its exercise. Ultimately, it placed faith in reason and sought to free human life from any oppressive agency based on authority alone. As John Garraty and Peter Gay have aptly said, it is from the Enlightenment that we "derived the notions of Individual Liberty, Political Rights, Equality, Democracy, and (to use the latest twentieth-century slogan) Participation."[6] These values are what characterize the West and its sensibilities today. The Enlightenment can also be seen as a product of the scientific revolution associated with such names as Francis Bacon, Nicolaus Copernicus, Galileo, René Descartes, and Sir Isaac Newton. Newton is often seen as a clear transition figure from the age of superstition to the age of Enlightenment. Newton, John Locke, and Francis Bacon are considered to be the torchbearers of the Age of Reason, the "English trinity" that inspired the Continental Enlightenment.[7]

Historians debated whether the Enlightenment should be seen as a single movement, or multiple related movements. In her book *The Roads to Modernity*, Gertrude Himmelfarb made a clear distinction between the British Enlightenment on the one hand, and the French and the American Enlightenments on the other. Not only did the latter two conclude with revolutions and the former with a reform, Himmelfarb emphasizes the plurality of the movement and shows that they are characteristically different.[8] The works of the French *philosophes* were known for justice and equality and the Americans stressed liberty. To these better-known features, Himmelfarb argues that the British Enlightenment added social

virtues as a character of the Enlightenment. While the British philosophers and scientists are known to be the torchbearers, the more seditious
French Enlightenment overshadowed the works of the British scholars.
Thus, one major feature of the Enlightenment emphasized by the British
scholars—social virtues of "compassion, benevolence, sympathy,"[9]—has
not been well recognized and does not figure as prominently in discussions of the Western age of reason. The expanse of the British Enlightenment also makes its version both porous and somewhat subtle to the
extent that some of what seemed to be anti-Enlightenment became a part
of the Enlightenment sensibility itself. Himmelfarb uses John Wesley and
the Methodists as an illustrative example. Though decidedly "enthusiasts"
in nature, which is contrasted with the Enlightenment thinking, Wesley's
comprehensive thought that combines feelings and reason, tradition and
freedom constitutes an important part of the Enlightenment. "Not the
Enlightenment of the French *philosophes*, to be sure," she clarified, "but of
the British moral philosophers."[10]

Lesslie Newbigin, a former missionary bishop in India and one of
the foremost missiologists of the twentieth century, debuted his thoughtful invocation of the missionary work in the Western secular society by
offering a profound critique of the Western Enlightenment. He uses the
term "conversion" to describe the Enlightenment experience in the West
as it transformed an entire worldview and way of thinking.[11] To Newbigin, this society that has converted to modern secularism through the
Enlightenment constitutes a new unbelieving missionary field for Christians. In his 1984 Warfield Lectures at Princeton Theological Seminary
titled "Can the West Be Converted?"[12] Newbigin developed his theological encounter with modern Western culture. After a careful analysis of the
values of Western Enlightenment, Newbigin calls for a new engagement
of the gospel with post-enlightenment Western culture. He argues that
religion in general, and Christian faith in particular, lost ground in the
post-enlightenment modern cultures where religion is eliminated from
the public sphere and constrained to the private realm of life. The domination by Newtonian cause-and-effect explanations leads to "the elimination of teleology" as an approach to life in the world. This purging of "the

category of purpose" as an explanation of existence nullifies the meaning of religion, especially Christianity.[13] The Enlightenment's axiom that every human has the right to pursue happiness replaces "the pursuit of the end for which the humans... exist."[14] So the religious quest for meaning in life is supplanted, the need for religion marginalized. Newbigin further argues that the noble obsession of science with "fact" not only fails to produce "value," the Enlightenment worldview marginalizes and perhaps eliminates values and purpose in existence.[15] This dominant version of Enlightenment rationality may be the result of and account for the eclipse of British Enlightenment social virtues overshadowed by the works of the French *philosophes*.

Following Newbigin's lead, David Bosch reviewed the Enlightenment's impact on theology and the understanding of Christian mission. Bosch lists six areas of Enlightenment influence on theology: (1) supremacy of reason in thinking theologically, (2) the application of the Enlightenment's strict separation of knowing subjects and known objects, (3) the elimination of purpose and its replacement with direct causality, (4) the distinction of fact and value, (5) the Enlightenment's tenet that all problems are solvable, and (6) autonomy of the individual.[16] These further influenced the missionary principles and practices of the modern missionary movement.

With the independence of many colonized nations and the birth of new ones in the twentieth century, the most common political form of nationhood adopted is the modern secular state. Newbigin stresses that "the phenomenon usually called 'modernization,' which is being promoted throughout much of the Third World..., is in fact the co-option of the leadership of those nations into the particular culture that had its origin among the peoples of western Europe."[17] The strong influence of Western modern civilization through political colonialism, education, and civil society propelled the leaders of the new nations to adopt the Western forms of nation-states. By the middle of the twentieth century, with the exception of some ethno-religious nation-states, the two contending forms of secular nation-states were socialism and democratic-capitalism. By the last decade of the twentieth century, the option had been narrowed to the latter after the fall of many communist states and the eclipse of socialist ideology itself by neo-liberal free-market capitalism. Have these new nations of the majority world (or Third World) reached their maturation as nation-states? Have they settled in what they ought to be? The process of culture change is a long one. It took many centuries for the West to develop its form of Christian identity and create a somewhat settled Christian corpus. There is reason to believe that most nation-states in the non-Western world have yet to reach the full maturation of their nationhood (if maturity is measured by so-called first-world cultural and economic standards).

The Enlightenment's influence grew as the Europeans expanded their worldwide reach through colonialism and Christian missions. While the relationship between the two is complex and difficult to simplify, they both served as vehicles of certain Western values, including religious and spiritual values. As the West felt the secularizing influence of the Enlightenment tradition deeper and deeper in its social and political life, it communicated those values to the non-Western civilizations and cultures through the ruling elites it cultivated in those communities. The reach of those values to the different societies of the non-Western world is difficult to assess as we see multifarious responses from the "rest." The phenomenon of world Christianity itself is a display of the surprising ways that non-Western cultures responded to Western civilization. As we will see in the remaining chapters, there are distinctive elements in the Christianity of the majority world that have somehow defied and resisted the Enlightenment worldview and ethos. At the heart of this defiant spirit is deep religiosity characterized by strong belief in the supernatural power of God. If Christianity has been passed on by the West to the Rest, how did such a defiant, and in some ways Enlightenment-challenging spirit become a part of the new forms of majority-world Christian faith? One explanation offered by scholars of world Christianity is found in the very dynamics of Christianity itself, manifested in its distinct forms of adaptability and translatability.

Behind what seem like impressive responses, non-Western societies processed and adapted Christianity and Western values through ongoing conversations with their cultural, social, and spiritual traditions. In much of the rest of this book we discuss the religious nature of the people of the non-Western world that will—surprisingly to some—demonstrate the limited reach and impact of Enlightenment tradition/ideology in the majority world. There is no doubt that Enlightenment thinking and practice has influenced and framed the values of the West (left and right, liberals and conservatives). But the impact of Western Enlightenment rationality on the non-Western societies has not been as strong as many assume.

The onslaught and persistence of the Enlightenment intellectual tradition through modern education is significant and measurable even if the direct impact does not seem to be as strong in shaping the mind-set and religious worldview of the non-West at this point. Forms of charismatic Christianity that largely color non-Western forms of Christian faith today can be seen as a kind of emblematic defiance of Enlightenment values. They may continue to challenge the Enlightenment tradition or become a channel of adaptation. At the heart of charismatic Christianity is the belief in a present and active Spirit of God who often acts supernaturally. As will be shown later, many majority-world Christians are charismatic by nature and most strongly believe in God's will to supernaturally reveal God's very self. The Pentecostal-charismatic Christianity that holds sway for these ascendant forms of Christian faith rests on the trust and confidence that God intervenes in the daily lives of God's people through miracles and healings. Such a faith in the Spirit and its supernatural activities is what many would say the Enlightenment sensibility has extinguished in the West.

The charismatic nature of popular Christianity in the majority world shows the obliviousness of the people to the core Western values passed on from the Enlightenment. If it is not a conscious agitation against the Enlightenment tradition, it may be a subconscious defiance borne by a combination of ignorance and an instinctive spiritual faith. It is true that the metaphorical tension of "town and gown" (non-academics and academics in a university town) exists in all societies, including the West. But the extent of the tension is wide and is multilayered in most societies of the majority world. While most educated elites are convinced of the evil of colonialism, for instance, many ordinary, uneducated people in the non-West do not share this negative view to the same degree. The obliviousness of the majority-world Christians to the post-Enlightenment rationalistic version of Christianity is founded in the inculturated form of Christian faith that constitutes their daily lives. The core of their faith in the supernatural works of God through the Spirit is a teaching and material conviction that defies the Enlightenment tradition. One wonders if the rise of world Christianity might redirect much of modernity by rejecting the Enlightenment challenge of cultured despisers to religion and religiosity. Time will tell if and how the emerging Christianity of the majority world might impact modernity and the world order born from the Enlightenment.

The Significance and Limits of the Modern Missionary Movement in the Making of World Christianity

At the core of what has been termed "world Christianity" is a dynamic movement of faith emerging in the global South and East after the collapse of Western political domination and colonialism. The end of Western colonialism closely relates to the crisis of missions resulting from major changes in global politics in the second half of the twentieth century. The crisis also signaled the eclipse of the modern missionary movement and the emerging new missiological concept under the rubric of "world mission." In this section, we will tell the story of the modern missionary movement and how it led to the emerging majority-world Christianity at the beginning of the twenty-first century.

The larger crisis that changed the course of Christian missions has been described in various ways. Timothy Tennent looked at this crisis through the lens of historical trends and identified seven "megatrends" that reshaped the missionary world.[18] James Scherer described it as a passing from one ("old") era to another ("new") "missionary era."[19] World Christianity arose on the heels of the fading modern missions movement and evolved into a new missionary conception of "world mission." By modern missions or the modern missionary movement, we refer to the passionate movement coming out of Europe and European immigrants in the "new world" proclaiming Christian faith to the whole world for the purpose of making new Christians. Because the movement occurred in the modern period and had a strong modernizing tendency, we call it "modern missions" or the "modern missionary movement."

The movement came about in "two cycles,"[20] to use Andrew Walls's term. The first cycle was Roman Catholic, beginning in the closing years of the fifteenth century and fading in the third quarter of the eighteenth century. The second, or Protestant cycle, began in the last years of the eighteenth century and gained momentum throughout the nineteenth century, peaking in the early twentieth century. Both movements underwent a conceptual and historical crisis and faded in the second half of the twentieth century to be replaced by a broader concept of mission accompanying the rise of world Christianity. The modern missionary movement waned and has mostly been replaced on the cusp of the twenty-first century by world Christianity with its new missionary practices.

The impact of the modern missionary movement is almost immeasurable. It changed the Christian world and resulted in the redefinition of Christianity itself. The very nomenclature of "mission" and "missionary" with their associated meanings was produced with, and by, the movement. Numerically and conceptually, no other period in history had done more to the expansion of Christianity than the modern missionary movement. What came to be called Christian mission and missionary work of course happened throughout the history of the church. But as historians of missions made clear, no prior century is comparable to the nineteenth century, especially in Protestant spheres of influence. Christianity expanded to more and wider regions of the world in the nineteenth century than at any other time. As a result of the missionary movement, by the twentieth century, "there was in the world a universal religion—the Christian religion,"[21] says Stephen Neill. "Christianity acclimatized itself," continued Neill, "in every continent and in almost every country"[22] by the third quarter of the twentieth century. The extent of Christianity's expansion in the nineteenth century is confirmed by historian Kenneth Scott

Latourette. In one of the most detailed and analytical studies of Christian expansion in the history of the faith, Latourette devoted three of the seven volumes to the nineteenth century, which he calls "the Great Century."[23] So three volumes focused on the nineteenth century and four on the remaining eighteen and a half centuries. There is consensus that the modern missionary movement produced the worldwide Christianity of today.

But the decline of this modern missionary movement from the middle of the twentieth century is not the end of missionary work itself, just the passing of a particular missionary conception characterized largely by Western modernization. The new concept of "world mission" and its theological moorings came to supplant the civilizing "foreign missions" of the West. Several milestones—including the evolution of a Christian theology of mission and the relativizing of churches—marked the transition from modern missions to world Christianity. The naming of the new Commission on World Mission and Evangelism of the World Council of Churches when it merged with the International Missionary Council in 1961 has aptly denoted this transition. The first world conference of the new Commission held in 1963 in Mexico City clearly demonstrated the passing of the Eurocentric "foreign missions" concept when it described Christian mission as an endeavor "from everywhere to everywhere." The meeting stated, "We therefore affirm that this missionary movement now involves Christians in all six continents and in all lands."[24]

When the Catholic Church began its missionary endeavor in the early modern period,[25] Protestants were preoccupied with defining their identity and their theological essence. Catholic missions accompanied and worked with colonial rulers. While Portuguese engaged in trade in their colonies in the East, Spanish colonies with their accompanying military power dominated the West politically. Catholic missions confronted historic religious traditions in the East with little success while Spanish Catholic missions succeeded in extending Christendom by amassing large numbers of converts to Christianity in the Americas.

Colonial attitudes on religion had largely changed by the late eighteenth century when Protestants began to engage significantly in missionary efforts. When William Carey, considered the father of modern missions among the Protestants, and his party first sailed to India in 1793, they were not permitted to enter the land as missionaries by the British East India Company, and they began their work as "illegal immigrants."[26] With Carey's formation of the Baptist Missionary Society, the Protestant missionary movement began and earned its distinctiveness as a movement of voluntary societies. The distinction we often make between mission and church has its historical origin in the independence of these missions as a voluntary movement. While the distinction contributes to the dynamics of mission and provides its ecumenical bearings, it also impeded the missionary movement by often marginalizing it from the main life of the church. Moreover, missions began among Protestants as endeavors of Christians on the margins. They were first produced by peripheral movements of Pietism in the seventeenth century and Evangelical Revival of the eighteenth century. The hold of missions on the church was never strong even after the movement earned a good reputation. An Anglican missionary-churchman and historian, Bishop Stephen Neill, complained that Protestant missionaries in the nineteenth century "had no strong sense of the Church at large."[27] The missional reach of these groups was impacted by this lack of "Church-sense"[28] in Neill's term. Andrew Walls stated the significance and limitation of modern missions this way: "The [modern] missionary movement is one of the turning points of church history; the whole shape of the Christian faith in the world has been transformed by it.... But the history of the missionary movement has never been at the center of Christian historical scholarship; like the practice of missions, it has been in the sphere of the enthusiasts, not of the main tradition."[29]

The gap between church and mission began to close slightly when denominational churches became involved in missions in the second half of the nineteenth century. Yet, missions either existed as small segments of the church or were absent from the life of most of the Western churches. It took many years for the missionary enterprise to impact the church meaningfully in the West. One way the gap came to be bridged was through the ecumenical movement. Because the missionary movement led to the ecumenical movement—especially through the World Missionary Conference of 1910 in Edinburgh, Scotland—the closing of the gap between church and mission also resulted from the efforts of the ecumenical movement. As a result of Edinburgh 1910, two major movements, the Faith and Order movement and the Life and Work movement, emerged and went on to merge in 1938 to form the World Council of Churches (WCC).[30] From Edinburgh 1910 arose the International Missionary Council (IMC), which until its merger with the WCC in 1961, was the acknowledged global forum of Christian missions. Developments in the global history of missions have been commonly traced through the development and themes of the IMC's major conferences. The IMC conference at Tambaram in India in 1938 was known for its church-centeredness.[31] After the Tambaram meeting, mission and church were no longer considered separately in developing ecumenical circles. This was the year the World Council of Churches formed with the merger of Faith and Order and Life and Work movements. The historic merger of the International Missionary Council and the World Council of Churches in 1961 may be seen as a culmination of the unification of the church and mission especially in Protestant ecumenical circles. Yet, despite this motion to unite church and mission in the international ecumenical movement, missions have largely been at the periphery of Protestant church life and work in the West.

From being a marginal movement in the periphery of the church led by dissenters at the beginning of the nineteenth century, the Christian missionary enterprise gained wide popularity by the middle of the century. In his careful analysis, Andrew Walls notes: "Within half a century, missions passed from being one of the enthusiasms of the evangelical to a cause supported by earnest ecclesiastics of every strand of opinion."[32] To illustrate the remarkable change in public opinion on missions, Walls quotes the sermon of Edward Steane preached on the fiftieth anniversary of the Baptist Missionary Society in 1842 where Steane challenged the audience by saying, "Who would prohibit the missionary from setting his foot on any shore that owes allegiance to the British crown? Where are the writers who affect to treat his self-denying labours with contempt? Where are the wits and reviewers who turn them into ridicule?"[33] By the end of the nineteenth century, the missionary movement had triumphed in the

Christian world. Yet, even as they gained wide popularity through their advocates in the churches, missions were far from occupying the heart of the church in the West.

Scores of missionaries dedicated their whole lives to the spread of Christian faith. They helped to form Christian communities and planted churches in different parts of the world. Most were trained on the job and learned lessons in the field. With a strong notion that the formation of Christian communities involved not only gathering new converts but also educating persons and developing communities, Christian missions became the main means for "civilizing" the indigenous peoples encountered. Education, health, and agriculture[34]—commonly prioritized in this order—were the main developmental means introduced by modern Western missions to the rest of the world. The mix of civilizational and religious motives is viewed by many as positive, but with caution and suspicion by others. Although rightly criticized as imperialistic, the Western educational system has become the most powerful unifying agent of global oneness. Missions' contribution in the diffusion of Western education is unparalleled, and its provision of basic medical care and the dissemination of Western ways of knowing is significant.

Punctured somewhat by two world wars and ensuing international political tensions, the modern missionary movement saw its zenith in the first half of the twentieth century. By 1915 when World War I was just underway, according to Dana Robert, 351 Protestant mission societies had about 24,000 foreign missionaries working mostly in Asia and Africa. The 109,000-strong native or indigenous workers who toiled alongside them outnumbered these missionaries. Roman Catholics had approximately 19,600 foreign missionaries of priests, lay brothers and sisters in Africa and Asia, and the number in Latin America was unaccountable as the distinction between missionaries and native workers could not be clearly made. Russian Orthodox churches also had at least 400 missionaries in Asia.[35] The numerical strength of Protestant missionaries almost doubled in about forty years. As estimated by the Missionary Research Library in New York City, there were approximately 43,000 Protestant missionaries working around the world by 1958.[36]

From being an almost exclusive religion of Europeans at the beginning of the sixteenth century when Roman Catholics began their mission, Christianity spread worldwide by the beginning of the twentieth century. Except for a few closed nations and regions—such as Afghanistan, Tibet, Nepal, and Bhutan—which resisted missionary entry by Christian missionaries, Christianity has reached most nations of the world. Stephen Neill notes, "The missionary 'occupation' carried out between 1792 and 1914 was so extensive and so effective that, in dealing with the period subsequent to 1914, it is only rarely possible to speak of absolutely fresh beginnings of Christian work in countries which prior to that date had had no contact whatever with the preaching of the Gospel."[37] By the end of the nineteenth century, more than one-third of the world's population had become Christian. Of the 1.6 billion people in the whole world in 1900, 558 million were Christians. This accounts for about 34.5 percent of the world's population.[38] As perhaps unsatisfying as the nature of its Christianity might have been, with 80 percent of its population baptized, South America was already considered "the only Christian continent in the Third World."[39] Beyond Latin America, Christianity had not penetrated the major populace of the other southern and eastern continents yet. However, it is fair to say that Christianity had been well seeded in Asia and Africa. By 1910, 2.4 percent of Asia's population was Christian, and more than 9 percent of Africans had become Christian.[40] European migrations to the Americas and Oceania (with their accompanying sometimes violent displacement of indigenous forms of faith) meant that most of the populations in these continents were Christian. Christian missions saw success in the sparse islands of the Pacific, especially in Polynesia and Micronesia early on, and Melanesia a bit later. But Christianity was still very much a religion of the Europeans. Europe and their "new worlds" in the Americas and Oceania held well over 90 percent of the world's Christian population.

The twentieth century is the most tumultuous century in the modern period. It is particularly so for Christians. The century began triumphantly with Christian missions climaxing as a movement when new ways and means of missionary cooperation were devised and utilized. Yet, as related numerous times, the European Christian root was being eroded by rising secularism and humanism. The outburst of global conflicts and wars and the shifting political configuration presented enormous challenges for Christian missions. New nations formed as a result of independence from colonial rule and rising versions of socialism and communism directly threatened missionary works in many new nations. China, which had one of the largest groups of missionaries at the time, expelled virtually all missionaries in the early 1950s, followed by a few other nations in Southeast Asia. India produced challenging voices against missionaries, including one from its national hero Mahatma Gandhi.[41] The rising anti-missionary sentiments produced what some called anti-conversion laws in the guise of freedom of religion acts during the 1960s. What has most affected the missionary work in India is the curbing of missionary visas from the late 1950s onward. The most devastating development against missions, however, happened in the Christian home front in the West under the rubric of what Lamin Sanneh calls "guilt complex."[42] By narrating his own experience, Sanneh shows that liberal Christians in the West were embarrassed to see a convert from another religion to Christianity as they seemed to presume that such a conversion can happen only under undue pressure.[43] In the postwar West of the mid-twentieth century, such a guilt complex seemed to be prevalent.

When the demand to preserve human rights, produced first by Enlightenment thinking in the West, was extended to the non-Western people and universalized in 1948 by the United Nations,[44] anything considered colonial or imperialistic became problematic and globally suspect. Critics of the missionary movement began to interpret all missionary works to be more or less imperialistic. Thus, even within Christian communities, the modern missionary movement came to be viewed largely as a colonial enterprise. While this critique—in some cases, demonization—of the missionary movement also produced a successful quest for a firmer theological understanding of the Christian mission, it also became largely responsible for the demise of the modern missionary movement as we know it. While such a verdict on the missionary movement was commonly accepted in liberal/progressive Christian circles and even by many conservative Christians, the Christian rank and file in the majority world could hardly understand or accept it. For many of them, Christianity is valuable and the effects of colonialism more complex than what secular humanisms and paternalistic Christian elites often made them out to be. And it was not lost on many of them that the missionary enterprise had largely been carried out by relatively conservative Christians in the West and the majority world. See chapter 6, for a discussion of the new missionary movements in the majority world.

Even as the missionary movement was conflated with colonialism and the missionary enterprise marginalized, Christian mission became grounded in firmer theological foundations. One notable development in the missionary thinking from the 1960s was a new holistic approach to mission. The first meeting of the Division (later Commission) on World Mission and Evangelism of the WCC in Mexico City in 1963 reconceived mission as an enterprise involving Christians from everywhere to everywhere. Bishop Anastasios of Androusia rightly stated that "Mission in Six Continents" became "the *leit-motiv*" of the meeting in Mexico City.[45] This meant there is no longer separation between missionary-sending nations and mission fields. This is what "world mission" means as adopted by the WCC for the name of its new division of mission, "Commission of World Mission and Evangelism." The concluding "Message" from the Mexico City meeting powerfully states, "We therefore affirm that this missionary movement now involves Christians in all six continents and in all lands. It must be the common witness of the whole Church, bringing the whole Gospel to the whole world."[46] This is a holistic understanding of Christian mission that anchored the missionary enterprise tightly to the church. It became the converging understanding of mission in the closing years of the twentieth century. Its influence on evangelical Christians is particularly notable as the evangelical Lausanne Movement[47] came to adopt it as its foundational theme. It was included in the Lausanne Covenant of 1974, and became the preparatory study theme of the Lausanne III conference in 2010 in Cape Town, South Africa. The emerging holistic missionary conception of the church is tied to the Trinitarian theology of *missio Dei,* which relocates the origin of mission from a foreign Western

Christian land to God's gracious act in Christ in the power of the Holy Spirit.

In the midst of the declining missionary movement and secularization of Europe, the second half of the twentieth century bore witness to a new emergence of Christian faith in the majority world. The demographic shift of Christianity by the end of the century was nothing short of a surprise, and Scott Sunquist appropriately calls the twentieth century "The Unexpected Christian Century." He begins his historical sweep of twentieth-century Christianity with these words: "No scholar—or as far as that goes, not even a madman—predicted that at the end of the twentieth century Christianity would not be recognized even as a cultural factor in Europe....No prognosticator predicted that more Christians would be worshipping each Sunday in China than in Europe or North America."[48]

What is surprising, Sunquist continues, is that most learned mission leaders predicted that "Africa would become a Muslim continent," and some "had pretty much given up on Africa." But "the opposite is true, for there are more Christians than Muslims in Africa today."[49] The African continent has become a powerhouse of Christian missional growth in many ways. As noted in the previous chapter, scholars had begun to notice this development and Walbert Bühlmann forecasted it in the 1970s. After Bühlmann, the "shifting center of gravity" from Christian Europe of the medieval and modern period to the majority world in the postcolonial globalizing world became a catchphrase for world Christianity. As the West becomes increasingly post-Christian, the global South joined by the East is raising a post-Western Christianity to write a new chapter, a chapter of [majority] world Christianity.

Chapter 3

CHRISTIAN MOVEMENTS IN THE MAJORITY WORLD

Part One:
Latin America and Africa

In the non-European Oceania, the movement to Christianity has been quite steady since the modern missionary movement of the nineteenth century. In Africa and Asia, the Christian movements came after the decolonization of the nations. Major movements to Christianity followed sociopolitical crises as the new nations struggled to stand on their own. In the case of Africa, the church faced a major sociopolitical crisis and a new beginning seemed to have come in the form of new charismatic and Pentecostal churches. Combined with the strong suggestion to inculturate the gospel in the African cultural contexts, African Christianity seemed to have emerged between inculturated charismatic Christianity and the modernizing orderliness of life. In Asia, the challenge came from socioreligious fronts and the political revolutions to which the churches gave divergent responses.

41

Vocal liberal critiques challenged the church to be opened to both religious diversity and political changes, though churches have been slow in that pursuit. Yet grassroots movements of charismatic Christianity have been emerging in recent decades in different nations, including the populous China and India. The story of Christian movement in Latin America, a continent considered Christian, is different. Beginning in the 1950s, Latin American Christianity has been experiencing a dramatic transformation. In the words of Todd Hartch:

> The change [in Latin America] has not been as obvious as it has been in other regions because the transformation has not been, as in Africa and Asia, the sudden and massive growth of a new faith. It has been rather a simultaneous fragmentation and revitalization that threatened, awakened, and ultimately brought to greater maturity a dormant and at times parochial religion.[1]

In this section of the chapter, we will offer an overview of the Christian movements in the majority-world continents in an effort to understand their nature and characteristics. Our attempt is not to offer a detailed narrative (as others have done), but to describe some of the stories of emergent forms of Christian faith that are changing the demography of Christianity, revealing the theological features and cultural, philosophical, and historical moorings. While we try to bring into view some of the common features of Christianity in these continents, we also recognize important differences among them and the distinctiveness of each. Even shared features such as European colonization were experienced very differently. Much of Africa was suppressed and governed as colonies with as little investment as possible by the colonizing nations. Missions cooperated with (and were co-opted by) colonial governments as they were used by these authorities to provide education. Many Africans, therefore, seem to have a more positive image of colonialists than people in some Asian nations.

Latin America, or for that matter the Americas, has never really been freed from colonial rule. It was the colonies themselves that gained independence from the parent nations. Because missionary efforts were originally part and parcel of the colonies, missions' resistance and struggle to change colonial systems were done (to some degree) from within these systems themselves. The campaign of Bartolome de Las Casas for the sake of the Indians is one example of an attempt to effect change from within.[2]

Asia had diverse colonial experiences among its many people in different regions. Because the colonialists faced not only an overwhelming and diverse population in Asia, but also established religious and philosophical systems, they did not employ a common approach. Unable to squash or overpower most of those established civilizations and people, the colonialists had to utilize different methods of governance. The long-lasting conflicts between colonial powers and the nationals in many places brought out adverse images of the colonialism. The relations between missions and colonialism in Asia are complex. They differ from period to period and place to place.

Latin America

We begin our survey of contemporary Christianity in regions of the majority world with Latin America. Our interest is in the Christian renewal movement experienced in the region since the 1950s. To Timothy Steigenga and Edward Cleary, the dramatic transformation of Christianity in Latin America is a part of the "remarkable and largely unforeseen religious transformations" that also extend to "other religious groups."[3] They call the movement in its entirety the *Conversion of a Continent*. Todd Hartch observes that the transformation of Latin American Christianity has not been as conspicuous as in Africa and Asia. For Hartch, the transformation of Latin American Christianity has been "a simultaneous fragmentation and revitalization that threatened, awakened, and ultimately brought to great maturity a dormant and at times parochial religion."[4] This unique renewal movement is confusing but genuine. While almost all people in Latin America were "Catholic just forty years ago, evangelical Protestants now represent approximately 15 percent of the population," note Steigenga and Cleary. They describe the complexity of this renewal: "While many Catholics are becoming Pentecostal, many Mainstream Protestants and Classic Pentecostals are also converting to 'health and wealth' neo-Pentecostal groups. At the same time, many Catholics have also joined more Charismatic Catholic congregations."[5] Offering some brief historical backdrop helps highlight this multifaceted change in contemporary Latin American Christianity.

The common heritage for all Latin American Christians is Roman Catholicism. Because of the dominance of the Catholic Church for five centuries, all Latin Americans share in the legacy of the Catholic Church's missional work. Enculturated Catholicism became the cultural frame for the entire continent. By the beginning of the twentieth century, more than 90 percent of Latin Americans were Catholic.[6] If there is colonial mission or imperialistic evangelism in the history of modern missions, the history of Latin American Christianity is perhaps the best example. Christianity was brought to Latin America by the invaders, and colonial conquest and Christianization went hand in hand. Some scholars contest the language of "conquest" in connection with evangelization of Latin America.[7] But Catholic priests participated from the earliest conquests of the region and at times utilized force to convert the indigenous peoples. In other words, the conquest was deeply connected to the evangelization or Christianization of the Western hemisphere as both the conquistadors and missionaries had mixed motives. The hemisphere was Christianized in less than a century—something that happened in part through the depopulation of the native peoples.[8] Operating with the medieval religious concept of *cuius regio eius religio* (the religion of the ruler, the religion of the ruled), the imposition of Christianity was seen as an essential part of the establishment of the political hegemony of conquering Spain and Portugal.[9] Indeed there were evangelistic protests against the inhuman treatment of the indigenous peoples by the invading Spaniards (e.g., Bartolome de Las Casas), but the dominant evangelizing force often propelled violent forms of forced conversion.[10]

As Ondina González and Justo González have rightly observed, from the very beginning the Latin American church has had two faces: the dominant, wealthy, and oppressive face that stands for the status quo, and a Christian face that stands with and for the oppressed.[11] Much of the history of Christianity in Latin America can be articulated between these two profiles. Although representations of each can be complex at times, often they are well depicted as the established institutional church versus the popular and informal form of Christianity, respectively. This polarized nature of Christianity persisted Latin America even as the religious landscape of the continent underwent tremendous change in the late twentieth century.

With all the nations in the region gaining their independence from Spain and Portugal by the second decade of the nineteenth century, sociopolitical changes gradually swept through the continent. The rise of new social classes, especially the middle class, and the struggle between liberals and conservatives colored much of the nineteenth-century political landscape. These changes are rooted in and had a lasting impact on church and state relations, with conservatives siding with the church and more voices offering a strong critique of the church. Protestant churches trickled into the continent slowly through migration beginning in the nineteenth century, and their modest presence never really posed any major numerical or theological threat to the Catholic Church until the rise of the evangelical and Pentecostal movements in the twentieth century.

Revolutions—among which the bloodiest was the Mexican revolution in the second decade of the twentieth century—brought about seismic and upsetting changes. Some of these revolutions contributed to the rise of Protestantism and a renewed awakening of the Catholic Church in the second half of the twentieth century. Liberal elites and revolutionaries often made use of Protestants to counter Catholic Church domination. This was also the case in Mexico when President Lázaro Cárdenas befriended an American evangelical Protestant missionary in 1936 leading to a partnership between Mexico and the Summer Institute of Linguistics (SIL), an evangelical missionary organization based in North America.[12] The partnership was largely responsible for the introduction and growth of Protestantism in Mexico which, after sixty years, has claimed 10 percent of Mexico's population.[13] But Protestantism was not the only expression of the growing religiosity of the populace. The simmering spirituality of the people waiting to explode could be felt in the early twentieth century in other ways, too. One development that exemplifies this growing spiritual awakening is the lay Catholic movement under Catholic Action, which came about in the first few decades of the twentieth century.[14] This lay movement, recognized and authorized by most local ecclesiastical authorities, aimed at putting "apostolic principles into action" by feeding the hungry, clothing the naked, and housing the homeless.[15] It inspired and provided opportunities for laypersons of different ages to be of service to the church in meaningful ways. In some ways, lay associations of Catholic Action paved the way for the basic ecclesial movement and liberation theologies in the second half of the twentieth century.

The Catholic renewal movement in the second half of the twentieth century was driven by several things. The increase in both expatriate clergy (mostly from Spain) and indigenous clergies and religious orders in the first half of the century[16] came alongside the rise of the lay Catholic Action movement. On the political side, the growing popularity of socialist ideology in the early part of the century posed a significant challenge to the church while military-backed dictators came to rule nation after nation from 1950 to 1975. "By the late 1970s," in the words of Todd Hartch, "Latin America seemed to be composed mostly of governments that oppressed their own people."[17] This sociopolitical crisis challenged and inspired the church to reach deeply into its spiritual resources as it negotiated difficult political conditions. Popular piety grew as the search for justice and concerns for poverty heightened. The first wave of Christian renewal came through "Prophetic Christianity" of the lay base communities and liberation theology of the intellectuals connected to their cause.[18]

The Christian base communities or Base Ecclesial Communities (*comunidades eclesiales de base* or CEB in Spanish), a grassroots faith formation movement, demonstrated and incited the piety of the people. It was popularized first in Brazil where some bishops utilized it as a means of evangelization and pastoral care. The early popularity of CEB in Brazil was also due to the support given by the country's president Janîa Quadros in the early 1960s. By 1963, there were at least seven thousand such small groups in Brazil.[19] CEBs significantly changed the popular understanding of the church, moving people to a deeper sense of ownership in the church's life. The CEB's "most common agenda," in the words of González and González, "included a time of sharing and solidarity, discussion and analysis of the social conditions in their own communities and their causes and possible solutions, prayer, and Bible study."[20] Some of these characteristics are familiar to most Protestants while others such as corporate social analysis may not be as important as they were for Catholic CEBs. The base ecclesial movement is spontaneous and diversified. Many groups were not formalized, and as González and González report, many groups became radicalized.[21] In politically repressive countries, there were some Protestant base communities.[22] And some of the Catholic groups were influenced and fed by Protestant resources and traditions. One well-known community was in Solentiname of Lake Nicaragua, led by Ernesto Cardenal. Quite like evangelical Protestant groups, this community did weekly Bible studies using a Protestant Bible translation in an engaging manner.[23] It produced a rich and unique volume comprising reports of what appears to be genuine reflections.[24] Perhaps, also influenced by some of the more radical socialist thinking of the time, the perspectives of the Solentiname group often leaned more strongly toward socialism. In the reflection on the Annunciation, for instance, Mary was concluded to be a "communist."[25]

The Second Vatican Council or Vatican II, which met in four autumn sessions from 1962 to 1965, was a watershed event that brought momentous changes in the Catholic Church around the world. Its impact for the Latin American church was profound, especially as it took place during a crucial renewal period of the Catholic Church in the region. As the council sought to update the church in relation to the modern world, most observers of the council agreed that it accomplished much more. The gathered bishops offered profound reflections on the crisis faced by the church in its alienation from the modern world. The church sought to change its posture from being formed primarily in the image of monarchic rule to that of a servant savior. From the popular experience and perspective, the most obvious changes include the use of vernacular in the celebration of the mass, a new emphasis on preaching, a central place given to Christ in the new theology, and changed attitudes to other churches (denominations) and religions outside the Roman Church.[26] If liberals were quick to take advantage of the new openness of Vatican II to the wider world, conservatives were resistant to the council's directives. In Latin America, the council spurred the ongoing search for the theological meaning of poverty and justice among key leaders and thinkers. It had a profound influence on the Bishops Conference of Latin America and the accompanying rise of liberation theology.

Since we will deal with liberation theology later in another chapter, a brief description of its emergence will suffice here. From the perspective of liberation theology, this Christian renewal was a growing "commitment" to the process of liberation.[27] As González and González have said, the emerging interest to find out the sociopolitical and economic causes of poverty in the hemisphere spurred a search for theological meaning that influenced deliberations of the Council of Latin American Bishops (*Consejo Episcopal Latinamericano* or CELAM) in a post–Vatican II atmosphere.[28] The long quest for relevance by the church came head-to-head with the social ills that captured the region. The second General Conference of CELAM, which met in Medellín, Colombia, took up the issue of poverty in the historical and sociopolitical context of Latin America. The conference produced sixteen documents analyzing human life and societal issues and the church's mission. While the aim was pastoral, the tone was social and somewhat political with the hope "for full emancipation, of liberation from every form of servitude, of personal maturity and of collective integration."[29] The Medellín document became foundational for liberation theology. In the words of Gutiérrez, "As regards doctrinal authority and impact, the most important text" for liberation theology was the Medellín documents.[30]

While politically conscious CEBs and liberation theology represented one aspect of Christian renewal in Latin America, the most conspicuous face of the renewal was on the Protestant front. Of course, Protestantism has different faces in Latin America, to use José Míguez Bonino's words.[31] It was the evangelical and Pentecostal Protestants, especially the latter, who experienced renewal and brought about significant increase in numbers from the 1960s to the present. While early studies combine Evangelicals with Pentecostals in bringing about Protestant dramatic increase,[32] some later studies singled out Pentecostals. The relation between Pentecostalism and Evangelicalism is quite complex.[33] Although the Pentecostal factor seems much larger in the renewal of Protestant Christianity in Latin America, the closeness between the two and the significance of evangelical contributions in the renewal means that it may not be helpful to draw too strict a line between the two in Latin America. As a subset of evangelical Christianity, no Pentecostal Christian can be non-evangelical. Yet, Pentecostals are also distinguished from Evangelicals. Due in part to the particular strength of the charismatic or Pentecostal features of evangelical Christians in the majority world, in this work we will use charismatic or Pentecostal Christianity as our main terms of reference.

"Charismatic Catholicism and Pentecostal Protestantism utterly transformed Latin America between 1970 and 2000,"[34] writes Todd Hartch. The Pentecostal explosion and the Catholic Renewal movement somewhat dwarfed the forms of renewal through liberation and base ecclesial communities. While the Catholic Church experienced a significant renewal, the net loss in the changing religious landscape came from the Catholic Church. Up until the middle of the twentieth century, the Catholics still comprised more than 90 percent of the region's population. As the Pew Research survey report released in November 2014 shows, only 69 percent of adults in the Latin America identify as Catholic.[35] Meanwhile as many as 84 percent of adults reported that they were raised Catholic.[36] Yet, the Catholic Charismatic Movement is as powerful a movement as Pentecostalism in Latin America. "Pentecostals and Catholic Charismatics," said Hartch, are "two heavyweights...fighting for the title of most influential religious movement in Latin America."[37]

The origin of the worldwide Pentecostal and charismatic movements is commonly traced back to the United States. Many studies credit the 1906 revival on Azusa Street in Los Angeles, California, under the leadership of William Seymour, as the origin of the Pentecostal movement. According to Cecil Robeck, who delivered one of the most thorough historical studies on the Azusa Street revival, "'Azusa Street' rightly continues to function as the primary icon expressing the power of the worldwide Pentecostal movement."[38] If there is a predecessor, it was in Topeka, Kansas, where Seymour received his training under Charles Parham. Credits for the movement were rarely given anywhere else. Similarly, the beginning of the charismatic movement among the Protestants has also been traced back to the charismatic experience of an Episcopal priest Dennis Bennet in Van Nuys, California, in 1960. On the Catholic side, too, the Catholic Charismatic Renewal (CCR) movement is also considered to originate in the United States. To use Andrew Chesnut's words: "The CCR specifically traces its genesis to the 'Duquesne Weekend' in February 1967, when some 25 students at Duquesne University in Pittsburgh...gathered for a spiritual retreat with two professors who had already been baptized under the direction of Presbyterian charismatics. Many of the students were baptized in the Holy Spirit and received charismata, making this the first event in which a group of Catholics experienced Pentecostal spirituality."[39]

Chesnut shows the continuing expansion of this wave to other colleges in the United States, and the significance of the international conference of CCR at Notre Dame University in 1974, attended by some 25,000 believers. The leadership at the conference of a Dominican priest Francis MacNutt (who contributed to the spread of the renewal movement in Latin America) is also noteworthy.[40]

While in no way meant to minimize the importance and influence of these early revivals, seeing these events as the pristine origins of a movement, and assuming that they spread from these places in the United States to other places around the world, is at best "misleading"[41] or at worst, imperialistic and ethnocentric.[42] Whether we use the term "Charismatic" to include Pentecostals, or we use "Pentecostalism" to include charismatic movements, both now appear as part of one global phenomenon with multiple origins around the same time. The connecting link from a revival movement in one place that is better *known* and *documented* than other connections does not mean it spread from that area to the rest. As we will see in the stories of Christians in Africa and Asia, the rise of Pentecostalism or charismatic revivalism is a worldwide phenomenon that touched Christians on every continent almost at the same time. Dana Robert's description helps us capture the global nature of these multiple origins:

In the midst of…international crises, news of spiritual awakenings also seemed to pour from every corner of the globe during the first decade of the twentieth century: from Wales in 1904; Los Angeles in 1906; Kedgaon, India in 1906; Pyongyang, Korea, in 1907; Valparaiso, Chile, in 1909, and rolling revivals in different parts of western Africa throughout the decade."[43]

Other lesser-known revivals may still be added to this list. The ability for this movement to impact people from different parts of the world comes not from the strength of one movement or movements in one area but in the readiness and commitment of people to receive what they believe to be the supernatural work of God.

A few months after the "Duquesne Weekend" in Pittsburgh in 1967, with no historical or personal connection to the Duquesne revival, Father Rafael García Herreros met and had many conversations on the Holy Spirit with a Protestant charismatic pastor, Samuel Ballesteros, in Bogotá, Colombia. "Eventually in the early 1970s," according to Edward Cleary, "Father Rafael received baptism in the Spirit."[44] The movement that began in the United States did greatly impact Latin American CCR, as did the one that began in Bogotá, Colombia. What characterized these charismatic Catholics? A description of the CCR in Buenos Aires in the 1990s explains that "Catholics were singing contemporary praise songs, engaging in 'spiritual warfare,' speaking in tongues, giving prophecies, interpreting prophecies, experiencing supernatural physical and spiritual healing."[45]

Pentecostalism is what changed the entire Latin American religious landscape in the closing decades of the twentieth century and the beginning of the twenty-first century. It took a while for the world to learn of this "quite extraordinary and little-known development."[46] A few scholars began to give serious attention to these developments in the 1990s, and today it is a well-known story. With already an estimated 141 million persons in 2000—with half of them in Brazil—Latin America has more Pentecostals than either Africa or Asia.[47] Seeing "varied origins" of different Pentecostal groups in Latin America, Juan Sepúlveda differentiates "Native Pentecostalism" from those of missionary origins.[48] The first Pentecostal church in Latin America was established in 1909 by an

American Methodist missionary physician Willis Collins Hoover in Valparaiso, Chile. Interestingly, the spark that lit the revival in Valparaiso came not from Los Angeles in the United States, but from Kedgaon, near Pune in India. A pamphlet from Pandita Ramabhai's ministry was passed to the Hoovers through Minnie Abrams.[49] According to Todd Hartch, by following the directions in the pamphlet, Hoover began speaking in tongues.[50] The church Hoover pastored received the stirring by the Holy Spirit in April 1909 with "many unusual and ecstatic manifestations." The manifestations include "weeping, laughing uncontrollably, groaning, prostration, rolling on the floor, people repenting and confessing of sin...seeing revelatory vision, singing and speaking in tongues."[51] The experience forced Hoover to resign from his position, and he, together with other pastors, founded Iglesia Metodista Pentecostal (Methodist Pentecostal Church) in 1910. Chilean Pentecostalism was indigenized from the very beginning and is distinct from (even if resembling) classical North American Pentecostalism.

One aspect of Pentecostalism, perhaps derived from notions of the freedom of the Spirit inherent in its teaching, is a frequent splitting into different churches. By the first decade of the twenty-first century, according to Allan Anderson, there were "over thirty Pentecostal denominations deriving from MPC [Methodist Pentecostal Church] forming some 95 percent of the Protestants in Chile."[52] While Chilean Pentecostals were of native origins, Pentecostals in Brazil and Argentina, the other two countries with high Pentecostal numbers, had their origins in the work of missionaries. In Central America, El Salvador became a center for the spreading of Pentecostalism in the region. Of the numerous Pentecostal denominations in Mexico, the earliest was started in 1912 by a Mexican woman, Romanita Carbajal de Valenzuela, who experienced the revival in Los Angeles.[53] Pentecostalism thrives in Brazil, which may now have the largest population of Pentecostals in the world.[54]

Todd Hartch made a helpful comparison between Pentecostals in Brazil and Bolivia. While the first missionaries to Brazil came without many resources or financial support, this actually benefited the mission since there was no measurable economic divide between missionaries and the native converts. With the arrival of more missionaries, tensions did rise, but subsided with the division of territories between nationals and missionaries. In Bolivia, on the other hand, a well-funded Swedish Pentecostal mission did not see success. As Hartch relates, "Only when the missionary presence waned or when movements independent of missionary control developed did Pentecostalism thrive."[55]

If the religious demography of Latin America did not change much during the past century, the face of Christianity certainly did. The number of Christians as a percentage of the overall population actually declined. According one account, Christians went from 95.2 percent of the population in 1910 to 92.5 percent in 2010.[56] Nevertheless, Christianity found new life late in the twentieth century, with religiosity growing as populations discovered new spiritual vitality. The decrease in the percentage of Christians, according to Timothy Steigenga and Edward Cleary, may have been caused by the very same phenomenon as Afro-Brazilian and indigenous religions experience new life.[57] From being an imposed religion in the sixteenth and seventeenth centuries, Christianity in Latin America is now enjoying a remarkable renewal in the new context of twenty-first-century religious freedom.

Africa

The Berlin Conference of 1884–1885 formalized what came to be called "The Scramble for Africa," an enterprise that made Africa a major object of European colonization. In the end, the continent of Africa was colonized almost in its entirety by Europeans, and the continent came to be divided mostly between Francophone and Anglophone forces. Yet, European colonizers hardly left a lighter "colonial imprint," says Martin Meredith, because the "colonial powers lost much of their earlier interest" when they saw no "prospect of immediate wealth" in much of Africa.[58] They shifted their methods to the most inexpensive way to govern: "Administration was thus kept to a minimum; education placed in the hands of the missionaries; economic activity was left to commercial companies."[59]

Between the late 1950s and the early 1970s, all the European colonies were freed one after another, and African nations became independent. The formation of the new nations and the process of nation-building and national developments following the various independence movements did not yield positive results. Instead, the social and political conditions worsened in the following decades. As Meredith describes in detail, from dictatorship to military coup, violent revolutions to tyrant leadership, nation after nation failed to prosper and eventually exacerbated impoverishment, in some cases creating extreme poverty.[60] J. W. Hofmeyr summarizes the situation of the 1970s and 1980s: "Between 1975 and 1990, the effects of poor leadership and militarization of the society became daunting as economies collapsed, abuse of human rights and ecology followed, civil society was decimated and corruption became rampant.... Poverty hit Africa and civil wars ensued with incredible brutality as caged rats ate themselves."[61] The economic decline in Africa was so steep in the 1980s that the decade came to be called "the lost decade."[62] Yet, it was in that same roughly ten-year span that the Christian movement reached its height.

Christian growth in the independent African nations is a stunning spectacle spurring great interest. Commenting on the impressive increase of 85 million Christians in fifty years in the continent, from 5 million in 1925 to an estimated 90 million in 1975, Adrian Hasting writes, "It is safe to say in no other continent during the last fifty years has Christianity shown so much growth and diversity."[63] So astounding is the growth in the subsequent decades that *World Christian Encyclopedia* estimates that the number of adult Christians grew from roughly 75 to 80 million in 1970[64] to more than 335 million in 2000.[65] In 1970, adult Christians on the African continent constituted about 17.7 percent, and by 2000, they comprised 42.7 percent of the continent's population. Lamin Sanneh writes, "By 1985, it had become clear that a major expansion of Christianity had been under way in spite of prevailing pessimism about the imminent collapse of post-independent states, and of waning confidence in the church in Europe."[66] The major growth of Christianity, says Sanneh, was among "the poor and the marginalized." By 1985, Sanneh continues, "There were over 16,500 conversions a day, yielding an annual rate over

6 million."[67] The expansion of African Christianity was incredible and unexpected, especially since the continent was going through its harshest period politically and economically.

The spectacular expansion of Christianity in the 1980s coincided with the proliferation of new independent churches, many of which are best characterized as being "in the evangelical and/or Pentecostal tradition."[68] It is easy to attribute the stunning growth of Christianity mainly or solely to this group. Hofmeyr, for instance, observed the following about mainline churches during the same period: "Mainline churches lost members and prominence to new churches that were growing and flourishing often at the expense of the mainline churches."[69] But the *World Christian Encyclopedia*'s statistics do not fully support this. They show that most churches experienced significant numerical growth in the period.[70] The Roman Catholic Church, the largest on the continent, grew from roughly 25.7 million in 1970 to 120 million in 2000. This is about a 368 percent increase in thirty years. The fastest-growing church (percentage wise) in this period, according to this encyclopedia, is the Anglican Church, which grew from about 4.5 million in 1970 to 42.5 million in 2000. The rate of this thirty-year increase is 844 percent. One Nigerian Anglican priest notes that many of those on the Anglican rolls are actively involved in Pentecostal churches too.

The Anglicans are closely followed by the independents,[71] which increased from 9 million in 1970 to almost 83.8 million in 2000, an increase of about 830 percent in thirty years. The Protestants, who others refer to variably as "mainline," increased from about 13 million in 1970 to 89 million in 2000, an increase rate of 585 percent. The truth is that all Christian confessions and denominations experienced major growth. Even the slowest-growing group included in the encyclopedia (the Orthodox Church) grew from 10.7 million to 35.3 million, an increase rate of 230 percent; this rate of increase is still much higher than the population growth rate of the continent. The entire population of the continent increased from 357 million in 1970 to 784.5 million in 2000, which is a 120 percent increase. The most conspicuous growth is in the surging Pentecostal-Charismatic churches.

Although Christianity continued to grow significantly in Africa, the rate of growth has declined since 2000. The data of adult Christians in Africa presented here in the chart, combines the report of *World Christian Encyclopedia* from 1970 to 2000 with the *Atlas of Global Christianity* between 2000 and 2010. This data shows that the rate of growth declined each decade considerably. In the case of the Orthodox Church, the first decade of the twenty-first century shows more than a 12 percent loss.

Africa's Adult Christians 1970-2010

Church Tradition	1970	2000	Approx. 10-Year Rate of Increase	2010	10-Year Rate of Increase/ Decrease
Anglican	4,489,000	42,542,000	848%	50,866,000	19.5%
Catholic	25,737,000	120,386,000	367%	169,495,000	41%
Independent	9,066,000	83,841,000	831%	98,819,000	17.9%
Marginal	380,000	2,427,000	539%	3,663,000	51%
Orthodox	10,745,000	35,304,000	230%	48,286,000	37%
Protestant	12,974,000	89,000,000	585%	137,207,000	54.2%
Christian Total	63,391,000	335,116,000 373,500,000[72]	429%	494,668,000 508,336,000[73]	47.6%
TOTAL Population of the Continent	357,038,600	784,537,686	120%	1,032,012,000	31.5%

What is noteworthy in the 2010 statistical report is that Protestants outpaced both independents and Anglicans. This is a surprise to most observers of African Christianity. One must recognize the enumeration difficulty when more and more Protestants become charismatic, increasingly resembling Pentecostal churches. Furthermore, it is easy to belong to more than one church tradition and be counted twice.[74] Though neither the *Encyclopedia* nor the *Atlas* reference the possibility of double counting, the reduction of total Christians in the two reports from the actual sum total of the reported numbers to the total reported (from the actual sum total of 373,500,000 to 335,116,000 in the *Encyclopedia* for 2000, and from

508,336,000 to 494,668,000 in the *Atlas*), may be accounted for by this phenomenon.

Despite the decline in the reported growth rate after 2000, the common perception that Pentecostalism and charismatic Christianity continues to grow in Africa is plausible. Because of the complexity involved in measuring growth rates with these groups and the possibility of double counting, categories like Pentecostalism and charismatic Christianity have to be used rather loosely as we have suggested before. The bulk of those categorized as "independents" belong to either Pentecostals or the broader charismatic family of Christians. Several studies on Pentecostal and charismatic movements in Africa attempt to clarify this complex history. The precise relationships among early Prophetic ministries, the so-called African Initiated Churches (or African Independent Churches), different forms of Pentecostal (older and newer) churches, and the charismatic movement are complex and difficult to ascertain. Kwabena Asamoah-Gyadu, a leading scholar on Pentecostal and charismatic Christianity in Africa, has articulated one of the clearest explanations of how all these movements relate closely and yet differ from one another.[75] The form of Christianity that came to be called the Pentecostal and charismatic movement originated with the work of those individuals commonly called "prophets," such as William Wadé Harris of the Gold Coast (now Ghana), Simon Kimbangu of Congo, and Joseph Ayo Bababola of Nigeria. While some of these are what Asamoah-Gyadu calls "precursors" of the Pentecostal movement,[76] the last one, Bababola, went on to be active in Pentecostal church leadership. These prophets challenged Africans to throw away their traditional beliefs and practices, including witchcraft and indigenous fetishes, and turn to the living God of the Bible. Yet, they operated within the African traditional faith regarding belief in the supernatural works of God. These prophetic campaigns were followed by the founding of several independent churches, which came to be clustered under "African Independent" or "African Initiated" or "African Instituted" churches with the popular acronym of AIC. Spirit churches in West and East Africa, Aladura (praying) churches in Nigeria, Zionist Churches in Southern Africa, and Kimbanguism in Central Africa are some of the better known

AICs.[77] Except for parts of Southern Africa, the prominence of AICs has declined and has been overtaken by Pentecostal churches since the 1970s. Like their prophetic predecessors, these churches emphasized healing with some shaped more by traditional African religious practices than those considered distinctly Christian.[78]

Pentecostalism is a fluid concept, referring to a denomination, a larger movement, and/or a stream within other forms of Christianity. While most AICs may easily be classified within the Pentecostal stream, not all fit well within the genre of Pentecostal Christianity. The Pentecostal movement in Africa has been classified broadly into Classical Pentecostal denominations and New Pentecostal churches. To capture all the families together in their distinct African features, Allan Anderson introduced the term "African Pentecostal Churches."[79] But the use of "Pentecostal" to distinguish some from others does not really allow such a grouping under Pentecostal churches. While some of the churches have their roots in the Azusa Street revivals of Los Angeles (USA), most are locally initiated. Like the Pentecostal churches in Latin America discussed above, local initiatives and adaptation rates are high even among those founded elsewhere. Most are truly indigenized. Among the larger groups, some—like the Assemblies of God—originated in the US, with others like Deeper Christian Life Ministry founded by Africans and spreading throughout Africa and other parts of the world. New Pentecostal churches are independent and autonomous in nature, and a number of them are classified to be "mega" churches because of the sheer size of the congregations. Beyond these two, there are trans-denominational Pentecostal fellowships whose impact is felt well beyond the Pentecostal churches themselves.

Not only are Pentecostal churches of various stripes growing in the continent, African Pentecostal churches have expanded beyond Africa. Afe Adogame classified African diaspora churches broadly into two: "those existing as branches of mother churches headquartered in Africa; and those founded by new African immigrants with headquarters in diaspora, from where they are expanding."[80] Two of Europe's largest congregations are founded and pastored by Nigerian immigrants. Embassy of the Blessed Kingdom of God for All Nations in Kieve, Ukraine, is founded and pastored by Sunday Adelaja, and Kingsway International Christian Center in London, Europe's "largest single Christian congregation" is founded and pastored by Matthew Ashimolowo.[81] While most African-initiated diaspora churches minister to African immigrants, Embassy of the Blessed Kingdom of God is different. "More than 90 percent of its 20,000 adult members [reported in 2006]...are indigenous Europeans"[82] even as its African-born pastor has struggled with strong opposition from both the Orthodox Church and the suspecting Ukrainian government.[83]

Many or most of the new independent Pentecostal and charismatic churches comprise former members of mainline or mission churches. While the mainline churches are often ridiculed as being on the losing side of this Pentecostal migration, statistics indicate they continue to grow significantly, even as they lose members to Pentecostal churches. Today, the term "Charismatic Christianity" has come to be used as a reference to a good number of these mainline Protestant and Catholic churches. The use of the term "charismatic" in Africa can be a bit confusing. Early on, the term was popularly used as a reference to the newer independent Pentecostal churches.[84] Today, the reference includes movements within the mainline Protestant and Catholic churches in line with its use elsewhere. As a Cameroonian Jesuit scholar Ludovic Lado exclaimed in the mid-1990s, "The recent proliferation of neo-Pentecostalism (or charismatic) churches in Black Africa has produced a complete reconfiguration of the landscape of African Christianity."[85]

What is called "charismatization" or "pentecostalization"[86] of mainline churches seems to have happened mainly as a result of lay members' desire and efforts. In a study on charismatic renewal in the mainline churches of Ghana, Cephas Omenyo identified such movements among Catholics, Anglicans, Presbyterians, Methodists, and Baptists.[87] A common process among Protestant mainline churches seems to be one of gradual study and adaption of their churches to the new movement. In most cases, charismatic renewal arises as a result of demands from within the church that are first cautiously observed and then gradually embraced.[88] The process in the Catholic Church is a combination of outside influence and local development. In his account of the Catholic Charismatic Renewal movement that began in Ghana in the early 1970s, Omenyo found three streams for its origin. The earliest of the three was in the participation by some Catholic youths in the Bible Study and Prayer Group, a charismatic community within the Presbyterian Church of Ghana in the mid-1960s. The second was through the participation of a Holy Spirit Sister in the renewal movement in the United States in 1971, with the third coming through a university student prayer group.[89] As in the Protestant mainline church, the Catholic Charismatic Renewal came into being, according to Omenyo, as a response to the felt need of Catholic Christians in Ghana. The experience of the United Church of Zambia seems a bit more dramatic. The heightening growth and popularity of Pentecostal-Charismatic Christianity, especially after a strong endorsement by the country's president Frederick Chiluba in the early 1990s, forced the United Church to come to terms with this movement's impact. In 1999, congregations were asked through a questionnaire about their views on charismatic worship. The outcome demonstrated that most congregations highly favored it. The Synod of the United Church of Zambia resolved to accommodate such a worship and prepared guidelines for it the same year.[90]

Not only have the worship services showed congregations' enthusiastic experience of the Holy Spirit in these charismatic churches, there are also practices of "healing and deliverance" that were previously exclusive characteristics of Pentecostal churches. The demand from people within some mainline Protestant and Catholic churches forced the adoption of such Pentecostal practices as faith healing and deliverance.[91] While many priests and pastors of Catholic and Protestant churches are flowing with the trend, some are known for their gifts and ministries. Among the Catholic, Monsignor Emmanuel Milingo, archbishop of Zambia, became an exorcist-practicing "healing and deliverance"[92] until he was removed due to opposition from other clergy in 1983. Even after he was recalled to Rome, he continued his charismatic ministries in Italy with some success.[93] And the Cameroonian Jesuit Meinrad Hegba, an African Catholic pioneer in charismatic Christianity, first experienced the phenomenon of charismatic renewal in the US and later testified to receiving the baptism of the Holy Spirit in the hands of leaders and members of the Assembly of God Church in Abidjan, Côte d'Ivoire.[94]

The story of Africa's growing Christianity is largely a story of Charismatic-Pentecostal Christianity. It is a story of a bottom-up Christian movement driven by ordinary people in the pews with a demand for an experiential spirituality that provides for their daily living needs. Although it commonly comes under the rubric of Pentecostalism, different church denominations and confessional bodies have all faced the people's demand and responded with varying degrees of adaptation or resistance. Meanwhile, the story of Christianity in Africa is larger than a display of enthusiastic religiosity. Secularization poses a serious challenge to this growing form of religiosity. Christian rationalists have resisted these forms of enthusiastic African Christianity. The tension between mainline Protestant churches and Charismatic-Pentecostal churches remains a major issue in Africa, perhaps more so than in other places. While this tension seems better accommodated in the Catholic Church, it persists there, too. Forms of rationalism—or a faith in human reasoning power—is a key to modern development in Africa and was introduced by the educational system of missionaries in the colonial period. While many so-called mission churches continue to bear witness to faith in reason and reasonableness as they have been taught, trending charismatic forms of Christianity challenge this sensibility—especially by resurrecting and resonating with the spiritual universe of primal, pre-colonial Africa. Even among many intellectuals, the hold of a faith in the power of the Spirit over other spirits appears firm. Belief in supernatural manifestations of God the Spirit, or at least its possibility, would seem near to most vital and growing forms of Christian faith in Africa.

Chapter 4

CHRISTIAN MOVEMENTS IN THE MAJORITY WORLD

Part Two:
Asia and the Pacific Islands

Asia is so diverse and complex that its different regions, cultures, and societies do not seem to share a common trait except being a part of Asia. The United Nations divides Asia into five[1] regions: Central, Southern (these two are often combined in statistical reports as South-Central[2]), Eastern, Southeastern, and Western Asia. Asia has the longest and perhaps the most complicated history with the Christian faith. Nevertheless, Christianity is a contested religion in most of Asia today. Western Asia (or the Middle East for Westerners) is the cradle of Christianity, but it has a complex mix of Christian traditions alongside some of the strongest critics of the religion in the world. Several Islamic nations in the Arabian Peninsula do not permit conversion to Christianity and do not allow Christian clergy to function in ministry within their borders.[3] Hindu nationalists fiercely oppose Christian conversion in India, and the communist policies in China, North Korea, Laos, and Vietnam have been, and continue to

63

be, a major impediment for Christian growth on the continent. With few exceptions (e.g., the Philippines), Christianity is a minority religion in most parts of Asia. The *Atlas of Global Christianity* estimates Christians in Asia to be 8.5 percent of the continent's total population.[4]

The United Nations reference of Oceania includes Australia, New Zealand, and the Pacific islands of Melanesia, Micronesia, and Polynesia. Australia and New Zealand are parts of the so-called European "new world" and have long been predominantly "Western" in culture and orientation. The history of Christianity in these two nations is to some degree an extension of Western Christianity.[5] As rich and dynamic as some of these forms of Christian mission are, we will not focus on these two nations in our survey but instead provide a brief look at Christianity in the Pacific Island regions of Melanesia, Micronesia, and Polynesia.

Both Central Asia and Western Asia, the heart of the growing Muslim world today, are also home to several Orthodox (both Chalcedonian and non-Chalcedonian) and Catholic Church families of ancient origins.[6] Christianity has been steadily declining in Western Asia. In the twentieth century alone, it decreased from 15 percent to 5 percent of the region's total population. Douglas Jacobsen notes that "roughly half of that decline can be attributed to the massacre of Armenian Christians that took place in Turkey during the early years of the twentieth century and to the mass exodus of Christians."[7] Today, scholars estimate "Middle Eastern church families" to be about 30 million; but only less than half of them, about 13 million, actually reside in the region.[8] The larger number are now living in North and South America, Australia, and Europe where they strongly maintain their church traditions and identities.

Movements to Christianity in recent times are occurring in parts of South, South-East, and Eastern Asia. These regions are the most populated areas of the world, and religiously the most diverse. In some parts of these regions, remarkable growth of Christianity is occurring while others witness significant activities or movements, even when numerical increase or change are not always conspicuous. In some countries, religious numbers are so politically sensitive that no impartial report can be expected. Political motives often prevent reporting of religious increase or decrease in some countries. Our attention to Asia will focus on those regions where Christianity is experiencing momentum and growth of varying kinds.

Eastern Asia

The twentieth century stands out as a century of dramatic changes throughout the colonial and postcolonial world. Two brutal world wars and the ideology-driven Cold War were followed by a new global consciousness and dramatic technological and economic advancement in terms of "globalization." The trauma of these changes and the brutality of the century were felt strongly in Eastern Asia. The defeat of Japan in World War II with the use of atomic weapons and the ideologically-based political division of the Korean people into North and South exemplify the pain suffered in this region.

The nations composing Eastern Asia—namely Japan, North Korea, South Korea, Mongolia, and China together with Hong Kong SAR, Macau SAR, and Taiwan ROC—share a common inheritance of Confucianism in their cultural heritage and the persistent influence of Mahayana Buddhism. As Edmond Tang has rightly pointed out, the Chinese, Japanese, and Koreans differ quite considerably in their response to modernization through Western expansion.[9] While China's struggle with modernization ranges from the xenophobic revolt of the Boxer Uprising to indigenized communism and "modernity in 'scientific socialism,'" Japan fought the West with the Western methods of market capitalism and military power to become an industrialized capitalist state. The two Korean nations share a history of imperial rule from the neighboring nations as one people and one nation. The end of World War II was the beginning of the division of Korea into North and South. The conflict between the two nations resulted in the Korean War of 1950 followed by deep tension between them. A symbolic gesture to declare an end to the war was held during an unprecedented summit between leaders of North and South Korea as recent as April 2018. While the North became communist first under Soviets' occupation in 1945 and then China's continuing influence, the South, in the words of Edmond Tang, is practically "a protectorate of the USA in all but name."[10]

Christianity reached China and possibly Japan as early as the seventh century in the form of Nestorian Christianity, but did not survive. The Catholic pioneer missionary to Asia, Francis Xavier (1549), reached Japan at the point of its political instability and had some notable success. Early Japanese Christianity, however, was wiped out in the succeeding generations, and China resisted foreign forms of Christian faith until Matteo Ricci gained limited access (1601) through his learned impression and accommodating Christian message. It took a great effort for Western power to force its way into China and Japan in the mid-nineteenth century, and Christian missions followed in the wake of this new access. After the efforts of Xavier, almost two centuries had to pass for Christianity to reach the Korean peninsula where it was first introduced through literature (1784), followed by the efforts of a Chinese priest (1795). The earliest Protestant missionary initiatives in Asia were through the Dutch Reformed Church, which sent the first missionary to present-day Taiwan in 1627.

Christianity in Japan is a story of advance and resistance since its first appearance in the sixteenth century. The Jesuits had an early success in relating Christianity to Japanese in the sixteenth and seventeenth century. But a new political climate resisted the new faith and Christianity was eventually outlawed and missionaries expelled in the early decades of the seventeenth century. After it was forced to open itself to the outside word in 1859, Western missionaries of the Catholic Church and different stripes of Protestants from Europe and North America plied their missional trade there with mixed results. Unlike the success in the sixteenth century, there has not been any major movement toward Christianity among the Japanese people. During World War II, to "facilitate [its] totalitarian control,"[11] the government forced a union of churches, and the United Church of Christ in Japan (called the Kyodan) was formed in 1941. The aftermath of the war saw a "boom" for Christianity when many people turned to church for spiritual support. Yet, the boom ended soon with rapid urbanization and secularization.[12]

About 2 percent of Japanese citizens declared themselves to be Christians in 2007 while the total number of church members of all denominations counts for just .89 percent of the country's population.[13] Forms of

Christianity that had made headway among the Japanese at the beginning of the seventeenth century—even showing some promising signs in the postwar decade—have not really advanced in terms of growth for the last two and a half centuries. Mark Mullins attributes this failure to "the difficult and complex political and religious situation" of Japanese society. The society has long established "a system of 'layered' religious obligations" that make up household Buddhism and communal Shintoism, complex and embedded forms of devotion that newer religious teachings cannot really penetrate.[14] The trend in Japan is to make nonexclusive religious commitments. This non-exclusive religious commitment is revealed clearest in the fact that Shinto dominated the birth rituals, Buddhism the rituals on death, and the "Christian Churches are becoming a significant competitor in the sacralization of weddings."[15]

If Christianity fails in numerical increase in Japan, it does not fail to impact the growing urban Japanese society. Christianity leads all other religious groups in education, sets great examples in social services, and makes a significant contribution in medical works. Though often criticized as a religion "for intellectuals," a good number of Japanese Christians are known for their missional and societal contributions. Japanese Christianity can appear at times to be dominated theologically by the Western theologies of Karl Barth, Emil Brunner, and so forth, as well as social gospel and Calvinistic evangelicalism.[16] Yet, Japanese Christianity holds its distinctive—"made in Japan," to use Mark Mullins's term[17]—character. Richard Fox Young has shown that Japan's distinct form of Christianity is best captured between the "top down" inculturation exemplified by Uchimura Kanzo's non-church movement in the Samurai tradition, and the "bottom-up" inculturation of Murai Jun's Pentecostal Spirit of Jesus Church.[18] The former is non-conformist to both the State and Western Christian tradition, and the latter deals with the ancestral question by turning "the ancestors toward Christ" with its distinctive "rite of vicarious baptism."[19]

In China, despite the government's restrictive policy on religion, Christianity is emerging as a major phenomenon since the closing decades of the twentieth century. "Christianity is now in vogue," declares Ying

Fuk-tsang as "'Christianity fever' (*jidujiao re*)"[20] is overtaking the society. This changed attitude toward Christianity (from resistance to appreciation) is sweeping Chinese society, especially among intellectuals—to the end that the official restrictive policy largely fails to hold in practice. This "Christian fever" is a part of what Tony Lambert calls total transformation, which took place in a matter of three decades.[21] The twentieth century was particularly turbulent for China as it experienced major sociopolitical reversals, with two revolutions (1911 and 1949)[22]—or three if we include the current shift from Maoism to socialist-capitalism—during this period. Different philosophies and ideologies vie for hearts and minds in China. Yang Huilan brings clarity to this contentious ideological atmosphere:

> The Confucian ethic, a historically dominating ideology in China, had been under fierce attack since 1949 and was almost exterminated during the Cultural Revolution. Socialist ideology, the other ideological pillar, has been severely questioned since the end of the Cultural Revolution.[23]

This oscillation between operative worldviews defines China's history in the twentieth century. The Christian community's experience reflects all these tumultuous changes, from being encouraged in numerical growth during the first four decades to finding their faith lives severely controlled under Maoist communism. This harsh suppression during the Cultural Revolution (1966–1976) has gradually morphed into forms of moderate control (since 1979) with a growing societal appreciation for Christian faith from many Chinese today.

With such a large and diverse nation, the changing religious landscape of China is difficult to capture. Over the years, studies are show that regional variances in religious compositions as well as differences between rural and rapidly growing urban populations need to be taken into serious consideration. Keeping such complexity in mind, we will try to create a portrait of the state of Christianity in China today. During the first half of the twentieth century, Western missionary works saw both its zenith and nadir in China. To quote Daniel H. Bays, "In the first half of the twentieth century, the foreign missionary movement in China matured, flourished, declined, and died."[24] Not only were there increases in missionaries, converts, and congregations, the indigenous and indigenized groups and churches also grew strong during that period. The True Jesus Church, the Jesus Family, and ministries and communities established around leader-preachers such as Dora Yu, Watchman Nee, Wang Mingdao, John Sung (Song Shangjie), and Marcus Ch'eng (Chen Chonggui) flourished. We mention these names as they continue to influence Chinese Christianity in the late twentieth century, both in China and around the world. For instance, the church founded by Watchman Nee and Witness Lee, came to be globalized today among the Chinese diaspora throughout Asia and around the world.[25] Everything changed for organized communities of faith with the establishment of the People's Republic of China by the Chinese Communist Party in 1949. To "purge" the "foreign [Western] imperialist influences" on the church, the new government insisted that the church be independent and patriotic. It expelled foreign missionaries and closely monitored the church's life and activities. At first, Protestants on the whole responded to the patriotic move positively, while Catholics resisted it. As time passed, strong resistance emerged among Protestants even as patriotic forms of Christianity entered the Catholic community. Until recently, Christians were sharply divided between those who submitted to the patriotic policy and control of the government (the Protestant's Three-Self Patriotic Movement and Catholic Patriotic Association [CPA]) and those who resisted it under the rubric of "house churches." With the moderation of the government's suppressive monitoring system and the growing popularity of evangelical and charismatic Christianity in both camps, tension between the two groups seems to have subsided—especially in urban churches. Following the 2005 Regulation on Religious Affairs,[26] with its provision to legalize all religious bodies,[27] tensions continue to ease between Christian groups.

The place of Christianity in China is multidimensional. First, the number of Christians actually residing among China's billion-plus people is still hidden in a cloud of controversy. The fast pace of Christianity's growth is undeniable. Nobody knows how many Christians are in China today. Counting Christians in a nation that is officially atheist cannot be neutral politically. Official statistics and estimated numbers are incredibly varied. Three different statistics published around the same time show very different numbers. The *Blue Book of Religions*[28] by the Chinese Academy of Social Science represents the official government statistics, recording the number of Christians in China as 28.75 million in 2010.[29] The *Atlas of Global Christianity*,[30] published in 2009, has the number at 115 million. The Pew Research Center placed the number around 68 million in 2010.[31] Most Christians seem to believe the number is much higher than what official statistics state, and even "conservatively," says Ying Fuk-tsang, the estimate is at least 40 million Protestants, and 12 million Catholics, and thus, a total of 52 million Christians.[32] The recovery of Christianity in China after the Cultural Revolution and the growing openness of the country to the rest of the world is celebrated by most Protestants, among whom rural quasi-Pentecostals and urban independent-evangelicals seemed to have grown the most.[33] Due to continuing internal conflicts between CPA and the "underground" Vatican loyalists, the Catholic Church has not grown as much as Protestant churches have since the 1980s.[34]

After the demise of the foreign missionary enterprise in the early 1950s, Christianity has been resurrected in quite a different form. It is Chinese Christianity in every sense, driven by Chinese Christians themselves in a distinctively Chinese spirit. To quote Lian Xi:

> Instead of bringing back to life a withered Western faith, the Chinese were fashioning a Christian faith that increasingly revealed continuities with indigenous folk religion....Like the latter, popular Christianity in both its Protestant and Catholic forms often emphasized healing, miracles, and similar abilities to harness the power of the spiritual world to the struggles of the common people.[35]

Surrounding China are territories closely related to Chinese culture(s) and history that benefit from a treatment of their particularity in the Christian mission story. These are the Special Administrative Regions of Hong Kong and Macau, and the self-administered country of Taiwan (Republic of China). Taiwan's relation with China is an issue beyond the scope of this study. While the history of Christianity in Hong Kong and Macau are closely related to the history of Christianity in China—as Hong Kong and Macau served as springboards for missions to China, the history of

Christianity in Taiwan has a longer, more complex and independent story. However, Christianity in each is influenced by the religious and political movements of mainland China. As a former Portuguese colony, Christianity in Macau is dominantly Catholic. Similarly, under British influence, Hong Kong has a relatively higher proportion of Protestant Christians. Hong Kong's status as a British colony became most conspicuous after China fell to the Communists in 1949. Refugees from China swelled to fill Hong Kong and the 1950s became a landmark period for Christianity in the former British colony. Hong Kong's population of 0.6 million in 1945 grew to "more than 2 million in the early 1950s, and more than 3 million in the early 1960s."[36] Among the refugees were many Christians and expelled missionaries as Hong Kong became a safe haven for Chinese missions and "a supermarket of denominations."[37] In 2006, there were more than 663,000 Christians, of which roughly 36 percent (or 243,000) identified as Catholic. Although Christians compose less than 10 percent of the population today, "Christianity in Hong Kong is vibrant and influential,"[38] declared Lo Lung-kwong in *Christianities in Asia*.

Formerly known as Formosa, which means "beautiful" in Portuguese, Taiwan today is dominated by Chinese who migrated to the island in different periods of China's history. The only exceptions are the indigenous people who comprises less than 2 percent of the population. Taiwan was the recipient of the earliest Protestant missions in East Asia under the Dutch regime in the seventeenth century. But the church did not survive after the collapse of Dutch rule in the 1660s.[39] The Presbyterian Church of Taiwan, originally founded by English and Canadian Presbyterian missionaries, is the main and historic Protestant church. As a result of political changes in China, Christian numbers grew rapidly in the 1950s to early 1960s.[40] While the rate of increase of the two largest bodies (Presbyterian and Catholic) has been steady, the independent churches are growing much more rapidly. The True Jesus Church, a Chinese Pentecostal group, is the second-largest Protestant church in Taiwan, followed by other Chinese mission churches: the China Protestant Baptist and the Local Church (or Little Flock) founded in China by Watchman Nee and later brought to Taiwan.[41] Other larger Protestant denominations are the Holiness Church

71

and China Free Methodist Church. Analyzing church growth between 1980 and 1990, Sha and Shen found that the most productive years were between 1986 and 1989. A growth of 44 percent through conversion (well above the 27 percent growth rate through natural/biological growth)[42] seems to mostly originate from and benefit the independent and Pentecostal churches.

Given Korea's fast pace of growth from the 1960s to the end of 1980—followed by a major world evangelistic missionary movement—Christianity in Korea at the beginning of the twenty-first century deserves special attention. Korean Christianity distinguished itself from the beginning when the first Catholic and Protestant churches formed through the efforts of native converts before the arrival of most missionaries. The Catholic community traces its beginning to 1784 with Yi Sung-Hun who was converted and baptized the previous year in China. The first Protestant church came into being in 1883 before the arrival of the first American missionaries the following year.[43] Like "a shrimp crushed in the fight of the whales,"[44] Korea has suffered the power struggles of neighboring nations for centuries. While Protestants experienced rapid growth from the 1960s to the end of the twentieth century, their growth has been plateauing or declining since the 1990s. Meanwhile Catholic Church growth has been closing the gap with Protestants since the late 1990s.

From a total number of 623,072 Korean Protestant in 1960, the demographic grew to almost 3.2 million in 1970, and to 5.86 million in 1980. A large part of the growth in the 1960s may be attributed to the Christian migration out of North Korea to South Korea following the establishment of an anti-Christian communist regime in the North. The greatest growth came between the late 1970s and the early 1980s. As Byong-suh Kim shows, the Protestant Church grew from roughly 3.75 million members in 1978 to 4.87 million in one year (1979), continuing its expansion to over 5.86 million in 1980.[45] Growth has subsided since the mid-1980s. Suspicious of Protestants' exaggeration of their numbers, Donald Baker used Gallup studies to estimate the actual growth rate.[46] He measured the declining growth rate from its peak in the early 1980s (almost 6 million) to 1.3 million in a five-year period (1984 and 1989)—with a further decline to around 1.1 million from 1989 to 1997. Meanwhile, the Gallup study estimated that Catholics grew from roughly 2 million in 1989 to 3.4 million in 1997, a growth of 1.4 million in the same eight years.

Various things account for the growth of Protestant churches in Korea. While conservatives tend to emphasize the strategic and spiritual dimensions of evangelism,[47] intellectuals and liberal scholars have identified sociopolitical factors. Much of the discussion may be summed up under three dominant and contributing factors. First, Protestant Christianity came to be identified closely with the Korean people through indigenization and leadership formation. Second, the charismatic nature of Korean Christianity from its early period seems to match the culture and ethos of the people.[48] Third, the evangelistic zeal of Korean Christians from the very beginning resulted in growth. The indigenous dimension of this growing faith community becomes clearer when Korean Protestant Christianity is compared with the Catholic Church in Korea. The choice of the term for God by Protestants was *Hananim*, which they claimed to be an indigenous term for "One God," whereas the Catholics have used a Sino-Korean *Ch'ŏnju* or "Lord of Heaven."[49] The so-called Nevius Method of mission[50] used by the Protestants was built on the indigenous church theory that aimed at establishing a self-supporting, self-propagating, and self-governing church. The method helped to implant first and foremost an evangelistic zeal among early converts. The Korean Protestant Church also had highly esteemed charismatic leaders from the beginning, including Gil Sunjoo (1869–1935), Kim Ikdu (1874–1950), and revivalist Yi Yongdo (1900–1933).[51] The use of Korean language for worship, especially for communal prayer and singing, contrasted with the Catholic use of Latin for the Mass (until recently), and was another significant factor in identifying Christianity with the indigenous realities of the Korean people. The Protestants' use and promotion of modern education and medicine was also a key factor in early missional successes. In addition, the experience of revival from an early period tied the new religion to the ethos of the people by building on the indigenous spiritual worldview.

As we will discuss in a later chapter, Korean Protestant evangelistic zeal has moved many homegrown missionaries into the wider world as the churches continue to invest heavily in global evangelistic missions. Meanwhile, the stagnating growth of Protestant churches at home in Korea seems to be taking its toll on this formerly vibrant missionary movement. An alarming missionary attrition rate reported in 2015 is by some accounts due to "the overall decline of churches in Korea, which represents a waning support base."[52]

Southeast Asia

When it comes to religious diversity, the ten nations comprising Southeast Asia may together constitute the most diverse region in the world. From Christian-majority regions of the Philippines and East Timor to Buddhism-dominated Thailand and Myanmar, from the Islam-dominated Malaysia and Indonesia, to atheistic communism of Laos and Cambodia, the region combines a variety of beliefs, including the extremes. The influence of various foreign powers and cultures including Indian, Chinese, Arabian, and European have left deep impressions in the region.[53] One must note that all dominant religions in the region that have also deeply influenced the art and cultures of Southeast Asians including Buddhism, Hinduism, Islam, and Daoism are foreign religions brought to the region. In addition to a general overview of the region, our attention will be focused on nations where more or less significant Christian movements are identifiable.

United as one nation until 1965 when the two separated, Malaysia and Singapore can appropriately be treated together, though they can be contrasted in several ways. Christians in Malaysia live "circumscribed" under a Muslim-led government[54] and a number of states have laws protecting Muslims from incursions by other religions. Singapore Christians on the other hand face a strong secular ideology. Singapore has pioneered economic success in the region and other nearby nations including Malaysia are following suit. Tension between Chinese and Indian migrants, on the one hand, and Malays who consider themselves indigenous (*Bumiputras*) on the other, largely influences the sociopolitical lives of the two nations, especially those living in Malaysia. Christian missions began as early as the colonization of the peninsula, first by the Portuguese and then the

Dutch. Missionary engagements were heightened from the beginning of the twentieth century when more confessional bodies and churches came to ply their missional trade in the region. Today, religious affiliations are largely based on ethnicity. To be a Malay is almost synonymous with being a Muslim while Chinese are mostly Buddhists or Taoists, and Indians Hindus. Most Christians in West Malaysia and Singapore are either Chinese or Indians. The majority of Malaysian Christians, about two-thirds, reside in the east Malaysian states of Sabah and Sarawak where Christians comprise a mix between indigenous people, Chinese, and some Indians.[55]

When it comes to religion, Singapore is "one of the strongholds of Christianity" in Asia, says Robbie Goh.[56] Christianity in Singapore grew by 14.6 percent in 2000 to 18.3 percent in 2010.[57] Malaysia's census report[58] shows no notable increase of Christians (9.2 percent of the population) in the same period. Churches are also growing in parts of East Malaysia, especially among independent tribal churches. Churches that have grown exponentially in the two nations are new, independent, evangelical, and charismatic-leaning churches.[59] The strength of Singaporean Christianity lies in its active and strategic missional roles. Because of the large proportion of missionaries sent out, some now call Singapore the "Antioch of Asia."[60] A report made in 2000 shows that Singapore sent out more than seven hundred missionaries. It also houses numerous international Christian organizations and mission agencies.[61] Robbie Goh suggests that sociopolitical factors account for the outward missionary investments of Malaysian and Singaporean Christians. Because domestic evangelistic activities are "circumscribed" by the Muslim-led government in Malaysia[62] and the "tightly-governed socio-political climate" of Singapore,[63] churches in the two nations naturally focus their energies outward on missions and evangelism.

Indonesia has the largest Muslim community (*umma*) in the world and the Christian community may also comprise the largest in a Muslim-dominated country.[64] Demographic and linguistic diversities have made it difficult to characterize the country religiously, and the immense diversity is also reflected in the proliferation of Christian groups into many (some 250) denominations including many ethnic subgroup denominations.[65] With approximately 70 percent of the Christian community, Lutheran and Reformed Protestant churches dominate Christianity in Indonesia. Catholics are active but relatively smaller in numbers. Christians are concentrated in varying minority-ethnic groups on different islands. While most of the central islands, including the most-populated island, Java, are predominantly Muslim, Christians are dominant in the northern Sumatra area of western Indonesia, and the east and northeast islands including Moluccas, northern Sulawesi, and the "Christian heartlands" of East Nusa Tenggara.[66] There have been mass conversions among these groups. The best-known story is that of the Bataks in Northern Sumatra. From the killing and supposed eating of the flesh of missionaries to the indigenous embrace of Christianity en masse, the Batak Christian story has marveled the Christian world.[67] Not only have the Bataks embraced Christianity and established strong churches, they have also actively contributed to the spread of Christianity.[68]

Indonesia is officially a secular democratic country on the basis of the political philosophy called Pancasila (Javanese for "five principles"),[69] which include the belief in "the one and only God." Muslim-dominated Indonesia is strongly influenced by Islamic principles. The Indonesian state recognizes six religions: Islam (composing 87.2 percent of the population), Protestantism (6.9 percent), Catholicism (2.9 percent), Hinduism (1.7 percent), Buddhism (0.7 percent), and Confucianism (0.05 percent).[70] Analysts are not convinced of these official census numbers. Robbie Goh opines the number to be closer to 80 percent for Muslims and 13 to 14 percent for Christians.[71]

Even as we continue to read phrases like "There is only one predominantly Christian country in all of Asia," that is, the Philippines,[72] or "The Philippines...the only Christian nation in Asia,"[73] East Timor (*Timor Leste*) emerged recently as the other predominantly Christian nation in East Asia. Both nations became dominantly Catholic as a result of centuries of colonization by Spain (the Philippines) and Portugal (East Timor). Because of the vast difference in population, just over 100 million in the Philippines[74] and less than 2 million in East Timor, clearly they are not of equal numerical significance.

The island of Timor in the Indonesian archipelago was colonized by the Portuguese in the third quarter of the sixteenth century. It became divided between the Dutch (West Timor) and Portuguese (East Timor) in 1859. The west later became a part of Indonesia and the east continued to be colonized by Portugal until 1975 when East Timor declared independence. Indonesia immediately invaded and annexed the region leading to conflict and war in which as many as 250,000 people are reported to have been killed. Following the 1999 UN-sponsored referendum, Timor-Leste became an independent nation on May 20, 2002.[75] While the World Bank report of 2005 showed 98 percent in East Timor to be Catholic, the Association of Religion Data Archive shows that 85.5 percent of the 1.15 million East Timorese identified as Christians in 2010.[76]

During its 375 years of colonial rule under Spain, the Philippines became almost exclusively Catholic. Christianization of the Philippines is said to have been completed in less than fifty years. "By the first decade of the seventeenth century," wrote Lorenzo Bautista, "most of the natives were baptized Catholics."[77] One unintended outcome of the positive response by the indigenous peoples, according to José Mario Francisco, is that they vernacularized Christianity and appropriated it for their own. This is a common occurrence when people convert en masse to a new religion. "Though missionaries took great care in transplanting Spanish Catholicism... the native asserted itself and similarly shaped this Catholicism," declared José Mario C. Francisco.[78] After the country was ceded to the United States of America following the Spanish-American War of 1898, Protestants jumped in to "Christianize"[79] the Filipino Catholics through their civilizing missions. Like the Catholics before them, Protestant missions' insensitivity to the strong nationalist sentiments of native Christians also led to schism. Nationalist sentiments connected to a deep religiosity produced dissatisfaction with colonial churches and produced such church movements as the Philippine Independent Church (Aglipayan Church), Iglesia ni Cristo (or Church of Christ), and Evangelical Methodist Church of the Philippines.

By the 1960s, churches in the Philippines converged under the banner of three or four main groups. After Vatican II, the Catholic Church experienced revitalization in the Philippines. Dispersed between socially active liberationist groups and conservative-charismatic Catholics, the Catholic Church remains strong and intact. Some Protestant mainline churches joined together in 1948 and formed the United Church of Christ in the Philippines (UCCP), which played an important role in the formation of the National Council of Churches in the Philippines (NCCP) in 1963. Conservative evangelical Protestants later formed the Philippine Council of Evangelical Churches (PCEC) in 1969. Independent churches such as Iglesia Ni Cristo and Aglipayan Church are popular and strong. Iglesia ni Cristo is the third-largest Christian group in the nation, exceeded in size only by the Catholic Church and the PCEC. A good number of Filipino Catholic theologians in the post–Vatican II atmosphere became more and more socially engaged finding their spiritual alliance in the progressive NCCP. Influenced by Latin American liberation theology, a "theology of the struggle" became the hallmark of Filipino liberation theology.[80] The contrast between NCCP and PCEC is demonstrated by the UCCP's call for a "moratorium" on new missionaries in 1974 while members of PCEC are "most hospitable to foreign missions," and are known for prioritizing evangelization and church planting.[81]

Charismatic Christianity of different stripes (including Catholics), certain evangelical Protestants, and Pentecostals, make up some of the strongest, most vital Christian communities in the Philippines. While most older Pentecostals are affiliated with the PCEC, newer Pentecostal churches are characterized by congregational independence. The two largest church members of PCEC in the 1960s were both Pentecostal churches (Assemblies of God and the Church of the Foursquare Gospel). But newer, large Pentecostal churches like Jesus is Lord and Bread of Life remain independent and have formed a new body called the Philippines for Jesus Movement.[82] Charismatic movements within the Catholic Church itself are quite strong. In fact, Francisco claims that "the charismatic phenomenon in the Philippines is predominantly Catholic."[83] Two prominent Catholic charismatic groups are "Couples for Christ," which pursues church renewal through families, and "El Shaddai" led by popular preacher Mariano "Mike" Velarde.

According to the Philippine Statistics Authority, the total population of the country crossed the 100-million mark in August 2015.[84] The 2010 numbers from the Statistics Authority show the top seven religious groups in the order of their numerical strength as follows:[85]

Ranking	Religion/Church	Total	Percentage (Approx.)
1.	Roman Catholic	74,211,896	80.58
2.	Islam	5,127,084	5.57
3.	Evangelicals (PCEC)	2,469,957	2.68
4.	Iglesia ni Cristo	2,251,941	2.45
5.	Other Religious Affiliation[86]	1,452,093	1.58
6.	Non-Catholic Protestant (NCCP)	1,071,686	1.16
7.	Aglipay	916,639	1.00

Earlier census reports show Catholic communities grew from 78.8 percent of the population in 1939, to 83.8 percent in 1960, and 85 percent in 1980, while older mainline Protestant communities have been in steady decline.[87]

Among the remaining nations of Southeast Asia, Christianity has a relatively strong presence in Myanmar (or Burma) and the Nation of Brunei. Christians in the Nation of Brunei are almost exclusively migrants, and their ministries are strictly circumscribed. As an Islamic state, Brunei prohibits evangelization.[88] In the changing political circumstances of Myanmar, on the other hand, Christians are active and growing. Although Christian faith has not significantly impacted the dominant Burmese population whose long-held Theravada Buddhism guided the nation for centuries, Christianity is the dominant religion among several ethnic groups—Karen (Kayah), Chin, and Kachin. The latest census report (2014) shows a stunning increase of Christians in Myanmar. From 4.9 percent of the population in 1983, the number of Christians has increased to 6.3 percent in 2014.[89]

Christians in Myanmar have suffered under a cold and constrictive government as well as the domination of the Buddhist majority. At its independence from British rule in 1948, Burma (now Myanmar) chose Buddhism as the state religion, which drew strong opposition, even in-surrectionist resistance from minority groups. After the military coup in 1962, the military ruling leader General Ne Win declared Burma to be a socialist nation isolating the country by its "Burmese Way of Socialism." Buddhism, however, enjoyed a privileged position under the military government while all Christian missionaries were ordered to leave the country in 1964.[90] By 1966, all foreign missionaries had left Burma/Myanmar. Ending the military rule by a landslide election victory of the National League for Democracy led by Nobel laureate Aung San Suu Kyi in November 2015, the first civilian government following more than five decades of military dictatorship was sworn into office on March 30, 2016. Myanmar is looking into a future of hope. What this means for Christians and the growth of Christianity in Myanmar is to be seen.[91]

Perhaps assisted by the political isolation of the nation, the Chin, Kachin, and Karen Christians have made Christianity as Burmese as any other Burmese religions.[92] Lian H. Sakhong has shown how Chin Christianity, like its kin Mizo counterpart on the Indian side, has rooted itself "in the socio-cultural tradition of the people."[93] According to Kachin scholar La Seng Dingrin, it was the assimilation of Christianity to the Kachin culture through translational processes largely using indigenous animistic religious concepts that a distinctively Kachin Christianity came into being.[94] In a study on the nineteenth-century interaction between American missionaries and an emerging form of Asian Christianity, Jay Riley Case made a similar case among the Karens that Karen Christianity exemplified a translated Christianity even challenging forms of American Missionary Christianity.[95]

The Pacific Islands

Before we turn to South Asia, it seems most appropriate to deal with Christianity in the islands of the South Pacific. In today's geopolitical categorization, the area is outside of Asia. It is a part of an area now named Oceania by the United Nations. As we survey vital Christian movements in the majority world, our interest lies in the spiritually vibrant Christian movements in the islands grouped under the three regions of Polynesia, Micronesia, and Melanesia. As mentioned above, dominant forms of Western Christianity in Australia and New Zealand are outside the purview of our discussion. Polynesia covers islands of the entire eastern section from Hawaii in the north to New Zealand in the south. Micronesia is in the northwestern section of the Pacific and borders the Philippine islands in the west, and Melanesia lies in the southwestern part bordering Indonesia in the west. By the beginning of the twenty-first century, all these island groups are predominantly Christian.

As an area, these islands may have the longest history of missionary works in the modern period, especially among Protestants. While several islands in Polynesia received some of the first missionaries of the modern Protestant missionary movement in the 1790s, other missional efforts had not begun until the close of the missionary movement in the 1960s on some islands of New Guinea in what is now called Melanesia. In other words, Protestant missionary work in these islands spanned from the beginning of the modern missionary movement until the end of the movement. As Ruth Tipton stated in her study of missionary works among the Nembi and Melpa people of Papua New Guinea, "One of the last areas of the world to be touched by Christianity was the South Pacific, and the Gospel did not reach some of the people living in the mountainous interior of the island of New Guinea until the 1960s and 1970s."[96] Yet, Protestant Christian missions in Polynesia can be claimed to be as old as the modern Protestant missionary movement itself. From the very beginning of the modern Protestant missionary movement in the 1790s, missionaries representing the London Missionary Society were already stationed in Tonga, Tahiti, and the Marquesas.[97] Success stories of Protestant missions may have come first from these islands. After initial hardships cost several missionary lives, the conversion of Tahitian chiefs led to the embrace of Christianity by most Tahitians. Similarly, with the conversion of Tongan chief Taufaahau under the Methodist missionary endeavor, the whole Tongan group had embraced Christianity by the 1830s.[98] Catholic missionary efforts, especially those by the Marists, also enjoyed success.

What missionary historian Stephen Neill calls a "less eventful history" of Christian mission in Samoa is particularly interesting for us today in connection with the story of world Christianity. The first entry of Christianity to Samoa may have been through a Samoan convert who was introduced to the Christian faith in Tonga, according to Neill. A visit by a missionary from Tahiti later, and the work of eight Tahitian teachers who were "left behind" by the missionary, bore fruit. "When the first European missionaries came to reside," continued Neill, "they found a Christian community of some 2,000 already in existence."[99] The work of these early converts in the evangelization of the islands was significant. Conversion to Christianity became a people's movement and Christianity was incorporated into the people's communal life. By the close of the nineteenth century, to be Tahitian or Tongan *was* to be a Christian.

By the beginning of the twentieth century, virtually all the people of Polynesia and a large part of Micronesia (three-fourth of the region's population) identified as Christian. Melanesia, which has the largest islands and population, was the least evangelized with just about 15.4 percent of the population embracing Christianity by 1910.[100] Missionary works continued on in Melanesia largely "built on the successes in Polynesia" utilizing Polynesian Christians as missionaries.[101] Displaying much greater diversity than Polynesia and Micronesia, Melanesia has some twelve hundred different languages and the societies were much more fragmented. Some missionaries noted the distinctly pragmatic mentality and communal characters of Melanesians. One major common characteristic of Christianity in most of the southern Pacific relates to the communal nature of indigenous people and the way Christianity has largely been incorporated into the local culture. From the so-called "cargo cult" to the "big men" leadership of communities, incorporation of Christianity into native cultures also yielded distinctively localized Christian characters. The communal characters of Christianity have also made denominational and confessional bodies prone to tensions and conflicts. As Ben Liua'ana relates, conflicts between Protestants and Catholics, the older churches (both Catholics and Protestant), and New Religious Groups is a common feature in the history of the churches in Melanesia.

Among the "issues facing Pacific Christianity" in the first decade of the twenty-first century, according to Ben Liua'ana, the challenge presented by New Religious Groups (NRG) is most dominant.[102] Sione Latukefu describes the rise of new religious movements in the Pacific region after World War II as an "invasion."[103] For stable, established churches closely identified with the communities for many years, the arrival of other Christian groups who are both active and attractive can be upsetting. In his study of the New Religious Groups in the Pacific Islands in the early 1990s, Manfred Ernst categorized NRGs into three groups: "established NRGs," "The most recent arrivals," and "Breakaways" from historic mainline and NRGs. The first group is the largest with about 14.6 percent of the population. It includes Seventh-Day Adventists, Mormons, Jehovah's Witnesses, Assemblies of God, and different evangelical groups. "The most recent arrivals" consists mainly of Pentecostals and charismatics and account only for 1 percent, with the "breakaways" making up about 2 percent of NRGs.[104] From this,[105] one can conclude that the dominant NRG was a combination of Seventh-Day Adventists, Latter-Day Saints, and Jehovah's Witnesses, who together made up just about half of the NRGs. About fifteen to twenty years later, observers recognize and note the dominance of Pentecostals and charismatics. In his study published in 2009, Liua'ana reported that Pentecostal and charismatic churches were the most challenging NRGs[106] (to traditional forms of Christianity), especially as they account for the largest increase in Melanesia in the twentieth century.[107]

South Asia

Within the region designated as South Asia by the United Nations, Christian movements are most identifiable in India, Nepal, Sri Lanka, and Pakistan. Because of their close historical connections with India, the story of Christianity in the other nations, especially Pakistan and Nepal, can best be narrated along with the story in India.

India has a rich, long, and uninterrupted history of Christianity, and broad generalizations serve to summarize the story. Contemporary Christian communities can be categorized according to their origins. First came the ancient St. Thomas (Syrian) Christians[108] whose tradition claims its origin in the first century. The second group is the Catholic Church, which began with the European maritime route discoveries to Asia at the end of the fifteenth century and the subsequent establishment of colonies. Vasco da Gama's landing in western India made India the first major recipient of modern Catholic missions in Asia. India also became the first sphere of Protestant missions in the east with the arrival of Bartholomew Ziegenbalg and Henry Plütschau in Tranquebar, along the coast in southern India. Enforced by William Carey's led missions in North India, through which Protestant missions as a modern movement unfolded, the Protestant mission became the third main Christian initiative in India. The fourth is an outcome of, yet nonetheless distinct from, the third, namely the dalit and tribal movements to Christianity. The name "dalit" is of recent origin as a reference to the people variously called "outcastes" (in reference to the traditional Hindu caste society) or "untouchables" as they were considered impure by Hindus. Historians have used other terms such as "depressed class" in the past. The name "tribal" adopted from the British rule refers generally to those Indians who lived in isolation from the Hindu majority and did not have contact (or regular contact) with the majority Hindus. The fifth group, Pentecostal and charismatic Christians, grew out of the first three, and is closely related to the fourth. It has a loose membership and freely connects with various Christian communities, yet is not unified in a singular church or tradition. There was one major phenomenon recognizable across some of these Christian groups, impacting them in one way or another. This is unfortunately (and inadequately) denoted by the misleading term "mass movements." More than half of Catholic Christians and as many as 70 percent of Protestants in India today trace their origin to these so-called mass movements toward Christianity.

For various reasons, it is not easy to determine a precise number of Indian Christians. According to the government census of 2011, the Christian population in India is a little over 27.8 million, which, out of the total

Indian population of 1.21 billion, counts slightly below 2.3 percent.[109] Other estimations consider this census number of Christians to be incredibly low. The *World Christian Encyclopedia* calculated the Indian Christians to be more than 62 million in 2000 (eleven years before the census report), which was 6.2 percent of the population at that time.[110] This is unjustifiably high. Ten years later, the *Atlas of Global Christianity* enumerated Christians in India to be 58.3 million, which was about 4.8 percent of the population.[111] In between these attempts to gather data came a statistic-guided prayer book, *Operation World*, which lists the percent of Indian Christians at 5.84 percent of the total population in 2010. Because many who claim to be Christian have also reported themselves as Hindus (for a variety of reasons), and a significant number adhere to forms of Christian faith yet identify as (or claim to be) Hindu, the line of identification for enumeration can be very unclear. Calculating the number of religious by tradition in general and reporting conversion/religious change in particular are very sensitive political issues in India. Thus, a wide gulf between what Christians tend to estimate and what official census enumerators report is not unexpected.

Among the different denominations in India, the Catholic Church appears to have the most reliable data. According to *The Catholic Directory of India 2013*, there are more than 17.5 million Catholics in India.[112] Based on the information that Catholics in India comprise slightly more than half of the Indian Christian population,[113] one can surmise the Indian Christian population to have been not less than 34 million in 2013. The charismatic movement within the Catholic Church in India is strong. Allan Anderson suggests the number to be as high as 5 million.[114] Pentecostalism, considered to be the fastest-growing Christian movement in the world at the end of the twentieth century, has a long history in India. Beginning with converts out of the Thomas (Syrian) Orthodox Church in the 1920s, Pentecostal preachers and leaders from Kerala and neighboring states initiated the diffusion of Pentecostalism in different parts of India. Today, as many as 25 percent of Protestants in south India are estimated to be Pentecostals.[115] However, the chance of double-counting is high as many active Pentecostals also maintain their membership in other churches.

In the religiously charged nations of South Asia, made up of a multitude of culturally autonomous communities, religious change or conversion from one religion to another has been a contentious issue. Insofar as Christian missions aim at making new Christians through the propagation of Christian teaching, missions efforts have been disliked by various leaders of non-Christian religions in India. Even an iconic personality and symbol of nonviolence, Mahatma Gandhi, was embroiled in the controversy of Christian conversions in India.[116] Within the first decade of India's independence, Christian missionary visas were restricted,[117] and a mistrustful major inquiry on missionary activities was conducted in Madhya Pradesh by the state.[118] As Manohar James has recently shown, the conclusions and recommendation of that "inquiry" have become the basis of the anti-Christian and anti-conversion propaganda of radical Hindu nationalists in the subsequent period.[119] The 1960s show the beginning of states enacting what Christians called "anti-conversion laws" under the guise of "freedom of religion acts," first in Orissa and Madhya Pradesh. The controversy intensified in the 1990s and continued well into the twenty-first century as more states have adopted and continue to adopt the law.

The contention against conversion is closely associated with the intellectual disapproval of "mass movements" to Christianity among the Dalit and tribal communities. The very idea of mass conversion seems to have created doubts about their authenticity. One of the most vocal and influential critics was India's influential leader Mahatma Gandhi. He once stated, "I do maintain that the vast mass of Harijans [his term for Dalits or the untouchable outcastes] . . . cannot understand the presentation of Christianity, and that generally speaking their conversion wherever it has taken place has not been a spiritual act in any sense of the term. They are conversion for convenience."[120] Such disdain like that expressed by Gandhi is contested and dismissed by most Christian scholars today. They conclude that Dalit and tribal conversions were as genuine as any conversion to Christianity.[121] In a monumental empirical study of the so-called mass movements, J. Waskom Pickett found that more than one-third (34.8 percent) claim their conversion to be of "Spiritual Motives"; about the same number (34.7 percent) acknowledged "Natal Influences" in their conversions, and only 8.1 percent showed "Secular Motives."[122]

A large portion of Christians in Pakistan are products of the same "mass movements" that occurred in India, with converts settling in Christian villages and Christian *bastis* (ghettos) in urban areas. As a minority (Christianity composes only 1.6 percent of the population) in this Islamic state, Pakistani Christian communities have been maintaining their strength in relatively isolated conditions. After the military coup under General Zia-ul-Haq in 1977, supported by Saudi Arabia and the United States, Pakistan has been further Islamized, adding to the marginalization of minorities (including Christians) from the broader society.[123] Increasingly, Christians in Pakistan have been targeted by radical Muslim groups and the Taliban. Miserable stories of Christian suffering in Pakistan have come to light in recent years.[124] In response to the Taliban Easter Sunday suicide attack of 2014, which killed scores of Christians, some expressed that "it feels like a crime to be Christian in Pakistan."[125]

Until the king of Nepal relinquished power in 2006, thus allowing the kingdom to eventually become a secular state, Nepal was a Hindu state. Strict Hindu rule seems to have arisen in the second half of the eighteenth century, and the monarchical constitution in 1962 declared Nepal to be a Hindu kingdom.[126] Accounting for this change, some suspect the influence of Hindu Nationalism in India.[127] The new constitution of the kingdom banned religious conversion: "Those who changed their religion and [those who] attempted to convert or baptize" others "were subjected to imprisonment."[128] An absolute monarchy prevailed until 1990 when the people's movement ("Jan Andolan") forced the king to begin the process of instituting a democratic form of governance. This was followed by political struggles between the monarchy, on the one hand, and Maoist rebels who began violent campaigns from the mid-1990s and the new political parties, on the other. The democracy movement continued its pressure on the king to relinquish sovereign power and make Nepal a secular state in 2008.

As recently as the 1990s, Christian missions were strictly curtailed. Only very few missions for social services were officially permitted. So Christianity essentially entered Nepal through Nepali diaspora communities. As Cindy Perry has shown in her voluminous well-researched study,[129] from the Nepali-dominated Darjeeling district of India's north Bengal and Sikkim to the various Christian-dominated states of Northeast India and some parts of North India, Nepali Christian communities sprang up. These new Nepali Christians became evangelists and church planters in Nepal. As the country became more and more open, Nepali Christian expatriate missionaries and evangelists were joined by other missionaries. From about fifty Christians in 1950, the Christian community grew to more than 100,000 in 2001 according to the official national census report. This represents 0.45 percent of the national population. According to a Nepali Christian scholar and leader, Bal Krishna Sharma, Nepali Christians doubted this number and some estimated the total Christian population to be closer to 400,000.[130] The 2011 national census report shows that of the roughly 26.5 million people in Nepal, there were 375,699 Christians, around 1.42 percent.[131] Compared to efforts by Christian statisticians, this is also remarkably low. A statistical-guided prayer book, *Operation World* estimated there were more than 850,000 Nepali Christians in Nepal in 2010, representing 2.85 percent of the total population. And the *Atlas of Global Christianity*, which identified Nepal to have the third-fastest growing number of Christian converts of any nation in 2010,[132] indicated the number of Christians to be more than 900,000 persons.[133] Although strikingly lower than the Christian estimation, the national census report shows a tremendous increase in the Christian population. According to *Operation World*, most Christians in Nepal are evangelicals, and a large portion (more than 72 percent) are charismatics, a good portion of which (roughly 28 percent) are Pentecostals.[134] Indeed, the Pentecostals were among the earliest to enter Nepal in 1951, and have contributed considerably to the growth of Christianity there.[135]

Like Pakistan and Bangladesh, Sri Lanka was a part of India until it became independent in 1948. Christianity's history in Sri Lanka is closely tied to changing colonial rule from the Portuguese (from 1505) to the Dutch (from 1602) and then to the British (from 1796; the British overtook the entire island in 1815). The Portuguese introduced Roman Catholicism and the Dutch brought Reformed Christianity. The harsh reactions against Catholicism by the Dutch ceased when the British took over the island and promoted freedom of religion. Other Protestant missions including the British Baptists, Wesleyan Methodists, American Congregationalists (American Board), Anglicans (Church Missionary Society), with Lutherans coming on board in the first three decades of the nineteenth century. Despite Dutch harassment and persecution and other Protestant colonial rule, the Catholic Church has grown to become the dominant Christian group. Sri Lanka has a significant history of Pentecostalism with the arrival of the Assemblies of God in 1914 and the founding of an indigenous Ceylon Pentecostal Mission in 1923—a group who broke away from the Assemblies of God.

Christianity as a minority of less than 8 percent came to face a hostile environment, especially since the 1980s. The rise of Buddhist nationalism combining anti-colonialism with a strong resistance to missional Christianity intensified efforts to suppress efforts to suppress evangelism in Sri Lanka. In 2004, nationalist Buddhist monks entered electoral politics under one political party. Although the party did not win many seats, it greatly influenced anti-conversion sentiments by introducing a bill to the Parliament that sought to curtail proselytizing efforts.[136] The bloody civil war between the government backed by the Sinhala majority and the minority Tamils ended in 2009 leaving a major vacuum for Hindu and Christian minorities. The 2012 national census shows that 70 percent of the population identify as Buddhist. Christians of all confessions comprise about 7.6 percent of the population. Of the 1.55 million Christians, more than 1.2 million are Catholics.[137] Christians of different theological persuasions have different views on the role of Christianity in Sri Lanka. G. P. V. Somratna of Colombo Theological Seminary opined that it was the lack of evangelism that led to the decline of Christian growth in the 1960s. He lauded the growth of evangelistic ministries after 1970 and saw its impact from the 1980s as "new evangelical missions emerged in all parts of the country."[138] The Jesuit Provincial of Sri Lanka, Jeyaraj Rasiah, on the other hand, blamed globalization, which aided "fundamentalist Christian groups" after 1977, for strengthening "mistrust and suspicions" against Christians and for fanning the flames of Buddhist nationalism.[139] The two appear to be referring to the same evangelistic phenomenon.

Chapter 5

CONTEXTUALIZATION, CONTEXTUAL THEOLOGY, AND GLOBAL CHRISTIANITY

When Christianity becomes the religion of people of different ethnicities, cultures, and regions (amid differing worldviews, each with its own ethos), how does a people/group make faith practices distinctly their own while allowing others to do the same? How does Christianity hold these different groups together amid their differences? Christian history teaches that this was never an easy lesson, yet the faithful learned and practiced a form of unity in difference. Christian faith is founded in part on the teaching that God's message of salvation in Jesus Christ is meant for *all* creation, and that the one God of Christian faith is God of *all*. It is addressed to *all* people, and calls *everyone* to God's transforming grace.

The universal nature or catholicity of the Christian faith requires means to access and understand the faith by people of all times, all cultures, and in all places of the world. Thus dissemination and meaningful communication of the faith are essential. As people of different societies, nations, and continents came to embrace Christian faith, they discovered that Christian teaching or theology bears within itself a way for all to possess the faith as distinctly their own (indigenous) and as a shared reality with others. For the earliest Christians, this is the work of the Holy Spirit (Acts 15:8-9).

Christian faith is not passed down from heaven, but passed from one to the other (Rom 10:5-17), and is thus a missionary faith. It is the common faith that connects and binds people of different times and communities of differing cultures. Christianity does not become worldwide by static enforcement of the teaching, but by the incarnational dynamism of the gospel it teaches. As Christianity became a worldwide phenomenon, Christians came to discern the dynamics of a faith strong enough to hold people of all cultures and nations together. In a way, this chapter is concerned with the realization of the gospel's dynamism in history as it is shared and owned by people of different cultures, nations, and continents. In other words, Christianity does not become worldwide in a "colourless uniformity," but in a manifold and diverse theology that corresponds to different contexts.[1] The various theological perspectives that represent different confessions, regions, cultures, and societies make up the world of Christian theology. The history of Christianity's expansion shows that authentic Christian faith maintains its life throughout its history by being adopted, indigenized, and contextualized. Our attention in this chapter focuses on the contextualizing dynamics of the Christian faith in history.

Contextualization—the Concept

The ugly neologism "contextualization"[2] was coined and introduced by an ecumenical organization for theological education in the non-Western world called Theological Education Fund (TEF).[3] The TEF used the term as the overarching theme of its third decadal mandate in 1972. The mandate of the previous decade was "indigenization," calling the Christian faith to be rooted in the culture of the people. Shoki Coe, a Taiwanese theologian and the chief architect of contextualization in the TEF explained the intention being "to convey all that is implied in the familiar term *indigenization*, yet seek to press beyond for a more dynamic concept which is open to change and which is also future-oriented."[4] If theology and missiology are to be distinguished based on their emphases and orientations, contextualization was first founded on missiology's field of cross-cultural communication. Missionary efforts to communicate the gospel meaningfully to people of different cultures led to various theoretical models such as accommodation, indigenization or autochthonization (being aboriginal), acculturation or inculturation.[5] The two terms indigenization and inculturation call for the integration of the gospel with local cultures, and they were employed distinctly and popularly by Protestants (indigenization) and Catholics (inculturation) from the 1960s. While still holding it as a "missiological necessity," TEF found indigenization to be "past-oriented" as it was associated with "traditional culture."[6] This is not to say that indigenous theologies failed to incorporate social and political changes then,[7] but only that the traditionalizing tendency inhibited theologians of the time—and contextualization became the way out.

In the postcolonial period of the non-Western world, a period characterized by revolutionary changes, the new dominantly "Third World" leadership[10] of TEF adopted contextualization for its promise to dynamically relate the gospel to both traditional cultures and the changing sociopolitical realities in the world. The holistic intention of the concept was difficult to comprehensively uphold and contextualization eventually came to mean different things to different people. As we will see, some use the concept within the narrow confines of cross-cultural communication of the gospel. For others, it signifies the liberative dimension of the gospel in relation to oppressive sociopolitical structures. Some of the uses of the term seem to defy the intention of the TEF to move away from the narrower notion of indigenization. A popular American missiologist and anthropologist, Paul Hiebert, for instance, used contextualization to relate the gospel "to the old culture."[11]

The inner dynamism of the concept has made it impossible to restrain contextualization in the way it was first introduced, or to confine it within the limits of missiology as it spread out into other realms of the theological enterprise. In the field of theological studies, it became a creative perspectival and conceptual tool. In biblical studies, the concept is applied to understand the life-setting or context of the stories of the Bible, relating the message meaningfully to the present-day reader. In addition to relating the gospel with culture, tradition, and sociopolitical changes, contextualization also came to name the fact that every interpretation is influenced and somewhat limited by its context. Lesslie Newbigin said this understanding distinguished contextualization from earlier discussions under such terms as "accommodation," "adaptation," and "indigenization." He stated that these other terms "sometimes seemed to imply that what the missionary brought with him [or her] was the pure, un-adapted gospel, and that 'adaptation' was thus a kind of concession to those who had not the advantage of having a Christian culture. But of course the truth is that every communication of the gospel is already culturally conditioned."[12] In other words, contextualization discloses the crucial role played by contexts in any genuine theological construction, communication, and reception. Today, any serious theologian understands the inevitable influence of, and limitation by, his or her context in any theological reflection.

Reviewing the discussions over the past decades, two parallel trends are discernible. One is a move toward doing contextual theology in which the act of theologizing is central. The other is contextualization of Christianity and deals with cultural dynamics for meaningful communication and reception of the gospel. The former is primarily about construction of contextual theology or *theologizing* in context and the latter emphasizes the *contextualizing* of Christianity or theology. For the sake of convenience, we will call the former "contextual theology" and the latter "contextualization of Christianity." Although "contextual theology" and "contextualization of theology" have often been used synonymously—and the difference between them is so subtle and not recognized immediately. However, as the discussion progressed, the differences became much more discernible. While there are writings to be rightly located on a continuum between the two, most studies clearly lean toward one or the other. Whereas contextual theologizing takes the sociopolitical conditions seriously, those advocating contextualization have been influenced by cultural studies employing specific anthropological methods. Robert Montgomery's observation that mainline protestant theological institutions relate more closely with sociological studies and conservative evangelicals emphasize anthropological methods (especially in its missiology)[13] may be related to these trends. As the two have diverged into separate trends, we will look at them separately. We examine the "contextualization of Christianity" approach first.

Contextualization of Christianity

The concepts of indigenization and inculturation were direct products of missionary endeavors, and they serve the missionary cause as important strategies. Contextualization, on the other hand, came out of theological education reform in a missionary context deeply influenced by missiological discussion. There was a reluctance at first to use the neologism "contextualization" among conservative evangelicals. The greatest fear for evangelicals was syncretism or compromising the faith with cultures. Evangelical scholarship in general is a latecomer when it comes to studying culture and relating it to the gospel. William Dyrness has vividly captured the attitude of evangelicals:

> Throughout their history evangelicals have displayed ambivalence toward their cultural context. The world was something to be won over in the name of Christ, or to be avoided as a source of temptation, but it could also represent a resource to be exploited in pursuit of their evangelical calling.[14]

The Fundamentalist-modernist debate may have also influenced North American evangelicals on this tension between gospel and culture. British evangelicals' positive influence in pushing their American counterparts to deal with the question should also be noted. It was the missionary use of culture in connection with communication of the gospel especially through Bible translation that led evangelicals to explore cultural questions and to tap anthropological methods for missions. North American evangelical influence has been dominant, and the works of Eugene Nida were crucial at the initial stage of the development. Following the pioneering work of the Kennedy School of World Mission at Hartford Seminary, some institutions such as the Catholic Theological Union in Chicago and the evangelical schools of Wheaton College and Fuller Seminary's School of World Mission and Evangelism dealt significantly with the question of culture in relation to Christian missions.[15] They were later joined by other institutions in the endeavor, including Asbury Theological Seminary and Trinity Evangelical Theological Seminary. The contributions of these schools are worth mentioning because of their global influence.

The Lausanne Movement, a collaborative movement of evangelical leaders and organizations for world evangelization,[16] exemplifies how a worldwide corporate evangelical voice came to embrace contextualization. The Lausanne Movement is considered the best example not only because it is the most representative organ of global evangelicalism today but also because the Lausanne Covenant explicitly dealt with culture in relation to strategies for worldwide evangelization.[17] What Dyrness calls evangelicals' "ambivalence" toward culture is recognized in the section of the covenant dealing with culture. While appreciating some of the culture to be rich in beauty and goodness, the covenant affirms that culture as a whole is tainted by sin and calls it to be tested and judged by Scripture. It acknowledges that "missions have all too frequently exported with the gospel an alien culture and churches have sometimes been in bondage to culture than to scripture."[18] The covenant is simplistic to assume the possibility of reading scripture independently from the reader's culture. It calls "Christ's evangelists" to "humbly seek to empty themselves of all but their personal authenticity."[19] As a follow-up, the Lausanne Committee organized the "Consultation on Theology and Culture" in Willowbank, Bermuda, in January 1978 where the issue was pursued further. Gathering the best evangelical scholars at the time—especially in biblical theology and missiological-anthropology—the consultation displayed rich scholarly reflection on various dimensions of the topic.[20] The Willowbank Report[21] brought together the common points in the most agreeable manner. The disagreements among presenters and diversity of ideas they brought may have confused those who look for clear guidelines, but the healthy clash of approaches and their common goal also helped to open up further thoughts and intellectual development for missiological and theological inquiries. In the Willowbank Report, one can trace the two lines of thought we have identified. While the first four sections are theological in nature emphasizing the biblical and hermeneutical dimensions of the task, the remaining sections are largely anthropological and pragmatic in nature.

The concept of contextualization in their distinctive interpretation was slowly embraced by other evangelical scholars. Charles Kraft rightly states that "by 1979, some of the more open evangelical thinkers started using the term *contextualization*. It was, however, still very suspect to the more conservative."[22] The "more open evangelical thinkers" in North America include scholars like Charles Taber, Charles Kraft, and later Paul Hiebert and other anthropologically-trained missiologists. The group found their counterparts among Catholics in Louis Luzbetak, Robert Schreiter and others in the Catholic Theological Union. Significant in the development of the contextualization of Christianity approach was the naming of a Professorship of "Contextualization of Theology" at Fuller Seminary in 1977. The entire issue of *Evangelical Missions Quarterly* of January 1978 was devoted to contextualization.[23] Henceforth, contextualization as a method employing the anthropological approach of cultural studies for the cross-cultural communication of the gospel emerged as a dominant missiological subdiscipline among evangelicals in North America. The theme is tenaciously advocated by the group Robert Priest calls "missiological anthropologists."[24]

What does contextualization mean for North American evangelical advocates? Scott Moreau attempts to answer that question with this description of contextualization:

> ... the process whereby Christians adapt the forms, content, and praxis of the Christian faith so as to communicate it to the minds and hearts of people with other cultural backgrounds. The goal is to make Christian faith as *a whole*—not only the message but also the means of living out our faith in the local setting—understandable.[25]

Here, the emphasis is on what Christians do with the Christian faith. Moreau provides a clear map of how different evangelical missiologists have theorized contextualization. Missiological anthropologist Darrell Whiteman seems to have made a similar point by stressing the receptors' side of Gospel communication. Two of the three functions of contextualization he proposed deal with this aspect. For the first function, he stresses:

> Contextualization attempts to communicate the Gospel *in word and deed* to establish the church in ways that makes sense to people within their local cultural context, presenting Christianity in such a way that it meets people's deepest needs and penetrates their worldview, thus allowing them to follow Christ and remain within their culture."[26]

Here, the manner of communication or presentation of Christianity is the key. The other function is about expecting reciprocity within the gospel exchange:

> ...to develop contextualized expressions of the Gospel so that the Gospel itself will be understood in ways the universal church has neither experienced nor understood before, thus expanding our understanding of the kingdom of God.[27]

This is a tall order and it will be difficult to claim any experience as "neither experienced nor understood before" by the universal church.

Charles Kraft, who is among the evangelical pioneers on contextualization, simplifies contextualization quite similar to Whiteman. To contextualize, he said, is to appropriate Christianity "to the *Scriptures*, on the one hand, and...to the *people* in a given cultural context, on the other."[28] For some evangelicals, Kraft's call to appropriate Christianity "to the *people* in a given cultural context" may be too compromising of the Scripture. Kraft, for his part, is critical of Western evangelicals' focus on knowledge and the subsequent failure to incorporate "spiritual power" in the process of contextualization.[29] To Paul Hiebert, contextualization cannot really be simplified and generalized. In calling for "critical contextualization" based on the theory of critical realism he sought complementarity between the truth of the Scripture and Christian tradition on the one hand, and "the local culture" including its "customary beliefs and practices" on the other hand.[30] This, he proposed can be reached by "exegesis of the culture" and "exegesis of the Scripture and the Hermeneutical Bridge."[31] The first major problem with Hiebert's proposal is that the hermeneutical bridge and the exegetical requirements are too complex for missionaries and pastors busy in the field. Second, Hiebert is quite critical of the emphasis on "contemporary cultural contexts" by early proponents of contextualization. In his stress to relate the gospel to the "traditional beliefs and practices" or "the 'old' culture" of the converts,[32] he seems to have fallen back to indigenization.

The works of these missiological anthropologists are helpful in making sense of charismatic Christianity in the majority world. Hiebert's theory of the "excluded middle" (which we will discuss later) and Kraft's works on "spiritual warfare" help to explain the religious and spiritual experiences of many Christians in the majority world. Yet, the form of contextualization developed by these missiological anthropologists also has some crucial limitations. First, the task of contextualization for this group is to provide meaningful connections between the gospel and traditional cultures for effective communication and reception of the gospel. It gives little or no place to complex present-day sociopolitical realities and changes that Shoki Coe and the TEF tried to address. If one compares this form of contextualization with what the TEF had proposed, this form may look closer to what the TEF group had categorized as "indigenization." Second, these missiological anthropologists all seem to give the dominant role to the missionaries as the "contextualizers" and the recipients of the gospel are treated merely as the object of contextualization. With few exceptions, most of them presume a certain theology of the gospel as a given, and the task is communication. It leaves little or no room for the projected recipients to theologize or synthesize the message on their own as inspired by the Holy Spirit. Even those among them who tried to move beyond modernism to postmodern anthropology treat contextualization objectively as the process of making the gospel understandable for other people.[33]

Against this objectivist treatment of contextualization, we ask, "How do people make the Christian faith their own?" In some ways, world Christianity shows how "the new Christianity"[34] of the majority world contextualizes the faith. In a recent book on contextualization in Asia, a group of evangelical scholars in the Philippines focus on reflections that tend toward contextualizing for themselves.[35] While maintaining the heart of contextualization as communicating the gospel, they also combine the objectivistic treatment with subjectivist reflections within their own context, with a particular stress on hermeneutics.

Theologizing in Contexts

Because the TEF's mandate was directed to "reform theological education,"[36] from the very beginning it tended toward "theologizing in context" rather than contextualizing Christianity. Asian Christian thinkers were at the forefront in the early history of missional contextualization, and the tendency to focus on theology was strong among them. As a part of its contextualization project, Christian Conference of Asia—the continent's representative ecumenical body—had been engaging sociopolitical issues theologically sometimes to the detriment of popular spirituality.[37] A Japanese missionary-theologian Kosuke Koyama explained this emerging phenomenon cautiously: "Authentic contextualization is a prophetic mode of living in the given historical cultural situation. It challenges the context and attempts to make critical theological observations."[38]

The last three decades of the twentieth century became an opportune time for contextual theology to flourish. Most ecumenical organizations in the non-Western world caught the contextual fever in various forms. In ecumenical circles where utmost stress was given to social action, contextual theology is reflected in theologies with various names, including Third World theologies, people's theology, and liberation theology. While a theology of religions and inculturation can be more general than specific, many contextual works have also appeared in this genre. Liberation theologies of various kinds like Latin American liberation theology, feminist (and womanist) theology, black theology, Korean Minjung theology, Filipino theology of struggle, and Indian Dalit ("subaltern") theology are the best-known contextual theologies in ecumenical circles. Yet, this is not to limit the ecumenists' contextual theology to liberation nor to say all liberation theologies are the same. A common theme among them all is understanding God's salvific call as liberation (or freeing) from the sin of oppression, bondage, or marginalization. As Elsa Tamez unequivocally puts it, these theologies see "liberation as the essence of faith itself."[39] Several of these theologies have also undergone a postcolonial twist in more recent years. Liberation advocates within the ecumenical body tend to represent the more radical segment of this body of literature. While the majority are radical and revolutionary in their approach to the politics and economics of oppression, not all Dalit, feminist or womanist, and Latin American liberation theologies would identify as "radical." In contrast to other forms of contextual theology, I will highlight the radical and revisionist forms of liberation theology first. We will deal specifically with Latin American liberation theology—which takes on both radical and evangelical forms—in the next chapter.

The common claim made by different forms of liberation theology is that this theology is shaped first and foremost by the concrete realities of oppression and marginalization. And with an emphasis on the experience of the historical reality of oppression, context is definitive. For Dalit theology, the context is the oppressive casteism; for South African theology, it is apartheid's legacy of racism; and for Minjung, it is the despairing people ("min" meaning people and "jung" meaning oppressed masses) struggling against institutional oppression by the elites (the Yangban). Oppression and victimhood of those experiencing exploitation become theological tools and interpretive keys to understanding God's saving efforts on behalf of the exploited. In Minjung theology, for instance, the concept of *han* is used to express the core of being Minjung, and thus an essential theological theme. Suh Nam-dong describes *han* as "an underlying feeling of Korean people. On the one hand, it is the dominant feeling of defeat, resignation, and nothingness. On the other hand, it is a feeling with a tenacity of will for life which comes to weaker beings."[40] Ironically, the term expresses the power of weakness. Quite similar is the choice of the name "Dalit" (meaning "being crushed" or "crushed people"). Theology also changes as the context is refined and redefined. For instance, arising out of the US civil rights movements, feminist theology emerged as a theology to liberate women from the bondages experienced under patriarchy. The context was feminism's articulation of women's oppression and the theology that emerges out of this context tends to be universally constructed for women.[41] Yet, as the theological formulations grew, feminism became both too wide and too narrow a context for meaningful reflection on all women's experiential realities. In the 1980s, ethnic feminist theologies reacted against Western feminism and refined the context racially and ethnically for themselves.[42] Today, we see various kinds of feminist theology such as Korean feminist theology, Hispanic (Mujerista) feminist theology, Asian/Asian North American feminist theologies, and others. Perhaps the most significant example of contextual reactions to the overgeneralizing of white middle-class feminist theology was that of African American women/theologians who created "womanist" theologies.[43] For these (and others), the specificity of one's social/racial/ethnic context refines and redefines the liberating work of theology.

As an action-oriented (or *praxis*) theology, liberation theology emphatically promotes resistance to what is perceived and named as injustice and oppression. Deeply humanistic in character, it is a theological construct or advocacy theology based on social analysis and undertaken by and on behalf of those perceived to be oppressed. It essentially becomes a theoretical reflection on social and political actions in which faith is placed primarily on human efforts (though usually understood as divinely aided) of political and social activism for liberation. In this regard, Paul Matheny's criticism is to the point: "Without faith in God the faith in transformation is shallow in significance. If political action is the goal of theological reflection then there is no role for the church or even for evangelism."[44]

To some of its critics, liberation theology placed too much emphasis on the social dynamics of oppression and injustice, and in so doing, unwittingly undermined faith in God's promise to be with people here and now as they benefit from the enjoyments of spiritual blessings in everyday life. Many poor Pentecostals testify to experiencing God's presence and relishing such spiritual blessings, even in the midst their poverty-stricken conditions. Liberation theologies presume structures of clearly dividing rich and the poor. Its famous maxim, "preferential option for the poor"[45] is built on the premise that the division between the rich and the poor is a given gap. But this gap is much more fluid in reality and the line between the two is quite porous.

The Ecumenical Association of Third World Theologians (EATWOT), which came into existence in 1976,[46] exemplifies this trend of liberation theology as a contextual theology. In its second conference in 1986, EAT-WOT collected commonalities and divergences among the various "Third World" experiences including minorities of the United States (African Americans and Native Americans). The commonalities boil down to "the people's resistance to oppression, racism, and dictatorships." It further states, "The fundamental common factor on all our continents is people in search of dignity, meaning, and fuller humanity."[47] On the divergence side, the meeting pointed out that "Asia and Africa are more challenged by cultural and religious realities while Latin America is more taken up with the socio-economic situation of the people."[48]

Dominant and vocal as radical forms of liberation theology are in many circles, it is not the only form of contextual theology in the ecumenical movement. In his book on contextual theology, Paul Matheny observes a less radical/socially-transformative contextual tradition that is clearly more confessional in nature.[49] Although Matheny tends to be too restrictive in his understanding of contextual theology in relation to ecumenical confessional theology,[50] his point and effort to rescue contextual theology from liberal revisionist captivity is both justified and significant. The theological tradition represented by ecumenical scholars such as "Paul Lehmann, Karl Barth, James Burtness, and Shoki Coe" that gave birth to contextual theology, he said, was "strongly confessional" in nature.[51] Thus, "the ecumenical force generated by contextual methods insists that theology remains biblical, confessional, and traditional."[52] Even if Matheny is too quick to identify confessional theologians as contextual by including theologians like Karl Barth, his point about the distinctly confessional character of early advocates of contextual theology in the ecumenical movement is well taken. The ecumenical movement through its world-wide or regional bodies has initiated various inter-confessional theological collaborations. Within and beyond such bodies exists a confessional ecumenism that holds diverse approaches and opinions of contextual theologies. The ecumenical approach to world Christianity is typified in the bringing together of different confessional, theological, and contextual voices without the surrendering of one's own confessional tradition.[53]

We noted the contributions of evangelical scholars spearheaded by missiological-anthropologists to the contextualization of Christianity. For a long time, evangelicals in the majority world bowed down before the leadership of Western evangelicals. Even though some of his arguments are unconvincing, what Soong-Chan Rah has shown about the cultural captivity of American evangelicalism to white Christian interests is undeniable.[54] Contextual theology has taught us that Western theologies were always contextual, but were erroneously thought to be universally meaningful, relevant, and useful. It is through the process of recognizing the distinct voice of others that one can give up domination and accept the status of one's voice as *one* among many others. This recognition of other theological voices took place sluggishly and reluctantly among Western, especially American, evangelicals. With a few exceptions mentioned below, non-Western evangelicals were for the most part slow in voicing their views too. They were too often characterized largely as worshippers of Western evangelical heroes. In recent years, especially with the decline of "White Christian America,"[55] the evangelical outlook has been changing.

In some non-Western evangelical circles, a few theologians and leaders have been vocal in offering a critique of their Western evangelical counterparts and in making bold contextual theological points. A small inconspicuous group called International Fellowship of Mission as Transformation (INFEMIT) has spearheaded evangelical theological works in the political, cultural, and religious contexts of the majority world. In addition to a number of collected studies from the fellowship led by Vinay Samuel and Chris Sugden, we find it worthwhile to briefly highlight the works of two scholar-leaders on contextualization from this thoughtful circle: C. René Padilla and Hwa Yung. René Padilla from Latin America can be bold and blunt. A critic of some Western evangelical missiological teachings such as the "homogenous unit" principle for church growth and the neo-capitalism of economic globalization, Padilla recognizes the subjectivity of interpretations in the understanding and communication of the universal gospel.[56] To Padilla, culture and personal faith play critical roles in the intercultural communication of the gospel. Asian evangelical theologian Hwa Yung identifies contextualization as the criterion for "missiological theology" in Asia and insists on evangelistic and pastoral contextualization that is both true to the context and faithful to Christian tradition.[57] While emphatic on communication of the gospel in contextualization, these theologians assert equal importance to theological construction in the sociopolitical and cultural context of the people.

As evangelicals came to embrace worldwide Christianity and its diverse multicultural character, they naturally came to recognize non-Western evangelical voices, distinct theologies, and leadership. Acceptance of other voices does not mean a validation of a cacophonous theology, but a recognition of the *polyvocal* nature of Christianity and its theology. For evangelicals, recognition of diverse theologies began with missiology and its contextualizing product. Highlighting a few recent publications shows this recent progression. Using globalization as a hermeneutical key, a group of evangelical scholars, including a few non-Westerners, published an impressive volume on theology in the context of world Christianity in 2006.[58] *Globalizing Theology* set the tone for further developments. Among the few historical studies on global expansion of evangelicalism in recent decades is *Global Evangelicalism*.[59] Here historians look at the distinct characters of evangelicalism in its expansion, theology, and consolidations in different continents. In addition to rich doctrinal studies from an evangelical perspective, *The Cambridge Companion to Evangelical Theology*[60] shows the emerging evangelical contextual theologies. Though the chosen theological contexts of discussions in some cases are a bit too broad for meaningful contextual discussions, several chapters of this companion are helpful initiatives. A bit more specific in dealing with particular (or local) theologies in their cultural contexts is the volume *Global Theology in Evangelical Perspective*.[61] The editors and some of the authors of the chapters are explicit in their contextual intent and the volume clearly marks the coming of age of evangelical contextual theologies.

The fear of syncretism or the compromising of the Christian faith with culture is on the wane among evangelicals. This is perhaps a result of the understanding that any reception of the Christian gospel involves culture and that every form of Christianity relates to a particular culture. There are theological constants that do not change even when they are received in different contexts. As long as these theological constants are faithfully kept, contextual understanding may take different forms. To compromise these theological foundations may result in syncretism, but a faithful keeping would solidify the Christian faith in a context. In their book *Constants in Context*, Stephen Bevans and Roger Schroeder list six theological constants for Christian mission: At the top of the list are two foundations they adopted from Andrew Walls' work: "the centrality of Jesus the Christ (along with his relation to the Father and the Holy Spirit) and the ecclesial nature of any missionary activity." To these two, they added another four: "Questions of *eschatology*," "the nature of *salvation*," "a particular [Christian] *anthropology*," and the place of human *culture* in theology and communication of the gospel.[62]

One significant contextual theological issue surfacing in some evangelical circles under the rubric of "insider movement" is the extent to which cultural and religious identity should be accommodated. John Travis (pseudonym) outlines six "Christ-centered communities" in Muslim contexts and calls them the "C1 to C6 Spectrum." The spectrum moves from "traditional church" (C1) with little or no relation to Muslim communities to "secret/underground believers" (C6) who worship Christ in isolation for fear of persecution.[63] Travis cautiously advocated C5 as a missionary strategy, stirring debate. C5 is described as "Christ-centered communities of 'Messianic Muslims' who have accepted Jesus as Lord and Savior" while remaining "legally and socially within the community of Islam."[64] "C5 believers" mostly participated in corporate Muslim worship and also meet regularly with other C5 believers. Unlike C6, C5 believers share their faith with other Muslims. What Jonas A. Jørgensen identified as "*Īsā Īmāndārs*" (or "faithful of Jesus") in Bangladesh[65] appears to be what Travis called "C5 believers." Their Hindu equivalent would be "*Khristbhaktas*" (or "devotees of Christ") who remain Hindu, but believe in the supreme Lordship and salvation of Jesus and actively worship him.[66] The debate as a result of the embrace of "C5 believers" by evangelical Christians is a sign of their seriousness on issues of contextualization.

Varieties of Contextual Theology

European theologians in the nineteenth and early twentieth centuries discovered the significance of the historical context of scripture in understanding the text. The German phrase *Sitz im Leben* ("life setting" or social context) became key to recognizing the context of the scriptural texts in the work of interpretation. But the interpreter's context (or *Sitz im Leben*) seemed to have been considered universally understood and relevant. The European theologies that were genuinely contextual and significantly related to their historical period of time were considered and taught as universal theologies relevant and meaningful to all people at all times. The time-bound nature of their theologies became problematic, but even more challenging was the growing awareness of the limitations of their contexts when Christianity became a worldwide religion. Stephen Bevans has rightly stated that "every authentic theology has been very much rooted in a particular context in some implicit or real way."[67] The new enterprise we call contextual theology both particularized theology by authenticating its sociocultural roots and universalized it by making theology an enterprise for every context of the world. Douglas John Hall is right in stressing, "No theological province of the *oikumĕnĕ* [the unified world] can be independent of the others. Every theological community, however, must work out its witness in dialogue with the particularities of its own sociohistorical situation.... Contextualization... is the sine qua non [indispensable and essential] of all genuine theological thought, as it always has been."[68]

Missiologists and theologians deal with contextual theologies in different ways. Robert Schreiter gave an early comprehensive treatment under the title of *Constructing Local Theologies*. He mapped out a complex system of how communities lived out their spirituality at the intersection of the church tradition and their cultures from which emerged a contextual (local) tradition in the form of a series of local theologies.[69] It seems that the emergent tradition or local theologies may sometimes arise spontaneously while theologians also intentionally construct such theologies. In the section "Mission as Contextualization" in his book *Transforming Mission*, David Bosch follows Justin Ukpong to identify two major types of contextual theology: the indigenization model and the socioeconomic model. The former is sub-typed into translation and inculturation, and the latter into the evolutionary and revolutionary (liberation theology). Bosch judged only inculturation in the former and revolutionary liberation theology as "contextual theologies proper."[70] The breakthrough of contextual theologies happened, Bosch said, at the birth of "third-world theologies" with the epistemological break they claim to have made. But the epistemological break he identified is largely limited to liberation theology.[71] Inculturation, the other form of contextual theology, is a relatively congenial approach that both inculturates the gospel or Christianity to the culture and also Christianizes the culture.[72] More recently, Dean Flemming identifies what the New Testament did to contextualize the gospel. Somewhat close to the German use of *Sitz im Leben*, Flemming looks at how the various families of New Testament writings use contextualization. He proposes "The Jesus model" in which Jesus "explained or exegeted (*exēgēsato*) the Father to us."[73] Not only did Jesus engage through his action but his very being is a model of contextualization according to Flemming.

The most comprehensive and useful discussion especially from a methodological viewpoint is Stephen Bevans's *Models of Contextual Theology*.[74] By bringing order to the "bewildering array of contextual theologies today,"[75] Bevans has done a great service to map out this complex world. Bevans classified the entire gamut of contextual theologies in a spectrum between an "experience-of-the-past" context and an "experience-of-the-present" reality.[76] Scripture and church tradition represent the past experience, and the present context is formed by the personal or communal experience of culture, social change, and social location.[77]

Using models ranging from "anthropological" (seeking to establish and preserve the cultural identity of a Christian)[78] on the extreme end, to "translation" (focusing on the Christian identity to preserve faith traditions), to a "countercultural" (seeking to "challenge and purify the context"[79]) at the other end of the spectrum, Bevans identifies six models: anthropological, transcendental, praxis, synthetic, translation, and countercultural. At the risk of oversimplifying this comprehensive work, let's describe each model in a sentence or two. Countercultural mission treats context with utmost seriousness, yet with a great deal of suspicion demanding its transformation or purification. Translation model is a basic contextualization model in which all other models are built. Its distinctiveness is in its contention that there is an authoritative text that is to be translated and this text together with Christian identity should be preserved in the translation process. Just opposite to the translation model in the spectrum is the anthropological model that starts in the culture and tends to preserve cultural identity in the Christian faith. Praxis model emphasizes the context of social change and how theology may effect change toward the good of the society. A synthetic model tries to balance or blend each of these models in a creative dialectic by bringing the best methods of each. Based on Immanuel Kant's transcendental philosophy, a transcendental mission model focuses on the active process required of a self-transcending subject, not context, to express religious and cultural identity.

By succinctly describing each model, Bevans systematically captures the multifarious forms of contextual theology and outlines them meaningfully. As the most comprehensive roadmap of how various types of contextual theology are constructed, Bevans's seminal book became a point of reference for most subsequent serious works on contextualization. The types of theology he brought together (as with many of the other works discussed above) show the composite functions of contextualization in the encounter of gospel and local culture. Together they demonstrate intentional and deliberate discussion of contextual engagements with the gospel in the life situation of Christians. They are largely formal in nature and characteristically academic. By saying "intentional," I mean they are intentionally constructed to be contextually relevant to the context. There is yet another form of contextual theology, one that arises spontaneously when popular Christians of the pew encountered the gospel in their daily lives. This kind of spontaneous contextualization has mostly been neglected by contextual theology in formal academic efforts. It is a theology constructed informally and instinctively by communities as they live out their faith in their day-to-day contextual realities. This kind of contextual theologizing is spontaneous (vs. intentional), communal or corporate in its engagements (vs. individual), and informal (vs. the formal thematic efforts of academic works). Contextual theology in this sense is manifest and witnessed in close relation to popular charismatic (Pentecostal) forms of Christianity, which we consider in the next chapter.

Chapter 6

CONTEXTUAL THEOLOGIES IN THE MAJORITY WORLD

We ended our discussion of contextualization and contextual theologies in the previous chapter by suggesting that there is a lesser known, informal, and instinctive contextual theology found in popular Christianity. This lesser-studied theological trend largely characterizes majority world Christianity and we will treat it as a part of "macro-contextual" theology,[1] to use David Bosch's term. We begin this chapter by highlighting some common macro-contextual issues faced in the majority world, and then turn the focus to Africa, Latin America, and Asia. To deal with the macro-contextual settings, we will have to make some gross generalizations.

Religiosity, Poverty, and Existential Tensions

As discussed in the previous chapter, contextual theologies are constructed in response to the contextual realities. We will identify three broad issues that are typified in the experiences of people in Latin America, Africa, Asia, and the Pacific Islands. They are (1) the religiosity of the people, (2) poverty and inequality, and (3) tensional existence.

111

Religiosity of the People

To state that Asia is religious would almost be an understatement. The birthplace of most of the world's living religions, traditional Asian societies lived and breathed religion, and modern Asian cultures continue to be deeply religious. In Africa, one of its most insightful thinkers and analysts, John Mbiti, states bluntly, "African peoples are deeply religious," and furthermore, they are "profoundly religious *in their own way*."[2] The indigenous primal worldviews of much of Africa and the Americas were deeply religious, and they are founded in beliefs about and dependency on supernatural powers. The indigenous worldviews that continue to shape the lives of average people are built on beliefs in spiritual-mystical powers. To Western secularized minds, they seem superstitious, but for the people in Asian, African, and Latin American villages, they are real and active in the daily lives of indigenous peoples. The extent to which such beliefs pervade their lives differs from community to community, but overall, beliefs in spiritual beings and their supernatural work/activity remain strong. Post-enlightenment, secular-trending societies of the West, and elitist alliances with secularists in the non-Western world, came to negate the impact of supernaturalism in local religions. Even so, religious experience in these regions continues to be deeply entrenched in faith in the supernatural.

In what Indian scholar Stanley J. Samartha criticized as "the Northern study of the Southern religions,"[3] Western meanings and values about all things religious have been imposed, jeopardizing and rendering invisible local cultural understandings. This is the case in point with Confucianism. Because Confucianism did not fully fit the mold of the Western religious nomenclature, it came to be seen as non-religious. C. K. Yang noted:

> Great Western Sinologues such as [James] Legge and [Herbert] Giles have emphasized the agnostic character of Confucianism. A later generation of Western scholars...assigned a relatively unimportant place to religion in Chinese society, leaving unexplained the universal presence of religious influence.[4]

Consequently, even "modern Chinese scholars," Yang said, "have developed the theme of the unimportance of religion in Chinese society to a much greater extreme."[5] As Yang and others argue, when Chinese religion is allowed to define itself, the religiosity of Confucianism and Chinese society becomes more than apparent.

Tissa Balasuriya, a Sri Lankan theologian, is critical of Western capitalistic influence in changing the spiritual norms and values of the non-Western world. Contrasting modern Western values and Asian religiosity, he states:

> Religion pervades the life of most Asian people. The creedal content of religions differs, but *there is a basic religiousness common to all.* It is even related to the forms of belief that antedated the intellectual synthesis of the great Asian religions—a profound animism and ritualism is found in the substratum of Asian societies.[6]

Asia continues to be predominantly non-Christian; Eastern Asia is dominated by Confucianism and Buddhism, Western Asia by Islam, South Asia by Hinduism and Islam, and Southeast Asia by Buddhism and Islam. Yet the Asian people's relationship to sacred power, their convictional life, ritual practice, and ordered forms of togetherness—in short, their religiosity—is virtually unquestioned.

In sub-Saharan Africa, a deep sense of primal religiosity is shifting from African traditional religions to Christianity. John Mbiti describes African religiosity as "the richest part of the African heritage." On Africa's religiosity, he observed:

> Religion is found in all areas of human life. It has dominated the thinking of African peoples to such an extent that it has shaped their cultures, their social life, their political organizations and economic activities. We can say, therefore, that religion is closely bound up with the traditional way of African life, while at the same time, this way of life has shaped religion as well.[7]

As we will discuss later, the shape and form of African traditional religions deeply characterizes virtually all versions of African Christianity.

In the case of Latin America, its sense of religiosity is a combination of late medieval Spanish *Reconquista* Catholicism; traditional religions inherited from the Aztec, Inca, Maya, and other smaller civilizations; and the African religions of slaves who were brought to the Americas by European colonizers. All the three traditions in the composition were deeply religious in character. Out of their deep religiosity, some resisted Christianity "usually in secret," while others syncretized old religions with their new religions.[8] This form of popular Catholicism came to define Latin American Christianity until recently. Peter Bakewell's description of Inca religiosity demonstrates the depth of the pre-Spanish Native American religiosity. He writes:

> These were an intensely religious people, or better, a people who were intensely aware of inhabiting a world crowded with bustling, fickle, often malevolent spirits. The great god Tezcatlipoca...was the creative force that gave children; but also a power that rejoiced to bring random, senseless destruction among humans. In general, the sacred forces, large and small, that crowded in on everyday life were threatening; only constant appeasement through many minor rituals would keep them at bay.... The fierce Aztec prohibition of drunkenness, except on proper celebratory occasions, was aimed not so much at maintaining decorous public order as at denying hazardous spiritual forces an open doorway into human affairs.[9]

Poverty and Inequality

The term "third world" is one of the most misunderstood and misused terms in popular parlance. The most common [mis]understanding embedded in this phrase is its pejorative ranking of last or least (or third). This understanding of hierarchical inferiority by rank is far from what representatives of twenty-nine nations in the Afro-Asian Conference of Bandung (Indonesia) had in mind in 1955 when they embraced "third world" as their self-identity.[10] Nonetheless, there is truth in equating the term with poverty and underdevelopment, if by development one means healthy economic, educational, medical, and governmental infrastructures. Today, the term "third world" is too often used casually as a reference to the developing nations of Asia, Africa, and Latin America. Some of these nations have overcome the negative connotations associated with being "last" in categories defining a healthy nation-state.

The United Nations Human Development Index confirms what the average person might suppose, namely the overwhelming majority of the least developing nations are in the continent of Africa, and a few in Asia.[11] Of the forty-three nations categorized as "low human development," thirty-seven are in Africa, four are in South Asia, and two are Pacific island nations. The majority of countries in the "medium human development" category are located in Africa, Asia, and Latin America, while the majority of those in the "very high human development" category are mainly in Europe and North America, with a few outliers in East and West Asia.[12]

Poverty can be a relative term and sometimes its clarity rests on its relation to inequality. The debate around poverty in relation to the phenomenon of globalization reveals that unless one's standing is seen in relation to others, the meaning of poverty can be difficult to clarify. Poverty alleviation has become an important global agenda in the twenty-first century, particularly for the so-called developed wealthy nations. Organizations like Make Poverty History and Global Call to Action Against Poverty have made it a recognized global issue. Yet, sustained attention and commitments seem lacking and the actual achievements are frequently dismal. The pledge made by wealthy nations in 2005 to cut poverty in half by 2015[13] produced results far below this goal.[14]

Writing about poverty in Africa, John Illife identified two levels: First, those who "struggle continuously to preserve themselves and their dependents from physical wants."[15] The majority of the poor living in Africa belong to this group. Second are "the poorest of the poor and destitute, whose poverty has reached an epidemic proportion."[16] For these people, the ongoing struggle to meet basic needs fails with devastating results. Though less in number than the "struggling poor," there are still many in this tragic category around the world.

As we will see, Latin American liberation theology was built on the recognition of poverty as a fundamental theological problem. What prompted the meeting of CELAM (Latin American Bishops' Council) in 1968 to take up the issue of poverty, justice, and social order, which in turn became the basis of liberation theology, were the queries on "the origins and reasons for poverty and inequity in the region."[17] Statistics show that what Adrian Hastings said about Africa in 1975 remains largely true in a number of nations. "A few rich and many very poor people—that is the common shape of Africa, white ruled or black ruled."[18] Almost a quarter of a century later, Ogbu Kalu saw the widening gap between the rich and the poor and the complicity involved in the persistency of poverty in Africa. He writes:

> The failure of the state in Africa is beyond economic explanation. Much of it is ethical. It relates to [the] ethics of power because some people have monopolized power and colluded with Western entrepreneurs to rob their people of both material resources and dignity. Admittedly, some of the arsenal were borrowed from primal cultural values.[19]

Despite some great economic success stories in East Asia, numerous Asian nations also experience extreme poverty. "Vietnam, Cambodia, Laos, North Korea, Bangladesh and Afghanistan...suffer from abject widespread poverty,"[20] rightly said Peter Phan. Millions in the nations of India and China, which are enjoying fast-paced development in recent decades, are subjected to similar devastation. In Asia, poverty is deeply connected to sociocultural realities and is endemic in some communities. Take, again, the case of Dalit people in India, whose religious subjugation by the Hindu caste system is the basis of their economic deprivation. In all Asian societies, women fare worse than men,[21] and among subjugated communities like the Dalits, women suffer double discrimination.

Tensional Existence

The last of the macro-contextual issues pervading the majority world is a conceptual one, namely the tension between tradition and change (or continuity and change). Such tension may be dismissed as a common experience of every society, but the previously colonized nations and those struggling to catch up experience it all the more. Addressing the contending realities of tradition and change is not so much about solving the tension, but rather understanding this tension as the framework and context of new forms of Christianity in the majority world. Tension between an indigenous people's cultural tradition and the impending forces of modernization is an important factor shaping the emerging Christian worldview. Modernization represents change that upsets the tradition by which people have been living, moving, and being. "If it [modernization] has sometimes been hailed as an exhilarating challenge to create new values and meanings, it has also often been feared as a threat to an existing pattern of values and meanings,"[22] states Robert Bellah. In cultures where traditions have been long held with their own distinct rational or philosophical explanations and defenses, change is harder to process and accomplish.

Topics and phenomena like contextualization, religious conversion, and globalization are all shaped by this tension between tradition and change. Recall, contextualization is about existence between the text (scripture and the church tradition) and the context (traditional cultures and social changes). In an attempt to give a philosophical explanation of the globalization process, Asha Mukherjee sees the interplay between culture understood as ever-changing, "always in a process, ever flowing," and an understanding of the world as "a finite, knowable bounded space" where differences and particularities are sought to be retained as much as possible.[23] These tensions characterizes the process we call globalization. Historically, the tension between the influence of the enlightenment tradition that defines much of modernity and modern educational systems, and the strong tradition of indigenous cultures and their accompanying ethos, has been the driving force that creates cultural identities in much of the majority world today.

Christianity often represents both change and continuity, and "Christianization" is characterized by this tension. In much of the present majority world where Christianity is rising, it came as a change agent, a transforming power. Yet, once established, like most traditions and institutions that persist through reified practices, it may (and does) resist change. The cycle of change and continuity, therefore, continues. And the tension between the "traditionalizing mission" (or mainline) churches and new ways of being church and doing ministry (including the challenge to embrace charismatic forms of faith) faces churches in the majority world every day. And as previously highlighted, it is almost impossible to differentiate

Pentecostals and mission (mainline) Christians in some countries in Africa (and other majority-world nations), as many on the rolls of Anglican (and other mainline churches) are active in Pentecostal worship and activities.

Macro-Contextual Theologies

At its tenth year and seventh international conference, the Ecumenical Association of Third World Theologians (EATWOT) identified the different kinds of challenges they faced in the so-called Third World. The final document of the assembly said, "From the very beginning there has been a different emphasis on the use and the quality of analysis for theologizing.... Asia and Africa are more challenged by their *cultural and religious* realities while Latin America is more taken up with the *socio-economic* situation of the people."[24] Ironically, it was only the "socio-economic and political challenges"[25] that they identified as their common experience, and economic liberation as the unifying theological solution. The document concluded, "Liberation is the common theme and central concern for all of us, because the central and common experience of all has been domination and oppression, whether colonial, racist, sexist, or capitalist."[26]

Indeed, vibrant cultures of rich, pulsating religious traditions define Africa and Asia. For Latin America the most important challenge has been socioeconomic. These three regions are confronted by many challenges, but each of these—ethno-cultural issues for Africa, religious challenges for Asia, and socioeconomic problems for Latin America—is a core issue. In saying this, we do not mean to diminish other issues among diverse nations, and this observation definitely comes with some essential caveats. Of course, political problems and the consequential socioeconomic issues are as vexing in Africa as they are in Latin America, if not more so. But cultural traditions and the accompanying religiosity seem to have the firmest grip on the people's worldview and ethos in much of sub-Saharan Africa. In southern Africa, forms of racism may have the equal or upper hand in people's minds. Similarly, to use religiosity and religious pluralism as the most dominant common issue in Asia is not to diminish the importance of ethnicity and economic struggles. Religiosity cannot be simply differentiated from cultural traditions, and socioeconomic challenges may be of primary importance for many Asians. The diversity of Asia is such that religiosity, cultural and religious pluralism, and political/economic realities may be given equal importance. Even if cultural issues are not as important as political and economic issues for the dominant whites and mestizos in Latin America, culture may indeed still be the defining factor and the most significant issue for many if not most of the indigenous people in the Americas.

It is not at all surprising to find that a theology of inculturation in Africa, a theology of religions in Asia, and political liberation theologies in Latin America are for each the most conspicuous contextual theological themes. While there is no exclusive "theology of the continent" (with "continent" loosely referenced) in each case, they indicate leading theological trends in these zones of world Christianity. Here, we will begin to briefly highlight these theologies within their contexts. This discussion is not exhaustive and emphasis is on the contextual nature of these theologies.

Liberation Theology in
Latin America and Beyond

If there is one theology to be identified with Latin America (South and Central America), it is liberation theology. In fact, the name was coined there. Roberto Oliveros articulates Latin American theologians' strong sense of possession regarding liberation theology vividly:

> When we speak of theology in Latin America, we must speak of the theology of liberation. Here, for the first time in the history of our sub-continent, a theology is appearing that belongs to us—a theological reflection incarnate in the situation of the persons and peoples of America.[27]

Liberation theology is a theology that reflects on the emancipation (freeing or being freed) of people from oppression or bondage. As noted in the previous chapter, there are various liberation theologies corresponding to particular forms of oppression or captivity addressed by God's liberating salvation. Latin American liberation theology arose out of a historical reality of the 1960s and 1970s as a part of a wider revitalizing movement of the church in Latin America. Faced by a particularly difficult situation

119

in the Cold War era when "military dictatorships and radical guerrilla movements spread throughout the region,"[28] and challenged by the rising Protestantism supported by the United States, "prophetic Catholicism" arose.[29] Liberation theology came about as a form of prophetic Christianity in this revitalizing movement.

To one of its founding theologians, Gustavo Gutiérrez, what distinguished liberation theology is its treatment of theology as "a critical reflection on praxis."[30] Thus, he defines liberation theology as "a critical reflection on Christian praxis in the light of the Word."[31] By praxis Gutiérrez means a mutual-feedback loop between action for justice and spiritual reflection. In his later work, he said praxis involves "a transforming activity marked and illuminated by Christian love."[32] He gives so much importance to praxis, that theology, in a sense, becomes secondary to praxis.[33] Liberation theology is defined by its struggle to liberate the oppressed and the marginalized in life, and is deeply colored by the theme of justice and resistance against oppression. In Latin American liberation theology's language, the oppressed are the poor, and the poor are the oppressed. The struggle of the poor and the effort to liberate them is the heart of this theology, and is best expressed in its famous phrase, the "preferential option for the poor."

In one of the best theological expositions of this phrase, Gutiérrez shows that the present-day worldwide historical experience of "the *irruption of the poor*," is the very context and framework of liberation theology. He argues that the option for the poor is God's choice to side with victims against forces that oppress, and Jesus' entire ministry displayed that option. The church, therefore, is characterized by an intentional poverty and solidarity from which it evangelizes.[34] In Jon Sobrino's words, "the theological locus...in Latin American theology...is constituted by the poor."[35] For Gutiérrez, liberation theology attempts to,

> reflect on the experience and meaning of the [Christian] faith based on the commitment to abolish injustice and build a new society; this theology must be verified by the practice of that commitment, by active, effective participation in the struggle which the exploited social classes have undertaken against their oppressor.[36]

This primary emphasis on commitment and active involvement in the abolition of injustice for the sake of the poor's freedom is common among all liberation theologians. According to Leonardo Boff and Clodovis Boff, "We can be followers of Jesus and true Christians only by making common cause with the poor and working out the gospel of liberation."[37]

Thus, liberation is not seen as one among different concepts of salvation, but as *the* concept of salvation. God is the God of liberation. Trinity is read as a communion of the three persons of the Godhead whose revelation is seen in the liberative salvation of humankind.[38] Christology in this trajectory bears even stronger marks of a liberation perspective on salvation. In his ministry, in his identification with the poor, and in his sacrifice on the cross, Jesus— the mediator of the reign of God— showed his uniqueness as liberator by confronting oppressors and overcoming oppression.[39] And Jesus left a liberatory example for his followers. Jon Sobrino uses the term "Christopraxis" to show the emancipatory aspects of Jesus' personhood, mission, and resurrection.[40] The Holy Spirit is experienced in community through the struggle of the poor and in human action for justice. The Spirit's presence in history is the presence of the reign of God, according to José Comblin.[41] The church has life only in the Spirit.

Even if Latin American theologians claim liberation theology as *theirs*, liberation theology is certainly not limited to Latin America nor to Catholic forms of faith. Protestants have been actively involved in the conversation and development of this theology. A rather distinct voice of both affirmation and critique comes from evangelicals in Latin America. By evangelicals, we are not referring to the historical *evangélicos* (Protestant denominations), but those who distinguished themselves with a theological evangelicalism. In the global evangelical movement (e.g., the Lausanne movement), Latin American evangelical theologians are known for their advocacy of social engagement while strongly maintaining their commitment to evangelical orthodoxy. Some of the representatives and spokespersons for this perspective are the late Orlando Costas, René Padilla, Emilio Núñez, Samuel Escobar, and the missionary theologian Andrew Kirk. In her outstanding analysis, *Contextual Theology for Latin America*, Sharon

Heaney has brought together the voices of these scholars in a dynamic conversation.[42]

The liberation theme as the main way to translate the concept of salvation in Latin America is both affirmed and appreciated by these liberationist–evangelical scholars and leaders. They clearly agree with the emphasis on a practical outworking of Christian faith and the concept of praxis. But they criticized the emphasis placed on historical praxis over replacing Scripture-generated praxis.[43] Similarly, they disagree with the Catholic liberationists' starting point of the historical reality of poverty and oppression and insist, instead, that priority should be given to the biblical texts. For Padilla, emphasizing historical reality and practice can easily reduce and subordinate the word of God to the historical context. Instead, he proposes "a hermeneutical circle between scripture and the historical situation."[44] Most interestingly, for Latin American evangelicals, "liberation" as propagated by Catholic and liberal Protestant (*evangélico*) liberation theologians "is too limited" and "too narrow."[45] In its stead, they suggest a more holistic concept of liberation true to their reading of the clear teaching of scripture.

For these evangelical readers, the liberationists' concept of sin is too narrowly confined to social and structural sins with too little regard for individual sins and corruption. It also disregards the eternal consequences of sin, all while minimizing the theme of repentance in its theology. A liberation understanding of salvation in this critique precludes divine initiative and undermines or dismisses the redemptive aspect of Christ's death. The words of Samuel Escobar reflect this evangelical concern for a more holistic understanding of liberation:

> Please notice that the simple liberation from human masters is not the freedom of which the gospel speaks. Freedom in Christian terms means subjection to Jesus Christ as Lord, deliverance from bondage of sin and Satan (John 8:1-38) and consequently the beginning of a new life under the Law of Christ (I Corinthians 9:19), life in the family of faith where the old human master becomes also the new brother in Christ.[46]

Escobar places a high value on the integration of spiritual and sociopolitical liberation:

> Not that he [Christ] says: "I come to announce to you a spiritual free-
> dom and because of that I do not care about your social, economic or
> political oppression." But rather he says: "I care about your oppression.
> I am with you in your search for a way out, and I can show you a deeper
> and most decisive deliverance that may help you to find a better way out
> of your social and political oppression."[47]

René Padilla's name is also associated with holistic mission or more pre-
cisely what is called "integral mission" (*misión integra*).[48]

Inculturation in Africa and Beyond

African theology is often described under two key themes: inculturation and liberation.[49] The former refers to the dynamic interaction
between the gospel and African culture. The latter, often termed "black
theology" is most popular in southern Africa and is closely associated with
black theology in North America. Not only do the two together constitute
African theology, the two are also integrated by theologians. Mercy Amba
Oduyoye, for instance, integrated these two perspectives skillfully and ef-
fectively in her discussion of African women's theology.[50] To her, African
theology cannot help being liberative *and* inculturated. For Jesse N. K.
Mugambi, inculturation and adaptation are variations of the dominant
liberative theology.[51]

The term "inculturation" is drawn originally from the sociocultural
concept of *enculturation*, and has been associated with Catholic missiological scholarship since the early 1960s. It became a popular ministerial
strategy for the post–Vatican II liturgical renewal in Asia and Africa. In
its simplest form, it means inserting Christian faith in a culture so that it
may become a part of the culture. Aylward Shorter argued such insertion
is only an initial phase, and that inculturation is "the on-going dialogue
between faith and culture or cultures." As a Christian enterprise, "it is the
creative and dynamic relationship between the Christian message and a
culture or cultures," he added.[52] Within the Catholic discussions in Africa,
some advocated adaptation approaches—especially for liturgies—while
others insist on a theological understanding of incarnational transformation. Tension between these two sensibilities was high in 1974 during the

123

Roman Synod Meeting of the Bishops of Africa and Madagascar. While Pope Paul IV's address followed adaptation, the bishops' declaration opted for incarnational theology.[53] As late as the 1990s, the tension persisted. The Congregation for Divine Worship and the Discipline of the Sacraments issued an instruction on inculturation in 1994 that used "adaptation" as a way of inculturation.[54] But such understandings have been challenged since the 1970s in Africa. The concept has been refined and more sophisticated definitions offered. Peter Schineller defines it as:

> the incarnation of the Christian life and of the Christian message in a particular cultural context, in such a way that this experience not only finds expression through elements proper to the culture in question, but becomes a principle that animates, directs and unifies the culture, transforming and remaking it so as to bring about "a new creation."[55]

Because the Christian message is always brought from one culture to another (transmitted from culture to culture as first embodied in the faith of Israel and in Jewish culture), inculturation is also an *inter*culturation.

In Asia, the plurality of religions and the popular religiosity of the people often present challenges to official or more rational forms of inculturation, said Peter Phan. From the Chinese Rite controversy in the sixteenth century, the works of Roberto de Nobili in seventeenth-century India, to popular religiosity in the Philippines, inculturation touches upon various aspect of the Asian Catholic life. In India, a liturgical renewal movement came about in the Catholic Church led by D. S. Amalorpavadass in the 1960s.[56] While the larger number of Indian Christians came from the Dalit and tribal communities who have nothing to do with Brahminic tradition,[57] the liturgical inculturation as represented for instance by the National Biblical Catechetical and Liturgical Centre, was largely directed toward Brahminic tradition.[58] The rise of subaltern theologies (dalit, tribal, and feminist-womanist) seemed to have overshadowed the movement. Peter Phan relates two major official studies on liturgical inculturation, the Lutheran World Federation's Nairobi Statement of 1996 and Pontifical Council for Culture's *Toward a Pastoral Approach to Culture* (1999), with popular religions and cultural devotion in postmodern

and postcolonial viewpoints. He concluded that the liturgical inculturation concept proposed by these official studies "is inadequate" and fails to
carry out "a fruitful dialogue between the gospel and culture."[59] Phan is
especially critical of the superficial "adaptation" approach of the Roman
document.[60]

Although not exactly the same as mentioned, the term "indigenization" was popularly used by Protestants as an equivalent term until the
1970s. Even though Protestants have largely embraced the concept of inculturation, not all Protestant scholars use the term. In Africa, the concept
of inculturation is a part of the larger issue of the gospel's interaction
with traditional religions and cultures. Some scholars have explicitly dealt
with the issue as what Ogbu Kalu called "the continuity of African primal
religion in African Christianity."[61] The pioneering scholar who may have
done the most in the study of the gospel and African traditional religions
and cultures is John Mbiti. Mbiti's theology involves dialectical relations
between biblical worldview and African religiosity and traditions in connection with the actual life of the church. In what Kwame Bediako called
"Mbiti's great Africana trilogy"[62]—*African Religion and Philosophy* (1969),
Concepts of God in Africa (1970), and *Prayers of African Religion* (1974)—
Mbiti intersected Christianity with African cultures in both biblical and
theological terms.

Mbiti seemed to reach the maturity of his theology on African culture in the mid-1970s. In his 1970 article, "Christianity and Traditional
Religions in Africa,"[63] he laid down what may be called a "fulfillment
theology" saying African religion is a preparation for the gospel that *fulfills*
it. African religions are "largely but not entirely compatible with Christianity,"[64] and thus are judged and saved by Christianity as they become
an enrichment for Christianity in Africa. Seven years later, his discussion
brought the gospel and culture even closer.[65] He clearly sees God's work in
the process and the gospel itself, according to Mbiti, "traverses" the culture
through which it is understood. It is only within their cultural framework
that people respond and are converted to the gospel. The gospel cannot
be implanted. "Let us say once and for all, as loudly as technology can
make it," he stated, "that IMPORTED CHRISTIANITY WILL NEVER

NEVER QUENCH THE SPIRITUAL THIRST OF AFRICAN PEO-
PLE."[66] Gospel, faith, and culture are the only tools needed to evolve a
viable Christianity, and Africa has plenty of them, he declared. Yet Mbiti
seemed unprepared to relate the gospel with the primal spirit world. For
instance, when he defends African religion from being animistic, superstitious, and ancestor worshipping,[67] he undermines their strong beliefs in
the power of multiple spirits and divinities. As Kwame Bediako critically
notes, the emphasis Mbiti and others place on African monotheism actually undercuts the African spirit world.[68]

Approaching the question of Africa's Christianity and its religious
and cultural roots in primal worldviews, Kwame Bediako argues that it
was the rich African primal traditions and ethos that helped Christianity thrive. "Historical studies of African primal religions have shown that
these religions, far from being 'passive traditional cosmologies,' have, in
fact, been dynamic institutions, able to adapt and respond to new situa-
tions and human needs in a society,"[69] he declared. For Bediako, African
beliefs in ancestors and spirits are not liabilities but assets for Christianity.
They are pathways to connect the biblical world and African traditions.[70]
Lamin Sanneh's work (dealt with elsewhere in this book) conceptualizes
the principle of translation as a way of incarnating Christ in the African
religious world.

Taking stock of how far along inculturation has actually occurred in
African churches (especially in the East), Laurenti Magesa conducted a
survey in 2002 in Kenya, Tanzania, and Uganda to find out how churches
felt about themselves "as truly African." A combination of Catholic
churches, African Independent churches (AIC hereafter), and Pentecostal
churches were selected as study sites where personal interviews and par-
ticipant observations were done.[71] Magesa summarized his overall findings
under (1) the practice of faith; (2) worship/liturgy; (3) healing and deliverance; (4) symbols, leadership structures and gender issues; (5) the Bible;
(6) ecumenism [together with interreligious dialogue]; and (7) theology.
The overall picture shown by these summary findings is that inculturation
has occurred, happening in varying and sometimes in stunning ways.

On the practice of faith, one major finding is the hiatus or gap between how people practice their faith at an instinctive subconscious level indigenously and how they perform the faith "according to official rules in concrete circumstances."[72] Examples of circumstances include illness, marriage and its procedures, and relationship with the ancestors and spirits. AICs are found to have succeeded the most in indigenizing worship, and styles of worship have often been cause for breaking away from mainline churches. In Kenya, the lack of emphasis on healing and exorcism in mainline Protestant churches is the most cited reason for breaking away to join independent churches.[73] In all three countries, it was clearly confirmed that healing is a high priority in religious life.[74] It therefore is no surprise, Magesa states, "that belief in spiritual powers remains an integral aspect of African religiosity even within the boundaries of Christianity."[75] The ancestors are seen to possess such powers, and there are evil and neutral spiritual powers to whom sacrifices and offerings are often performed. Such practices go on "quietly but frequently in all Christian churches in the East African region."[76]

Mission and mainline churches place great importance on theological and ministerial training. But in AICs, leadership positions were awarded until recently "on the traditional basis of chronological and social elderhood, or through some sign of divine choice."[77] This last point, sign of divine choice, is important—especially when one looks further into the new Pentecostal movements. Personal charisma and claims of mysterious spiritual connectedness to the Holy Spirit through divination, prophecy, power of exorcism, and so on, are common in most churches and especially in Pentecostal and independent churches. Compared to AICs, mainline churches are also often slower to accept women in leadership positions.

The clear difference between mainline churches in Africa and AICs, according to the findings of Magesa's study, is on the way the Bible is treated or interpreted. "Whereas most AICs understand the Bible literally as historical truth, the mainline churches tend to bring a more sophisticated approach to it, not undervaluing it, but not considering it a factual history either."[78] The literal biblical interpretation of AICs is done contextually through allegories "substituting more directly Africa and her experience for that of biblical Israel."[79] Surprisingly, the study found that most interviewees were favorable to ecumenical relationships. Most stunning, perhaps, is the ignorance of many mainline church leaders on African theology.[80] It is unsurprising that AIC leaders are not aware of theological developments in Africa since they are not academically trained. But mainline clergy who have received advanced education in the academic study of philosophy, Bible, and theology are (or should be) expected to be informed about African theology.

Asia and Theology of Religions

With even a casual glance through some collected studies by both evangelical and more liberal Christians in Asia, one sees the dominance of a theology of religions approach to Christian faith in the region. Almost half of the chapters of *Asian Faces of Jesus*,[81] a collection of essays by Asian theologians, deal with understanding Jesus in relation to non-Christian religions. Papers and findings from "the first conference of evangelical mission theologians from the Two Thirds World" (Bangkok, Thailand, March 22–25, 1982) were published under the title *Sharing Jesus in the Two Thirds World*.[82] There are five papers written by Asian evangelical theologians, and all of them deal with theology or Christology in relation to other religions. Christianity's relationship with other living religions is indeed a dominant issue in Asia, and Asian scholars continue to champion a theology of religions approach. Other theological themes like inculturation and liberation are also very important for Asian Christians, and distinctly Asian versions of these ideas are colored by the region's profound religiosity and religious diversity. To Peter Phan, inculturation, liberation, and interreligious dialogue are "the three tasks of the church's mission" in Asia.[83]

Missionaries were among the first to encounter other living religions and cultures. Matteo Ricci in China and Robert de Nobili in India were among the first to accommodate non-Christian religious practices in their missions. Adaptation to the cultures and religions of Asians was a major turning point in the history of Catholic missions in general and the work of the Jesuits, in particular. Ricci's accommodation to various aspects of Confucianism and de Nobili's Sannyasin adaptation to Hindu Brahminism led to the long "Chinese rite controversy"[84] in the Catholic Church, which they eventually lost to their opponents. Yet they succeeded in making this agenda a Christian one, setting the stage for further development. For missionaries, the goal in the study of other religions was to understand their beliefs and worldviews for effective communication of the gospel. The pioneer Lutheran missionary to India, Bartholomew Ziegenbalg, had a practice of promoting interreligious dialogue developed out of deep appreciation for the Tamil culture of his time.[85] The translation work of the Serampore trio (William Carey, Joshua Marshmann, and William Ward) exemplified the use of non-Christian religious worldviews to communicate the gospel. Although the intent of the missionaries was exclusively the meaningful communication of the gospel, they also laid important foundations for the Western study of non-Christian religions.

It was natural for converts from other religions to use the concepts, symbols, and thought forms of their previous cultural and religious life. Even those who outwardly opposed their old forms of faith could not help carrying the deep-seated elements of their old viewpoints over to the new. In the Catholic Church, Vatican II was the watershed moment for missional understandings of Christianity among a world of other religions. Not only were other Christians accepted as fellow believers, but the council also affirmed the possibility of salvation for those who do not know the gospel. The Council consented to the possibility of salvation for those "who without fault on their own part do not know the Gospel of Christ and his Church, but seek God with sincere hearts, and under the influence of grace endeavor to do his will as recognized though the promptings of their conscience."[86] This foundational affirmation in the church's ecclesiology is dealt with in further detail in the Council's *Declaration on the Relation of the Church to Non-Christian Religions (Nostra Aetate)*.[87] The council did not affirm other religions as ways of salvation, but showed the possibility of salvation for their adherents.

Interest in the theology of religions increased as people of different faith traditions came to live side-by-side in a globalized world. A theology

129

of religions evolved out of this proximate reality of religious pluralism. The term "plurality" refers to a condition of existence where religions crisscross in various ways through their adherents. It is not a mere multi-religiosity in which different religions may exist independently even in the same place and at the same time. Religious pluralism evolved from the coexistence of religions and their eventual mutual recognition, and in some cases, cross pollinizing hybridization. It rests on an environment and social structure that values the freedom of religion. Unfortunately, religious pluralism has also been used as a reference point for the relativist theological position of radical pluralists. In this work, we reserve the term "religious pluralism" strictly to name a condition of existence in which people of different religions mutually recognize one another's religions.[88] A turning point in the theology of religions through changes in the Christian attitude toward other religions came about in the third quarter of the twentieth century, a development that can be traced back to the 1960s. Asian Catholic theologians explored the theological implications of Vatican II in dealing with other religious traditions, and much of the development among Protestant and Orthodox Christians came through the initiatives of the World Council of Churches (WCC). While radical theological directions taken by some Catholic theologians could not be contained or supported by the Vatican, the form and theology of interfaith dialogue proposed in the WCC was often controversial and met with strong opposition.

At the heart of the controversies was the relativistic *pluralist* theology which insisted on its particular form of interreligious dialogue. Understandably, pluralism and interreligious dialogue emerged in opposition to attitudes of Christian triumphalism. However, the way that concepts of interreligious dialogue and religious pluralism emerged was unfortunately quite polemical and divisive. While most Christians came to recognize the need to have a new attitude and posture that is humble and less aggressive in its propagation of Christian faith, there came a class of pluralistic theologians who challenged the Christian claim that Jesus is the only savior under the rubric of religious pluralism and interfaith dialogue. The confusion between religious pluralism and pluralistic theology was unsettling for many. Using a classification articulated by one theologian, they sorted out all Christians as either "exclusivists," "inclusivists," or "pluralists"[89] with the last group valued highest in the presupposed evolving order of progression. This categorical compartmentalization seemed to be most acceptable for those who found themselves on the polar ends of this classificatory scheme, that is, the self-identified pluralists and exclusivists. For most others, such a siloed categorization scheme fails to capture the on-the-ground experience of actual religious pluralism. What Lesslie Newbigin said about his distinct position using these three categories is shared by many:

> [My] position which I have outlined is exclusivist in the sense that it affirms the unique truth of the revelation in Jesus Christ, but it is not exclusivist in the sense of denying the possibility of the salvation of the non-Christian. It is inclusivist in the sense that it refuses to limit the saving grace of God to the members of the Christian Church, but it rejects the inclusivism which regards the non-Christian religions as vehicles of salvation. It is pluralist in the sense of acknowledging the gracious work of God in the lives of all human beings, but it rejects a pluralism which denies the uniqueness and decisiveness of what God has done in Jesus Christ.[90]

In recent years, theologians have revised these categories. Paul F. Knitter broadened the categories and gave a much more nuanced description of views that are not mutually exclusive of one another. He compiled the different views under four models: a replacement model (total and partial replacements), a fulfillment model, a mutuality model, and an acceptance model.[91] Alongside Knitter's work, Timothy Tennent proposes a set of four positions from an evangelical perspective, that he believes are "more descriptively accurate" than inclusivism or exclusivism, and that may be easily affirmed by those subscribing to these positions.[92] Tennent's descriptors of pluralistic theology are: revelatory particularism (in place of Knitter's replacement model); universal particularism (for Knitter's fulfilment model); dialogic pluralism (for Knitter's mutuality model); and, narrative postmodernism (for Knitter's acceptance model).

Pluralistic theology made its presence felt most strongly with the publication of *The Myth of Christian Uniqueness: Toward a Pluralistic Theology of Religions*, in 1987. This book is a collection of writings advocating "a pluralist position," which one of its editors described as "a move away from insistence on the superiority or finality of Christ and Christianity toward a recognition of the independent validity of other [religious] ways."[93] The same editor claims the new pluralistic theology of religions to be "a new turn—what might be called a 'paradigm shift'" in a Christian theology of religions. Typically, pluralistic theology contested the exclusivity of traditional Christian claims that God's salvation comes only through Jesus Christ and it condemned the belief that Christian faith is superior to other religious teachings. The logic of interreligious dialogue according to this theology is that only by accepting the salvific possibility of other religions can there be meaningful dialogue. If Christians think that other religions have no valid teaching, there can be no meaningful interaction with them worth calling dialogue. Confused by this controversial theology of religions, many Christians seemed to have either opposed it outright or ignored the proposition as a costly compromise of Christian faith. The most significant and reasoned response came in an appropriately titled *Christian Uniqueness Reconsidered: The Myth of Pluralistic Theology of Religions* from a group of theologians who opposed "the pluralism" as defined by the self-defined pluralists as "the only viable option for Christianity in the modern age."[94] Among the contributors, Lesslie Newbigin's work[95] provides an example of a viable alternative understanding of interfaith dialogue and religious pluralism. Newbigin strongly recommends an honest and genuine dialogue and cooperative projects with other religions through which Christians will tell the story of Jesus and the Bible in words and witnessing actions.[96] He said:

> The purpose of dialogue for the Christian is obedient witness to Jesus Christ, who is not the property of the church but the lord of the church and of all people and who is glorified as the living Holy Spirit takes all that the Father has given to humankind—all people of every creed and culture—and declares it to the church as that which belongs to Christ as Lord.[97]

Liberal theologians from Asia were at the forefront of this new pluralistic theology of religions upon which they proposed interreligious dialogue as a new form of ministry. The only non-Western contributors to *The Myth of Christian Uniqueness* were Asian or persons of Asian origin. The WCC project in interreligious dialogue was initiated and led by Indian scholar and faith leader Stanley J. Samartha, one of the contributors to the collection. He was succeeded in the WCC office by Sri Lankan Wesley Ariarajah. While many Western evangelicals were silent on the issue until the 1990s, some Asian evangelicals joined the conversation boldly. In their 1982 contributions to the meeting of Evangelical Mission Theologians of the "two-thirds world" previously cited, Asian evangelical theologians engage teachings of other religions in relation to Christ and converse with the propositions of other Christian confessional traditions. Vinay Samuel and Chris Sugden outline interreligious dialogue from an evangelical viewpoint and define dialogue with other faiths as:

> being open to other religions, to recognize God's activity in them and to see how they are related to God's unique revelation in Christ.... The goal of dialogue [is] to affirm the Lordship of Christ over all life in such a way that people within their own context may recognize the relevance of that Lordship to them and discover it for themselves.[98]

Asian evangelical scholars continue to develop this theology and refine their positions. Among the list of "important concerns in the contextualization process in Asian theology" by Hwa Yung is "dialogue with Asian religions." He offers a critique of the "two extreme positions" of "total exclusivism" and "salvific inclusivism" that accept "all religions as equally valid ways to God and salvation" and finds a biblically faithful position in between. From a similar viewpoint, Vinoth Ramachandra engages in a stimulating conversation with, and a rich analytical-theological response to, three of the finest Asian liberal theologians: Stanley J. Samartha, Aloysius Pieris, and Raimundo Panikkar.[99]

Between the pluralist and evangelical position is a broad spectrum that defies any easy sorting. Analytical-thinker M. M. Thomas of India, for instance, wants to see the unfolding of the divine purpose in the pluralistic secular history of India "with the unique Christ event...as its clue."[100] Thomas has also done one of the finest studies on the theology of religions by comparing the theologies of two Indian thinkers, Raimundo Panikkar and Paul Devanandan, as a way of witnessing to Christ.[101] Thomas dialectically relates Panikkar's trinitarian universalist theology with Devanandan's proposal for transformative interreligious dialogue in the common quest for the new humanity, as one example of the rich theological ideas fermenting in India.

Even as Asian evangelical scholars have engaged theologically with other religious teachings and outlined a theology of interreligious dialogue, their Western evangelical counterparts still defied such move. In fact, as Harold Netland has pointed out, all the major evangelical meetings in the 1960s and the 1970s that converged into the Lausanne Movement "have almost nothing to say about non-Christian religions themselves."[102] The Lausanne covenant of 1974 mentions interreligious dialogue only negatively by stating, "We reject as derogatory to Christ and the gospel every kind of syncretism and dialogue which implies that Christ speaks equally through all religions and ideologies." Here the most likely reference is some of the pluralistic voices in the WCC's initiative on interreligious dialogue. But, as Netland said, "There is no suggestion in the Covenant that there might be appropriate forms of dialogue,"[103] such as what Samuel and Sugden later proposed. Evangelical theologians began to consider a theology of religions and interreligious dialogue only in the 1990s when a new class of evangelical-inclusive scholars such as Clark Pinnock[104] and John Sanders[105] challenged the soundness and cogency of traditional Western evangelical exclusivism. Today, religious pluralism is accepted by most as a new fact of our time, and interreligious dialogue is trending as ministerial and missional witness among many evangelicals.

Charismatic Theology of Popular Christianity in the Majority World

Through their skillful empirical research and phenomenological approach, social scientists have contributed significantly to the study of world Christianity, especially in charismatic-Pentecostal studies. Such scholars as David Martin, Harvey Cox, Stephen Offutt,[106] and others have made pertinent observations on the religious practices of the people, glimpsed the lived religion (beyond the performed religion) of people in the pews, and made good sense of popular religious phenomenon especially when such a religion experienced special momentum. Among historians, Philip Jenkins is an exception in capturing Christianity in the global South as a social phenomenon.[107] In the previous chapter, we mentioned the contributions of anthropologists, particularly missiological anthropologists. The work of some represented by this group have helped us understand significant aspects of world Christianity. Paul Hiebert's theory of "the excluded middle" deserves a special mention, which we will discuss later in this chapter.

One definitive form of world Christianity in the majority world is the so-called charismatic or Pentecostal movement. Our accounts of new Christian movements in Latin America, Africa, and Asia in the previous chapters clearly indicate the significance of charismatic-Pentecostal dynamics in the emerging reality of world Christianity. While not denying the popular term "Pentecostal-charismatic" or "charismatic-Pentecostal," I will use "charismatic movement" as a broad, encompassing term that includes Pentecostalism, African independent churches, and other such movements in historical mainline churches. As a subset of worldwide evangelical Christianity, charismatic Christianity and its core Pentecostal movement may also be named charismatic evangelicalism, or, as Amos Yong cleverly puts it, "penta-evangelical" Christianity.[108] Kwabena Asamoah-Gyadhu's suggestion of "pneumatic Christianity" accurately describes the main character of this form of faith. As a global movement, Vinson Synan and others appropriately call it "spirit-empowered Christianity."[109] To stress the Pentecostal identity of the movement, David Martin calls the charismatic movement Pentecostalism's "penumbra."[110] As shown in our earlier survey, charismatic Christianity is the heart of the new Christian movements in the majority world. An essential feature of the movement is its grassroots character exemplified in the lives of new Christians in Asia and Africa, and among the renewed Christians in Latin America.

At the heart of this new Christianity in the majority world is a belief in the spirit of God who is active and powerful amid other spiritual forces.

Here lies the fault line between this new charismatic Christianity and the old Western Christianity. For the new charismatic Christians, Jesus Christ has defeated the malignant spirits and Christians share his victory by the infilling of the Holy Spirit that empowers believers. The Holy Spirit is not something to be merely believed objectively, but is alive to be experienced and followed in real life. Faith in God is not only a rational persuasion that God exists and works redemptively, it is also a faith conviction that God wants to save, heal, and empower his people *in their present lives*. For most Christians in the majority world, to believe in the salvation of Jesus Christ is to experience him in life—including his healing—and to follow his teaching and guidance in the power of the Holy Spirit.

Paul Hiebert makes a convincing argument that Western Christians are unable to apprehend the spirituality of Christians in the majority world. He explains Western missionaries' failure to understand the spiritual realities of Indians among whom he was ministering by noting the difference between the Western two-tiered view of reality and the three-tiered view of reality characterizing Indian religious experience. The Western two-tiered view comprises theistic other-world or transcendental godly realm in the upper level, and the present world where we live, the world of empirical science at the lower level. Indians, Hiebert suggests, have another level between these two, namely the unseen world of spirits where spiritual being and forces exist that cannot be directly perceived.[111] This middle-level realm exists in this world but also beyond this world, and is connected to the transcendental realm. The West has excluded this middle realm intellectually since the seventeenth and eighteenth centuries by abandoning or minimizing its belief in spiritual beings. This excluded middle level, the world of the spirits, is what explains the difference between Indian and Western frameworks. The Indian three-tiered view, Hiebert asserts, is similar to the biblical view. As Hwa Yung has rightly noted, this worldview "actually applies throughout much of the "two-thirds world," even among those who seemingly have been secularized by Western education."[112] And according to Kwame Bediako, the success of the ministry of William Wade Harris in West Africa in the early twentieth century came from his functioning "in a spiritual universe," which arose out of his "primal imagination."[113] Harvey Cox has also rightly pointed out this primal spiritual character of the Pentecostal-Charismatic movement[114] in contrast to modernized Christianity of the West.

Global charismatic Christianity is a grassroots spiritual movement in which people express their spirituality in meaningful ways. It deviates from the intellectual movement and more cognitive forms of faith dominating much of the West that emerged out of the Enlightenment. The rationalism of the Enlightenment movement and its kindred secularism swept the Western world nearly clean from any belief in spiritual beings. As discussed in chapter 2, the Enlightenment was a movement that is based upon a strong faith in the descriptive—some would say exhaustive—power of human rationality. It sought to free human beings from superstitions, authorities, and anything that might impede the exercise of human reasoning power. It is suspicious of any claims or anything that cannot be scientifically explained. Thus, it (intellectually) bracketed or even eliminated the spiritual realm. The intellectualization of theology after the Enlightenment is deeply influenced by this reigning rationalism. Romanticism of the nineteenth century which addressed the irrational aspect of human nature somewhat neutralized the hyper-rationalism of the Enlightenment, and largely saved theology from the suppression of rationalism. Even then, belief in supernatural entities and miracles has little or no place in rationalistic intellectual theologies of the West. Typical is the view of William Phipps, who bemoans the survival of supernaturalism in Christianity. The supernatural Jesus found in the gospels, for Phipps, was a creation of the early Christians and evangelists. The authentic gospel of Jesus comes from Paul, according to Phipps, as Paul "refused to pander to seekers of unnatural happenings, and never wrote about Jesus working miracles."[115]

Enlightenment-driven Christianity has, according to some, stripped supernatural miracles from its understanding of the Christian faith. Bible stories of miracles performed by Jesus are treated as mere addenda to the message of the bible. Charismatic Christians are reclaiming such stories as real and resonant with the Holy Spirit's activity in their lives today. The rise of charismatic Christianity also came to contradict the secularization theory of Western liberalism. Built on the intellectualization phenomenon of the modern world, secularization theory asserts that "modernization necessarily leads to a decline of religion, both in society and in the minds of individuals."[116] As scholars studying Pentecostal-charismatic Christianity have testified, charismatic Christianity together with its kindred evangelicalism is part of the religious resurgence that disproves and discredits secularization theory as explanatory of modern religious experience.[117]

More often than not, contextual theology gives greater weight to the context of intellectuals and the "cultured despisers" of faith and not the popular context of the ordinary faithful in constructing its theology. Yet by its very nature, contextual theology is supposed to be a popular theology. Whether or not a theology represents popular aspirations and beliefs is a test of its contextuality. Popular Christianity is usually defined in contradistinction to institutional religion.[118] It is characteristically elusive in that there really is no common belief or practice that defines popular religion and that most popular religious movements frequently grow into powerful institutions even to the point of losing their popular essence or experiential base. Charismatic Christianity, and especially Pentecostalism, emerged as a grassroots popular Christian movement. As we have discussed in chapter 3, Pentecostalism did not begin in the Azusa Street Revival of 1906 alone; it arose as a part of the larger grassroots charismatic awakening that happened simultaneously in different parts of the world at the beginning of the twentieth century. And most who identify with its vitality and power believe its continuation as a grassroots movement will be determined by the sustenance of its charisma.

Some characteristics of popular religion provide points of departure for understanding charismatic Christianity. The phrase "popular Christianity" is sometimes used to emphasize the continuation of pre-Christian or non-Christian elements in popular practice. The term "popular religion" also highlights the liveliness of a religious practice, where average people pray, worship, and live. It refers to the religion that is close to the people's heart and to which they can relate instinctively.[119] Its marginality and people-centeredness are the key identifiers. The survey findings on inculturation by Laurenti Magesa discussed earlier in this chapter show forms of popular inculturation in Africa. The gap Magesa discovered between the indigenous practices of faith—and the faith performed according to the official rules—shows the tension between the instinctively expressed indigenous faith of popular Christianity and the imposed institutionalized faith. Inculturation can be done in an imposing manner, but genuine inculturation grows out of the people as a spontaneous expression of faith. Therefore, we submit that charismatic popular Christian theology, as fluid and ambiguous as it may be, is as contextual a theology as other forms of contextual theology we have discussed.

Again, the concept of contextualization attempts to relate the gospel to both traditional culture and the changing sociopolitical world. If indigenization, inculturation, and interfaith dialogue intend to interact with traditional cultures and religious beliefs, liberation theologies will likely relate more with present political and socioeconomic realities. If inculturation does not come from the people as a spontaneous faith expression, its genuineness as an inculturation is doubtful. Similarly, liberation has to be the experienced liberation of the people. Liberation theology is supposedly a theology of the people in that it claims people as the subject of its theology. In the brief sketch we have provided on liberation theology in Latin America, we have shown that it was born out of the socioeconomic and political oppression of the poor people who elicit its theology. The goal of the theology is the people's freedom from such exploitation. Recall Korean *minjung* theology directly relates to the people—as "min" and "jung" mean "people" and "mass of people." Here the mass of people as the subject of history and theology is understood in opposition to the ruling elites.[120] Again, the choice of *han* as the subject of *minjung* theology and the Dalit theology's choice of *dalit* (meaning "crushed" or "oppressed") to signify the marginality of the people for whom the theologies are constructed indicates the nature of the theology as an articulation of God's remedial calling to change the material experiences of people living under oppression.

There is no doubt about the intention of these liberation theologies to be genuine theologies of oppressed people. The question, however, is if the people's spiritual aspirations and visions are represented in the theology or if these theologies are prescribed theologies of what intellectual theologians believed to be good for the people based on economic and philosophical analysis. Either in their initial or developed stage, contextual liberation theologies become theological prescriptions for the people in need. This is not to suggest that such theologies are totally devoid of grassroots connections, but rather to note that if a theology does not arise out of the heart of the people, it easily turns into a mere *prescription* theology for the people. There is a real historical tension between humanistic liberation theologies that prescribe a this-worldly liberation of the poor, on the one hand, and, on the other hand, the spiritually imbued charismatic theology that is built on the people's vision and experience of the Holy Spirit in their hope for a heavenly liberation as well. Here, the difference is also what experts think is good for the people and what the people long for. In the opinion of intellectual experts, what transpires among the people such as other-worldly spiritual longings and emotional expressions of their faith experience may not be good for the people as they are not rationally proven or faithful to the tradition. Again, popular inculturated faith does not always produce a reasonable belief in the eyes of official and institutional versions of the faith. And some may even criticize aspects of popular beliefs as simply convictions based on convenience.

The rise of charismatic-Pentecostalism in the twentieth century is a testimony of the power of a religion that connects to the worldview, ethos, and psycho-social outlook of the people. Even as some charismatics may think of themselves in otherworldly terms, they are truly contextual, as their form of spiritual otherworldliness itself is a contextual expression of their spirituality. As important as the issues of poverty, oppression, and exploitations are, the theology and actions propounded by liberationists on these issues do not always relate to the grassroots religious aspirations of ordinary people—be they feminist for women, Latin America for the poor people, Dalit for the outcaste, or *minjung* for the exploited laborers. While these theologies tend to look for a this-worldly humanistic liberation, popular Christianity as expressed in the charismatic movements tends to privilege the spiritual rather than the material and humanistic, finding present spiritual joy in the hope for freedoms that also come in the afterworld. Simon Chan makes a helpful differentiation between "a theology of human experience" of liberation theologies and "a theology grounded in ecclesial experience" found in charismatic Christianity.[121] The contrast between the two forms of contextualization is quite clear in Korean Christianity, according to Sebastian Kim. The two are represented by *kibock sinang* ("faith of seeking blessings") and *minjung* theology. While the former, a dominant character of Korean Christianity, came out of Korean revival and sees spiritual blessings as the clue for the nation, *minjung* liberation theology seeks to meet the people's material needs.[122] The contrast may have explained the disconnect between liberation theology and the rise of Pentecostal and charismatic movements in Latin America.

Literal in their understanding of the Bible and biblicist in their attempt to follow the exact letter of the Bible, charismatic Christians rely on what they believe the Bible teaches. Yet, as Laurent Magesi mentioned in his survey findings, their applications of biblical teachings are done in the most contextual way. Commenting on R. S. Sugirtharajah's statement that "there is at present an explosion of interest in Third World biblical interpretation," Philip Jenkins asks "which of these voices [conservative or liberationist] accurately represent the thought of the wider Christian community in those societies"?[123] The conservative voice may be closer to the popular voice, but a popular Christian voice has a distinction that is hard to articulate and defies reduction to categories of conservative, liberal, and liberationist.

Chapter 7

CHRISTIAN MISSION IN THE NEW WORLD OF CHRISTIANITY

We closed our discussion of the modern missionary movement in chapter 2 by noting the shift from the post-Christian West to the rising post-Western Christianity in the global South and East. Picking up from the discussion of Christian mission in that chapter, we will continue to deal with the modern missions followed by the rising world mission movements and the dynamics of world Christianity that have helped to redefine the meaning and practice of Christian mission in the twenty-first century. What does it mean to do mission in the new world of Christianity? How has mission been done by the new Christians from the global South and East? What continues and what has changed from the modern missionary movement? We will first highlight some conceptual changes in the world of Christian missions, and then look into the developments of mission in the majority world, especially among Protestants. It is not possible to tell the story of missions in all the countries of the majority world? Our modest aim is to underline significant developments of Christian missions in regions and nations where such developments are conspicuous. We will select a few such regions, choose one or two missionary organizations, and do brief case studies.

Chapter 7

Changes in Missionary Conceptions

The crisis of mission experienced in the second half of the twentieth century that we briefly discussed in chapter 2 was caused in part by the decolonization of many non-Western nations together with the consensus demonization of colonialism. No easy generalization can be made on the relationship between modern missions and colonialism. What was broadly true is that modern missions functioned under the general "friendly protective umbrella" of colonial rules.[1] The extent to which mission efforts related to colonial rule differ from place to place and time to time. Even the work of one missionary, William Carey, shows contrasting pictures of the relationship between the two enterprises. Carey entered India illegally as a missionary, and had to leave the British colony to work in the Danish colony of Serampore with his colleagues. However, Carey later worked for the British colony as a professor of Indian languages in Fort William College, which trained officers for the British colonial administration. Later missionaries in India such as C. F. Andrews and E. Stanley Jones contributed enormously to the cause of the Indian nationalist movement.

As noted, decolonization and rising nationalism in the non-Western world radically changed the world of Christian missions, bringing to a close the era of modern missions. Independence and the new pride in national identities were accompanied by the resurgence of non-Christian religions.[2] The challenges faced by Christians were not primarily the non-Christian religions of the people, but the Western political ideologies of communism and humanistic secularism that provided significant opposition to Christian faith and mission. The struggle to free mission efforts from Western domination and the colonial legacy was hard fought. Indigenous church leaders in the non-Western world were caught between the moral questioning of missional work for its colonial collaborations and the call to protect the integrity of indigenous forms of Christian faith. Confronting charges against Christians and missionaries that they were the watchdogs of colonialism, these leaders also had to educate Christians in the pew against unhealthy reliance on foreign missionary resources. The call for a missionary moratorium and the ensuing controversy demonstrated the complexity of the situation.

Some church leaders in the majority world called for a moratorium on missions by a temporary withholding of foreign missionaries and funds in order for the indigenous churches in the non-West (mission fields) to discover their own identity and demonstrate self-reliance. Several leaders including Emerito P. Nacpil of the Philippines (Asia), José Miguez-Bonino of Argentina (Latin America), and John Gatu of Kenya (Africa) voiced such a call. The clearest and most-sustained argument was issued by John Gatu. If Nacpil's call to "go home" and Migueze-Bonino's "stay home" left a question mark to the missionary enterprise in general, Gatu seemed careful in calling for the withdrawal of all missionaries "for a period of not less than five years for each side to rethink and formulate what is going to be the future of their relationship."[3] We should also note that similar concerns (though not in the form of moratorium) had been voiced in other places. The National Christian Council of India had reconsidered the role of missionaries in a consultation as early as 1961. It asked such questions as "Is he [i.e., the missionary] needed? If needed, for what purpose? What sort of missionary does the Indian Church need now?"[4] Thus, by the 1970s, the question of foreign missionaries' role was not new in the larger context of the Christian world. Gatu, then general secretary of the Presbyterian Church of East Africa, first issued his call at the "Mission Festival '71" of the Reformed Church of America at Milwaukee, Wisconsin, in October 1971;[5] and then pressed on the call at the WCC Committee on Ecumenical Sharing of Personnel in 1972;[6] the All Africa Conference of Churches (AACC) in 1974; and at the Lausanne Congress of World Evangelization the same year (1974).[7]

At his presentation in the Mission Festival '71 in Milwaukee, Gatu stunned the audience of twelve hundred or so in the auditorium. He declared:

> We cannot build the church in Africa on alms given by overseas churches, nor are we serving the cause of the Kingdom by turning all bishops, general secretaries, moderators, presidents, superintendents, into good, enthusiastic beggars, by always singing the tune of poverty in the church of the Third World.... But I am saying that we in the Third World must liberate ourselves from the bondage of Western dependency

by refusing anything that renders impotent the development of our spiritual resources, which in turn makes it impossible for the church in the Third World to engage in the mission of God in their own areas. . . . I started by saying that the missionaries should be withdrawn from the Third World for a period of five years. I will go further and say that missionaries should be withdrawn, period.[8]

Marvin Hoff describes the immediate response as follows:

People filed out of the auditorium . . . in stunned silence or hushed conversation. Some broke into tears in their groups, feeling rejected in their deep call to serve God in mission. Some wrestled genuinely with this thunderbolt challenge from a servant of Christ. A special workshop was quickly organized to provide for discussion of this unexpected challenge to a new commitment in mission.[9]

In his reflections on the Festival, John Hesselink said, "Some, I suspect, will condemn the whole Festival as a failure, if not a betrayal of the cause of 'missions' because of the strident, negative note heard rather frequently."[10] In the festival, "the dominant [negative] impression," he said was "the burden of the address by the Rev. John Gatu, General Secretary of the Presbyterian Church of East Africa."[11]

Gatu seemed to have fine-tuned his call in his later addresses, indicating that the moratorium should be a temporary one. At the AACC, his call received mixed responses as "there is no real agreement either to its meaning or as to its desirability,"[12] reported Adrian Hastings. The impact on the Lausanne Congress appeared to be mild but quite significant.[13] Part of Lausanne Covenant article 9 states, "A reduction of foreign missionaries and money in an evangelized country may sometimes be necessary to facilitate the national church's growth in self-reliance and to release resources for unevangelized areas." The WCC's Ecumenical Sharing of Personnel passed the baton to the Bangkok Conference of the Commission on World Mission and Evangelism in 1973. The Bangkok Conference agreed with Gatu's call but recognized it is not applicable to every situation.[14]

Different Christians understood the moratorium call differently. Many evangelicals resisted it at first for fear of ceasing evangelistic mission work altogether. Other missionary advocates both in the West and in the majority world opposed the idea of ceasing interdependence among churches. Gatu defended the call and persuaded many doubters. Those who questioned the practice of evangelistic mission interpreted the call to end the evangelistic missionary enterprise as well overdue. What this call signified was of utmost importance for the history of missional efforts. Gerald Anderson pointed out that though "shortsighted and simplistic" in approach, the moratorium call was significant.[15] First, it indicates "that the 'younger churches' have come of age," and we should be thankful. Second the call is one of "integrity—for both sides," the so-called Third World churches and the missionary-sending Western churches. Robert Reese concluded that the moratorium was seen "as either a threat to world mission or the dawn of a new and better era." Writing in 2014, he opined that "the moratorium represented a symbolic milestone marking the end of a colonial mission paradigm and the beginning of the current postcolonial era in missions."[16] It clearly marked the end of Western "foreign mission" paradigm, and the beginning of "world mission" in which churches from all continents and nations are invited to participate in God's mission to all the continents and regions of the world.

The moratorium on mission exemplified the larger crisis in missional sensibilities that prevailed from the middle of the twentieth century for decades. The crisis became a purging instrument and a change agent for the concept of mission. The crisis offered a corrective to the enterprise of mission from its colonial collaboration and complicity, generating a period of theological creativity. The most important theological development of the period was the relocation of the foundation of the missionary enterprise to the Triune God's redemptive mission (*missio Dei*) of the world and the entire creation. Among the conciliar Protestants, the concept of *missio Dei* began to surface at the International Missionary Council's enlarged meeting in Willingen in 1952. After the failure to produce an agreeable statement on the Theological Basis of the Missionary Obligation of the Church (the theme of the meeting), a Statement on the

Missionary Calling of the Church was produced and accepted. The opening sentence of section 2 of the Statement on the Missionary Calling of the Church says, "The missionary movement of which we are apart has its source in the Triune God himself."[17] Here the postcolonial concept of *missio Dei* began to take shape.

Karl Hartenstein first used the term *"missio Dei"* to describe the main theological emphasis of the meeting in his report after the conference.[18] From there, the term circulated and gradually gained wide acceptance. The concluding sentence of the Statement on the Missionary Calling also became key in this emerging missional sensibility. It says, "There is no participation in Christ without participation in His mission to the world."[19] If being Christian means participation in Christ, every Christian is obligated to be a missionary. This theological grounding of the missionary enterprise is not foreign to the Orthodox Church for whom salvation (*theosis* or deification) consists in the participation in, or being drawn into, the divine communion of the Triune God.[20] This perspective has theological consonance with the Catholic conciliar efforts of Vatican II that developed the notion of the *missio Dei* based on a redefinition of the church. The Council's Dogmatic Constitution of the Church (*Lumen Gentium*) redefined the church "as 'the people made one in the unity of the Father, Son, and Holy Spirit' (LG4)."[21] This, according to Stephen Bevans and Roger Schroeder, became the basis for the Trinitarian missionary understanding of the council as developed in its document on mission *Ad Gentes.*[22]

David Bosch identified a major paradigm shift in missiology in the crisis of mission in the mid-twentieth century.[23] American Lutheran mission historian James Scherer was even more specific. On how the missionary crisis was accompanied by the birth of a new theology of mission, he states, "Before 1950 the study of the 'theology of mission' in today's sense hardly existed. The discipline was not considered necessary."[24] From the 1960s, theology of mission as a discipline began to take shape practically with the publication of the first comprehensive study on the theology of mission, *The Theology of the Christian Mission.*[25] The most comprehensive and thorough study of the theology of mission in the closing years of the twentieth century was Bosch's own *Transforming Mission*. Bosch's book continues to be one of the most influential missional texts to this day. His discussions of a biblical theology of mission and historical paradigms of missional justification are exceptionally insightful and meaningful. What makes Bosch's work stand out, however, is how he brilliantly captures what he calls the various "Elements of an Emerging Ecumenical Missionary Paradigm." Beginning with the church and its missional nature, he lists thirteen elements of the new missionary paradigm.[26] The list demonstrates the richness and wealth missiology of missiology. Although he included *missio Dei* as one of the elements of the new paradigm, really Bosch's entire treatment of the theology of mission rests on this concept. A major lacuna is the absence of Pentecostal-charismatic Christianity in the discussion, which, by the time Bosch's book was published in the early 1990s, had already exerted wide influence.

Overall, Bosch takes a synchronic approach in discussing the theology of mission by identifying a number of key elements. Taking a slightly different, somewhat diachronic approach, Stephen Bevans and Roger Schroeder recapitulated the continuing development of a theology of mission. Examining the historical development of missionary thinking of different confessional bodies including Catholic, Orthodox, conciliar Protestants, and evangelical and Pentecostal Protestants, they show how missiology converges into a complex character at the end of the twentieth century. They propose to capture the various strands of the theology of mission together under "prophetic dialogue" for the beginning of the twenty-first century. As simple as it may first appear, this also shows the complexity and nuance of the theology of mission. For Bevans and Schroeder, mission must be both prophetical and dialogical at the same time. Can dialogue and prophecy go together? If the ministry of prophecy is understood as the pronouncement of God's word without diluting the message or negotiating the content, is there a room for dialogue? Bevans and Schroeder rightly assert that our world demands we engage in dialogue around the meaning of authoritative pronouncements. Yet no authoritative understanding can be reached without considering the view of the neighbor whose confession and beliefs are different from ours. While the authority of the prophetic message may not be negotiable, our understanding of the authoritative message is highly negotiable. There are nonnegotiable theological constants [for example, "God is love"], yet the understanding, interpretations, and practices of those constants are contextual. Our pluralistic world demands that we listen to one another's confessional voices.

Missions from the Majority World

It is intriguing to note that around the same time that missions conceptually changed from being a "foreign" enterprise of the Western churches to the "world mission" of the global church in the 1960s, Christians from Africa, Asia, and Latin America began to engage actively in missional new efforts. A holistic understanding of mission as "the whole Church taking the whole Gospel to the whole world" seems to be penetrating the global church as Christians from the majority world are taking their place. The numerical increase in the number of Christians in Africa was largely the result of active engagement in evangelistic missions by grassroots African Christians themselves. This growth sowed the seeds of even more indigenous missional growth. It is of great interest that Christians in Asia, the least Christian of the continents in proportion to the population, seems to be most active in missions. Today, the tiny nation of South Korea, where Christians comprise only a quarter of the population, sends out the second-highest number of missionaries in the world, next only to the United States.[27] The enormous growth of the Christian faith in the world's two most populous nations of China and India is only matched by the vigorous evangelistic missionary activities of its indigenous Christians. Because of the large number of missionaries sent out in recent years, Singapore has been called the "Antioch of Asia."[28] A report made around the year 2000 shows that Singapore sent out more than 700 missionaries. It also houses numerous international Christian organizations and mission agencies.[29]

In accounting for the story of missional efforts from the majority world, it can be difficult to decide where to begin. Most Western missionaries during the modern missionary movement worked with the so-called "native evangelists." It would be unfair to discount the contributions of those native evangelists. In many cases, they were the pioneers who penetrated the frontiers and led to the conversions of many. Overshadowed by Western missionaries, they were commonly denied the status of "missionary."[30] Who is a missionary and who is not? The issue becomes even more complex today as the discrimination between missionaries and native peoples continues even in newer missionary enterprises. Thousands of missionaries are working in India today, and almost all of them are Indians. They are native in the sense that they are Indians; but many of them do crosscultural boundaries while others remain culturally native. Similarly, most "missionaries" in China today are Chinese and many are culturally native to their zone of missional work. Meanwhile, in numbering Korean missionaries, the Korea Research Institute for Mission (KRIM) counts only those sent from South Korea serving outside South Korea.[31]

When Peter Wagner described the early story of missions in the majority world as follows, he does not seem to be mindful of the difference between the designations of "native evangelists" and "missionaries":

> In the 1820s, for example, missionaries like Josua Mateinaniu were hopping from one island to another in the Pacific. This is one reason why Oceania is almost entirely Christian today. In the 1830s, some Jamaicans, led by Joseph Merrick, pioneered the missionary movement to the Cameroons. By 1884, Methodist missionaries were going out from India to Malaysia. In 1907, Korean Presbyterians began sending missionaries, among the first being Kee Pung Lee. One of history's most effective missionary societies, called the Melanesian Brotherhood, was organized in the 1920s in Oceania.[32]

While most native evangelists were not given the "missionary" title, there were many who deserved it. Bishop Samuel Ajayi Crowther, for instance, could not be discounted from being a missionary of the Church Missionary Society. A freed slave who made his home first in Sierra Leone, Crowther joined the Niger expedition and later led the Yoruba Mission to his native state and had a long missionary career in his home state of Nigeria.[33] Even if strict "cross-cultural" and "cross-religious" works are used as the norms, native Christians were involved in cross-religious and cultural missions from an early period. As early as 1910, the small Mizo Christians of Northeast India sent a few missionaries to the neighboring Manipur.[34]

From such early humble beginnings, the missionary endeavors of the majority world church grew. Active engagement in missions in large measure came about following the great influx of people converting to Christianity in the third quarter of the twentieth century.

In a study conducted in 1972, a group of scholars led by Wagner found about 3,404 Protestant missionaries sent by 210 mission agencies from the majority (non-Western) world.[35] By 1980, the number of missionaries had reached 13,238 and the mission agencies had increased to 749.[36] Larry Pate estimated some 137,170 Protestant missionaries in the world in 1990. Of these, about 48,884 were missionaries from the majority world, including 46,157 missionaries sent by missionary agencies of the majority world and the remaining 2,727 by Western missionary agencies.[37] As the number of missionaries from the majority world outgrew missionaries from the West, the Christian world began to pay more attention to forms of Christianity in the global South.

Since the beginning of the twenty-first century, it has become increasingly difficult to find reliable statistics for mission efforts and missionaries, especially in the majority world. And, again, many Christian leaders seem to disagree on who qualifies as a "missionary." Numerous mission agencies from the majority world today continue to differentiate "missionary" from "native evangelist" as was done popularly in the modern missionary movement. Yet, their experience of evangelistic missions does not always support distinguishing missionaries from evangelists. I'll recount a personal experience to clarify the point. In the summer of 2013, I was privileged to meet with representatives of a few indigenous mission agencies in Jos, Nigeria. During the discussion, it became clear that there was tension in the understanding of what constitutes "mission" and "missionary." Those serving with students in the universities who had numerous success stories of conversions from other religions and those serving cross-culturally among non-Christian ethnic tribes had different priorities and understanding. The discussion evolved into a debate on what constitutes "Christian mission."

The main distinction between the roles of missionaries and evangelists appears to be between *cross-cultural* mission and *evangelistic* mission.

While the former diffuses the gospel, the latter is a contagious movement that grows by attracting people to Christian faith. This is quite similar to the distinction between "Traditional Evangelism" and "Pentecostal Evangelism" in Latin American Protestantism.[38] I tried to explain to the group that both understandings constitute mission proper, especially in our contemporary understanding. I am not sure to what extend I succeeded, and I do not think I convinced all participants with my plea that we should value both forms of mission. Many of the charismatics and Pentecostals grew by way of attracting congregants into their lively worship services. They are often accused of indulging in "sheep stealing" as their growth includes shifting members from other congregations. But spontaneous Pentecostal/charismatic growth also results from attracting non-Christians or inactive, unchurched Christians. This form of growth is attractional in nature and may not involve deliberate frontier crossing of cultures or religions. The faith spreads contagiously through the emotional and spiritual affections of people drawn to these congregations.

In order to highlight the missional sensibility of these new indigenous Christians of the majority world, I will offer some selected stories of missionary movements in the three continents of Asia, Africa, and Latin America. Not meant to be an exhaustive study, these selections are mostly from Protestant Christianity and exemplify the new wave of missions. Parallel movements are happening in other traditions. In fact, the Catholic Church has been experiencing remarkable globalization with the balance of its reach and influence tilting toward the majority world in recent years.

Each region of the majority world has distinctive characteristics that are manifested in the way the missionary movements there originated and developed. Whereas there are far too many mission organizations in different parts of Asia and Africa working on their own, the new missionary movement among the evangelicals in Latin America is organized under one broad organization called COMIBAM. Therefore, we can get a good picture of the developments in Latin America through the story of COMIBAM. To get a glimpse of the new missionary movements, we will study one or two mission agencies or cooperative organizations in Asia and Africa.

Asian Missions—Stories from South and Northeast Asia

Asian Christians have a long history of engagements in mission. The Marthoma Evangelistic Association of India was formed in Kerala, India, in 1888 and is claimed to be the first of such indigenous evangelistic endeavors in Asia. [39] The association sent out missionaries among non-Christians in other parts of India. Despite being a small minority, Japanese Christians have made a significant contribution to mission efforts in other Asian countries. Because of the high number and diversity of missional efforts there, we will look at more stories from Asia than other continents. After overviewing Chinese evangelistic missions, we will examine cases from India (South Asia) and South Korea (Northeast Asia).

In much of Southeast Asia, diaspora Chinese Christians have great influence. From such great Chinese evangelists as Dora Yu, Watchman Nee, Witness Lee, Wang Mingdao, and John Sung, Chinese evangelists have made great impact within China and among diaspora Chinese communities in Taiwan, Malaysia, the Philippines, Singapore, and beyond. The rapid growth of the unregistered Protestant house churches from the 1980s was in part caused by the works of these diaspora churches. Today, indigenous Christians in China are heavily engaged in evangelistic missionary works within China and beyond, and the Chinese churches in places like Singapore, Malaysia, and the Philippines have been doing powerful and profound missional work in Southeast Asia and beyond. Within China, as the tensions between the registered churches of the Three-Self Patriotic Movement (TSPM) and the unregistered congregations (popularly called "house churches" although most in the cities are no longer meeting in houses) are decreasing in China's urban contexts, the theological differences between the two continue. By and large TSPM officials held liberal theological views while a good number of Christians in registered TSPM churches and most unregistered churches hold to a conservative or even fundamentalist theology.

A brief comparison between what Bishop K. H. Ding (Bishop Ding Guangxun) wrote about "evangelism" in 1983 and how Peter Xu, founder of the Word of Life (house church) movement from the 1960s to the 1980s, thinks of evangelism demonstrates their different missional perspectives. Defending TSPM's identification with the Communist Party and calling the Chinese church "post-liberational," Ding insists that the evangelistic message in China is "reconciliation in Jesus Christ."[40] He discounted suffering as an essential part of being Christian and said "suffering may hinder as much as help people in their approach to God."[41] Provokingly, he said, "Our job is to awaken our people to behold and rejoice and adore him, and let every spark of color be brought out everywhere. Evangelism is not only to bring Christ to men and women and to bring about repentance; it is to an extent to bring him out of them."[42] Peter Xu, on the other hand, understood evangelism to consist in God's forgiveness of sin as wrought by Christ at the cross.[43] To him and the movement of the Word of Life congregations, the theology of the cross is the center of Christian faith and suffering is an essential part of being Christian.[44] An itinerant evangelist during the height of China's Cultural Revolution in the 1960s and the 1970s, Xu became a leader and connecting link among "revival furnaces" of house churches from the 1980s. In his 2004 interview with Yalin Xin, he stated, "At the time when it was extremely difficult to connect with fellow Christians, 'revival furnaces' did not have horizontal relationships. Their relationship was vertical and independent. Because I was a 'wanderer,' who had no home to return to, I became a connector and a seeker."[45]

1. Korean Missionary Movement and the University Bible Fellowship

In the history of Korean Christianity, the "Nevius method" or the "Ross-Nevius method"[46] was credited for the success of Christian missions. The method emphasized the training and utilizing of every convert to evangelize others. The Korean Church was a missionary church from its early years and its missionary engagement has expanded tremendously since the 1980s when it shifted from being a "missionary-receiving church" to a "missionary-sending church."[47] A number of statistical studies have been done on Korean missions. While the Korea Research Institute for Mission (KRIM) seems generally conservative in its counting, the Korea World Missions Association's (KWMA) statistics show larger numbers especially after the year 2000. Statistical reports of the two were the same between 1979 (KRIM, 93 missionaries) and 1996 (KWMA, 4,402 missionaries), then differed from 1998 when KWMA reported 6,804 missionaries and KRIM has 5,948 missionaries.[48] I will mostly follow the more conservative count by KRIM and occasionally compare it with KWMA's numbers.

The greatest rate of growth in the missionary force was seen in the 1980s when the number of missionaries jumped from 93 in 1979 to 1,178 in 1989. Between 1986 and 1989, the number of missionaries more than doubled from 511 to 1,178. This sudden spike has been credited partly to South Korea's hosting of the Olympic Games through which the populace was introduced to the wider world, and due to the fact that travel became much easier for Koreans. The increase from 1,645 in 1990 to 8,103 in the year 2000 is just as impressive, if not more so, as the previous decade, though the average annual growth rate of missionaries was just 17.2 percent[49] was much less impressive. According to Steve Sang-Cheol Moon of KRIM, various factors contributed to the explosive growth of Korean missions in the 1980s and the 1990s including the following:

…the rapid growth of the Korean church up into the 1970s, the churches' conservative theological orientation, a culture of sacrificial giving and support for missionaries, government policies that allowed for unrestricted travel[s] and stays overseas, and a surplus of seminary graduates who could not find ministry opportunities in Korea.[50]

The increase of missionaries from 8,103 in 2000 to 19,373 in 2011 shows a further decline in the average annual growth to 10.5 percent. By 2013, according to KRIM, the number of Korean foreign missionaries reached 20,085 spreading to 171 countries around the world.[51] From this point, Korean missions seem to stagnate. At the end of 2014, according to KRIM's finding, there were 20,467 missionaries working in 163 countries.[52] The findings of Moon and others of KRIM are not corroborated by Timothy Park's report based on KWMA statistics. In sharp contrast to the report by Moon, Park states that 1,317 new missionaries were added in 2013, and 932 new missionaries in 2014.[53]

Korean missions are of differing kinds. From tent-making missions on college campuses to rural and urban church planting, from strictly preaching the gospel to educational and diaconal ministries, the majority of works relate to theologically conservative missionary works. Yet, there are also a few radicals whose missionary orientation is social in nature and humanistic in purview. In Timothy Park's calculation, more than 35 percent of the Korean missionaries are involved in church planting, which shows a high view of the church.[54] Steve Sang-Cheol Moon analyzed the missionaries in 2013 and noted several important characteristics. "A large majority of Korean missionaries (81.3 percent)," he said, "were involved in traditional soul-wining ministries, including Bible translation, church planting, discipleship training, educational ministries, itinerant evangelism, and theological education."[55] His statistical analysis shows that there are more women missionaries (53.7 percent) than men, more interdenominational agencies than denominational agencies, and almost all (96.2 percent) are university graduates among whom 37.5 percent have postgraduate degrees.[56] An estimated 363 million US dollars "[were] channeled through mission agencies of Korean missionaries" in 2012.[57]

Major economic growth experienced by the country had a tremendous impact on missionary efforts. Missions and missionaries have also drawn criticism as the primary mode of missionary activity changed from mission out of poverty to mission out of affluence. From allegations of spiritual pride to playing the role of neocolonialists, some missions and missionaries suffered the reproach of critics. The decline in the rate of growth of missionaries is also accompanied by other issues. The 2015 report of KRIM shows a rather high number (304) of missionary attrition, and it says as many as 267 missionaries withdrew involuntarily.[58]

In a comparison between missionaries sent by denominational churches and nondenominational societies from South Korea, Eun Soo Kim identified "10 Largest Sending Denominational Mission Boards" and "10 Largest Sending Mission Societies." At the top of the mission societies is the University Bible Fellowship while the General Assembly of the Presbyterian Church in Korea (Hapdong) occupies the top place among the denominational boards.[59] A brief case study of the University Bible Fellowship (UBF) reveals an important aspect of Korean missionary endeavors. The selection of UBF is not meant to suggest that it represents Korean missionary movement as a whole. In fact, the opposite is true to an extent as UBF has typically distinguished itself from many other Korean missions. Yet as Rebecca Y. Kim has argued, UBF typifies Korean evangelicalism, which is characterized by conservatism and fundamentalism, intense devotional life, and being hierarchically organized. "Despite the influences of American Christianity, UBF is...very much a *Korean* evangelical organization,"[60] said Kim. One feature of UBF that interests the present volume is the emphasis it gives in doing missions in the Western Hemisphere, especially in the United States.

Founded during the volatile period of South Korea in 1961, UBF is a lay-based tent-making missionary enterprise focusing on discipling college students through Bible studies, prayer, and a disciplined life. With an effort to instill hope through these Bible studies to a despairing student community, Samuel Chang-woo Lee and an American missionary, Sarah Barry, founded the fellowship in Kwangju in September 1961.[61] Its early prayer catchphrase "Bible Korea, World Mission" summarize its two major emphases: Bible study and world mission. In 1977, the two leaders moved to the United States and made Chicago the headquarters of the UBF while much of the human resources continued to be drawn from South Korea. From then on, UBF came to be known most popularly for its ministry to evangelize or re-evangelize the West through campus ministries.

From his founding of the fellowship until his death in 2002, Samuel Lee ruled the fellowship as both an autocratic authoritarian leader and a caring fatherly figure. At the heart of the ministry is an intense practice of Bible study and prayer done by missionaries to interested students. Missionaries are encouraged to trust the Holy Spirit to guide and help every work and event of the ministry. Converts are expected to join the fellowship, to grow in their spiritual life, and climb the fellowship's ladder of membership and leadership. Simple living and a disciplined life of devotion to the fellowship and its mission are demanded. Although missionaries are unpaid and expected to support themselves, their unquestionable loyalty as a family and/or individual is demanded. Unmarried members are encouraged to marry another member, and such marriages are called "marriage for mission." Children of missionaries are often referred to as "second generation 'missionaries.'"[62] In homes of missionaries, one would find displayed the "spiritual rules" of Samuel Lee together with his picture.

In North America, the fellowship became controversial for several reasons, including Lee's heavy-handed leadership style and the organization's militaristic style of governance.[63] The aggressiveness of its evangelism; its isolationist style of existence; its top-heavy leadership, steep hierarchy, and high demand from members has drawn intense criticism. Samuel Lee often severely criticized those who left the fellowship.[64] At one time, UBF was considered a cult by some and lost its membership with the National Association of Evangelicals.[65] It regained its NAE membership in 2008 after a good bit of campaigning through American evangelical leaders and scholars. In Rebecca Kim's opinion, much of these criticisms and allegations of cultlike behavior are results of a cultural clash between UBF's hyper-Korean evangelicalism and American individualist culture.[66] Yet, strong criticisms were also made by formers members of UBF and other non-UBF church leaders. In 2000, almost half of UBF staff members staged a protest and demanded "reform."[67]

After Lee's death, UBF is said to have become more democratic and mainstream while also losing the intensity of its evangelistic enthusiasm. Despite its heavy investment with intense zeal to evangelize, UBF missions in North America show no tangible results.[68] Rebecca Kim suggests several reasons including the hardness of secular American college campuses as a mission field, the "deficiencies" of the Korean missionaries to meet that challenge, and the clash with the dominant white culture and its sense of racial superiority.[69]

2. Indigenous Missions in India

The clash between foreign missions in India and Indian nationalism dates back to Mahatma Gandhi, who grew increasingly critical toward

Christian missions during his tenure as the leader of the Indian nationalist movement for independence from British colonial rule. In response to the question of whether missionaries would be welcomed to the future independent India, Gandhi made a controversial statement in 1931:

> If they [missionaries] confine themselves to social and economic uplift they would be [welcome], but if they did as they are now doing, namely using hospitals and schools for the purpose of proselytizing then I should certainly ask them to withdraw. One nation's religion is as good as another nation's. Certainly India's religions are not inadequate for her needs. India needs no spiritual conversion.[70]

As radical Hindu nationalists continue to protest against Christian missionary activities in India, it has become very difficult for foreign missionaries to even enter India. The development that led to the curtailment of missionary visa dates back to the first decade of Indian independence. In 1955, the government of India set up a new policy (which it called the "new procedure") on admission of foreign missionaries. It states, among other things, that "those [foreign missionaries] coming for the first time in augmentation...or in replacement [of the existing missionaries] will be admitted into India, if they possess outstanding qualifications or specialized experience" and if Indians are not available for such posts.[71] This marked the beginning of doors closing for foreign missionaries to India. The task of evangelizing India fell to Indian Christians themselves. Today, India is experiencing a major renewal of missionary movement carried out by Indian missionaries. And in November 2016, *Christianity Today* published a special report on Indian Christianity, calling it "the World's most Vibrant Christward Movement."[72]

Beginning in the 1950s, some small missionary efforts by Indian Christians eventually grew into a significant movement by the beginning of the twenty-first century. These new missionary endeavors joined hands with the few older indigenous missionary efforts. In the history of Indian Christian missionary engagements, the Marthoma Evangelistic Association has been sending out missionaries and is believed to be the first organized indigenous missionary endeavor in the country.[73] Through the leadership of V. S. Azariah, the Indian Missionary Society (IMS) was started in

1903 in Tamil Nadu. Two years later, a group of seventeen young Indian Christian leaders, again led by Azariah, formed an interdenominational National Missionary Society (NMS) on Christmas day, 1905, in Serampore near Kolkata of West Bengal. As stated in the original constitution of the society, the NMS was established "to evangelize unoccupied fields in India and adjacent countries."[74] The two societies continue their work to this day. At the beginning of the twenty-first century, the IMS had at least 635 missionaries in twenty states.[75]

While these new indigenous missions were popularly known to have minor distinctions, other indigenous missionary works were closely related with foreign missions and missionaries. For instance, in 1910 a group of Mizo converts from today's Mizoram were sent as missionaries by Watkin R. Roberts (who voluntarily accompanied Welsh missionaries to Mizoram) to southern Manipur with whom began the "Thado-Kuki Pioneer Mission."[76] The Mizo Presbyterian Church expanded its field of missions with more missionaries and formed the Synod Mission Committee in 1953.[77] In its report at the end of 2016, the Synod Mission Board showed that it had 2,534 workers in its mission fields.[78] Similar mission endeavors were made by other Mizo churches including the Baptist Church of Mizoram, which had close to 1,000 missionaries in 2015.[79]

Indian missionary movements intensified from the late 1970s and early 1980s largely maneuvered by denominational and para-church missionary organizations. Spiritual renewal movements within denominational churches as those in the Tirunelvelli Diocese and the South Kerala Diocese of the Church of South India, the Presbyterian and Baptist churches in Mizoram, and the Nagaland Missionary Movement of the Naga Baptist churches led to new missionary endeavors. Not only do these churches carry out active mission works, they spawn voluntary mission work through various para-church organizations. Many of the independent nondenominational or interdenominational mission organizations are supported by members of these churches.

In the rise of nondenominational or interdenominational mission works, a major catalyst of the missionary movement was the life and work of the Evangelical Fellowship of India (EFI). The fellowship's role in the movement was a combination of both direct and indirect influence. The story of two leading nondenominational mission organizations, the Friends' Missionary Prayer Band and the Indian Evangelical Mission, offer examples. Started informally from a students' prayer group in the Tirunelvelli area of Tamil Nadu in the late 1950s,[80] the Friends' Missionary Prayer Band grew into a strong and viable mission "movement,"[81] becoming the largest Indian indigenous nondenominational mission with 835 missionaries and 729 local evangelists.[82] The Indian Evangelical Mission was formed as the mission wing of the EFI in 1965 to reach the un-evangelized areas of India and to challenge the Indian churches to mission.[83] Like several other ministerial arms of the EFI, it has grown into a strong independent missionary organization with some 580 missions staff persons.[84]

The growth of Pentecostal-charismatic churches in India during the last three decades of the twentieth century was the result of the active evangelizing works of its missionaries and evangelists. According to P. T. Abraham of Sharon Pentecostal Fellowship, "In the decade [of] 1970, twenty-one, and in the decade of 1980 another twenty-four more agencies were started. In 1988 there were 3,661 missionaries working with PCM [Pentecostal-charismatic churches] agencies."[85] As the Pentecostal-charismatic missions grew, it became impossible to trace the numbers because of their independent and diversified nature. Closely associated but quite distinct are the indigenous independent churches, most of which are charismatic in character. P. Solomon Raj has been researching this group as well, and at the beginning of the twenty-first century, he found and studied "73 indigenous mission groups in four coastal districts of Andhra Pradesh."[86]

It is impossible to know how many Indian missionaries are working in India today. But it is clear that there are more missionaries in India today than ever before, and almost all of the missionaries are Indians. According to K. Rajendran, there were 543 Indian missionaries in 1972, a total which has grown to 12,000 in 1994.[87] Although it does not represent all Indian missionary endeavours, the story of the India Missions Association is indicative of the growth of Indian missions. Like IEM and FMPB we have mentioned, India Missions Association (IMA) grew out of the initiative of the Evangelical Fellowship of India (EFI). More specifically, it was formed by five mission agencies as a networking agency for mutual cooperation following the All India Congress on Missions and Evangelism organized by the EFI in March 1977 at Devlali, Maharashtra. It is not a missionary society in itself, but an association or "a national federation of missions" for partnership, for sharing of resources, training, and research. The mission of IMA is to assist "missions and churches in the proclamation of the Good news and in making disciples of Jesus Christ among all peoples, languages, and geographical areas through members who partner to share resources, research, and training by their effective accountability and care of their personnel."[88]

By 1990, IMA's membership had grown to 44,[89] and almost doubled to 86 in 1995 with almost 12,000 missionaries.[90] In addition to providing cooperation among the members, it demands its members be open and accountable to "assure credibility."[91] By 2000, IMA had 130 member organizations, and at the end of 2016, the number grew to 254 members spreading over 25 Indian states and Union Territories whose total workers has crossed 60,000.[92] Since there are far too many missionary organizations outside of IMA, IMA is only one indicator of the growth of the Indian missionary enterprise. The fact that there are more than 60,000 Christian workers associated with IMA who are intentionally witnessing to Christ in India demonstrates the vitality of indigenous missionary movements in India.

African Missions—A Nigerian Example

The tension we have described before between cross-cultural diffusional missions and contagious attractional missions in Nigeria typifies what is going in most nations in sub-Saharan Africa and beyond. Many of the recent conversions to Christianity in Africa may have been directly linked to the second strategy, that is, contagious evangelistic mission, but the harder task of sowing seed among non-Christians through cross-cultural missions is equally important. There is a third way of missionary engagement that is quite close to contagious evangelistic mission, and is gaining acceptance especially as an African way of doing mission. This is an evangelistic mission by way of migration and diaspora communities. Since the primary engagement is with and among migrant communities and secondarily with others, its missionary dimension is often inconspicuous. Yet, the missional contributions of African diaspora Christian communities in witnessing to the gospel in the secular Western societies is becoming more apparent.

African Christianity today is impacting the world through its diaspora communities, especially by challenging and reviving secularized Westerners to a passionate and vital form of Christianity. Among the three ways of missional engagement, Africa's contribution in cross-cultural mission may be the lowest, but has the longest history. According to *Atlas of Global Christianity*, African churches have sent out fewer numbers of missionaries than Asia and Latin America. With a total of 20,700 African missionaries according to the *Atlas*,[93] African missionaries constituted a meager 5 percent of the world's missionaries in 2010.[94] Highlighting the diasporic missionary efforts of African Christians within and beyond Africa, the Congolese missiologist Fohle Lygunda li-M asked what the *Atlas* meant by "African missionaries." He wrote, "In what sense and for what purpose are they presented as 'African missionaries'?"[95] Fohle li-M advocated those working among migrants to be included as missionaries as well.

In the history of Protestant missions in Africa, the contributions of African Christian missionaries from Sierra Leone is most noteworthy. To quote Andrew Walls, "For nearly half a century that tiny country [Sierra Leone] sent a stream of [African] missionaries, ordained and lay, to the Niger territories.... It is cruel that the missionary contribution of Sierra Leone has been persistently overlooked, and even denied."[96] Founded as a Christian colony of freed slaves by the anti-slavery evangelical "Clapham Sect" led by William Wilberforce, Sierra Leone became an early Christian center for emancipated slaves. It was from here that much of West Africa received its early missionaries.

Protestant Christianity in Nigeria began with the Sierra Leone–based missionary works and among the pioneers was a Nigerian freed salve by the name of Samuel Ajayi Crowther. Freed from a Portuguese slave trading ship in 1822, Crowther became a Christian three years later. Educated as one of the earliest Africans to receive a college degree, he became a school-master.[97] Known to be a great orator and a good linguist, Crowther joined the Niger expedition of 1841 through which his personal qualities and leadership skill were recognized, placing him on a preparation track for ordination. After his ordination as a missionary of the Church Missionary Society (CMS), Crowther became an advocate and leader for a new mission in Yorubaland in today's Nigeria. The Yoruba mission established a Christian settlement in Abeokuta. It was here that Crowther was reunited with his mother and sister from whom he was snatched away by the raiders more than twenty years earlier. His mother and sisters were among the first to be baptized in Abeokuto.[98] Crowther became the leader of a missionary team composed entirely of Africans from Sierra Leone stream-ing through the Niger Delta. His translation of the Bible to Yoruba was the first by an African, and he wrote the first book in the Igbo language.[99] His long missionary engagement with Muslims in northern Nigeria led him to advocate what may be called a dialogical approach marked by "the patience and the readiness to listen."[100] As a part of the indigenous church experiment by Henry Venn of the CMS, Crowther was ordained a bishop in 1864. But Crowther's episcopate was not a happy one as he came to face opposition and resistance from younger missionaries. Andrew Walls tells the story of Crowther's last days:

> There is no need here to recount more than the essentials: the questions arose about the lives of some of the missionaries; that European mis-sionaries were brought into the mission, and then took it over, brushing aside the old bishop (he was over eighty) and suspending or dismissing his staff. In 1891 Crowther, a desolate, broken man, suffered a stroke; on the last day of the year, he died. The self-governing church and the indigenization of the episcopate were abandoned.[101]

Crowther was not the only African pioneer missionary from Sierra Leone. There were other outstanding missionaries including J. C. Taylor, an Igbo man who opened the Igbo mission at Onitsha of Igboland as a part of the Crowther-led Niger mission.[102] They all were imperiled as an

African missionary initiative by the new European-dominated mission efforts.

Indigenization of Christianity in Nigeria and other African nations had to take a different route in the form of African church movements such as those led by Prophet William Wadé Harris and the Aladura Prophetic churches in West Africa. A number of these movements resisted the European-dominated Christianity introduced by missionaries of the modern missionary movement. Missiologically, this line of indigenous Christian movements pioneered the contagious evangelistic mission we have described before in Africa. When it comes to cross-cultural missions, however, Africa took a much longer time to develop indigenous missionary agencies. In Nigeria, the African Missionary Society, which later changed its name to Evangelical Missionary Society (EMS), is considered to be the first indigenous missionary society.[103] The indigenous foundation of the beginning was a bit shaky as it was the result of the challenge thrown to the Evangelical Church of West Africa by its parent body the Sudan Interior Mission (SIM). At SIM's motivation, the society was established in 1948 as the missionary body of the Evangelical Church of West Africa. The stated primary objective of the society is this: "to pass on the missionary vision and philosophy to the indigenous Christians."[104] By 1988, EMS had 729 missionaries, and ten years later it grew to 1,002.[105]

By the 1990s, Nigeria had the largest number of missionaries in sub-Saharan Africa. In 1982, six indigenous evangelical missionary agencies including EMS and CAPRO ("Calvary Productions")[106] together founded a cooperative networking organization called Nigeria Evangelical Missions Association (NEMA). NEMA is defined in its mission statement as a service-based platform to enable the Nigerian church to carry out her missionary work. It assists and seeks to empower churches and mission agencies in the proclamation of the gospel and the making of disciples among all people, languages, and geographical areas.[107] The association grew over the years and by the end of 2016, it has eighty-two member-organizations.[108]

CAPRO—*The Story of an Emergent Mission in Nigeria*

In his book on the story of CAPRO, Isaac Oyebamiji made an interesting statement. He wrote:

> CAPRO did not come into missions by a deliberate well-thought-out plan of what they [the leaders] were going into. Rather they came into it by responding to the need and doing what they believed was the will of God for the Church. It was the burden of the unsaved and the zeal for evangelism that was in the mind of the founding fathers but it was missions they found themselves in.[109]

In fact, it was another organization that explained to CAPRO that CAPRO was a missionary organization. During his visit to Gambia looking for ways to serve youth, Amos Aderonmu—the first full-time staff member of CAPRO who later became the international director—came in contact with Worldwide Evangelization for Christ International (WEC International). As he explained what CAPRO was doing, the missionaries of WEC International explained to him and convinced him that what CAPRO was doing was, in fact, "mission."[110] The spontaneous evangelistic witness of young zealous Christians eventually led to the establishment of a strong cross-cultural missionary agency. The partnership developed with WEC International, which was to be formalized later in 1984,[111] was to have a lasting impact on CAPRO. The following story of CAPRO draws mostly from Isaac Oyebamiji's account in his book *Travail and Triumph*. We choose to highlight CAPRO for its indigenous nature and for its combination of the two types of missions we described above, namely contagious evangelistic missions and cross-cultural missions. CAPRO started as the former and discovered itself to be the latter, especially with the help of WEC International.

The immediate context for the founding of CAPRO was the spiritual movement among students, particularly the charismatic revival that broke out at the University of Ibadan in 1970.[112] The larger campus ministries led by such organizations as the Fellowship of Christian Students, the Christian Union, and the Student Christian had connected Christian evangelism efforts and students. The revival spread from University of

Ibadan to other universities, and by 1975, it had spread to most universities in the country. Furthermore, the introduction of National Youth Service Corps also contributed to the expansion of the revival's impact. The Christian youths who were serving in the northern (Muslim-dominated) state of Kaduna under Youth Service Corp organized a Christian crusade in the city of Zaria on Christmas day 1974. The crusade was attacked by a Muslim mob and the evangelists were stoned (50). If the crusade was a failure, the spirit behind the crusade did not fail as they now learned that public preaching from a rostrum does not work in Muslim context.

The leader of the group Bayo Famonure was led to a period of reflection and prayers to realize his vision for ministry in the Muslim-dominated area of northern Nigeria. He was joined by Aderonmu who had a similar burden to evangelize Muslims in northern Nigeria. After much prayer, a few others joined them. The small group met on April 25, 1975, in Zaria, marking the birth of CAPRO as a prayer initiative for the evangelization of Muslims in northern Nigeria and the Francophone West Africa (50–51). The name "CAPRO" originated as an abbreviation for Calvary Productions. Famonure had started a Bible study and drama group while teaching in a higher school certification and named it "Calvary Theatre." He also had a dream to establish a filming industry for evangelism to be called "Calvary Foundation" (49). One can trace the line that led to the naming of Calvary Productions. But the acronym CAPRO became its popular name, and later the name changed to Calvary Ministries while CAPRO remains as its popular name. At a time when "evangelism" and "mission" were popularly distinguished, the founders understood their ministry to be evangelism until they were persuaded that they were also a mission society. The organization evolved into a significant indigenous cross-cultural missionary agency.

CAPRO is one of the largest indigenous mission agencies in Africa. By the first decade of the twenty-first century, CAPRO "has missionary works in 20 African nations, two nations each in Europe, the Middle East, and North America."[113] Tesilimi Lawanson divided CAPRO's first thirty years into three phases. He named the first phase (1975 to 1988) "Informal Organization Stage," the second (1988 to 1997) "Consolidation and Structuring Phase," and the third (1997 to 2004) the "Expansion Phase."[114]

In its early years, the leaders envisioned CAPRO's method of ministries to be city-wide, open-air evangelism. It gained popularity mostly among students who provided the lifeblood of the organization. The National Congress on Evangelization later in 1975 helped to redirect CAPRO for ministries to "unreached people's group." The first of such unreached people groups identified was Maguzawa near Zaria. Attention was also redirected to need outside of Nigeria, particularly Niger Republic. A gospel crusade was held for the first time in Niger in 1977, and the same year the Calvary Bible Institute was also started in Zaria offering courses on evangelism. A visit to Gambia the following year led to a self-discovery of CAPRO as a missionary agency and a missionary nurse was sent to Gambia in 1980 in partnership with WEC International (56–57). In 1980, the two founding leaders Famonure and Aderonmu visited the headquarters of WEC International near London. At the advice and encouragement of WEC International leadership, Famonure drafted the Guiding Principles of CAPRO, which were adopted the following year. It also started a research wing and a training school for mission (58–59).

The Guiding Principles clarified the mission of CAPRO as reaching the unreached, particularly Muslims, with the aim of establishing "an indigenous body of believers [which] will be able to stand and disciple others" (60). All missionaries and staff are "contractually obliged to the Guiding Principles."[115] Altough Lawanson named the stage "informal," with the adoption of the Guiding Principles in the mid-1980s, it had become quite formal. Financially CAPRO supported itself with the meager donations mainly from student members in the early years. Scarcity of funds and difficult life did not deter the missionaries from what they were doing (63–64). They lived together as a community first in Zaria, and then constructed a campus of huts at a location believed to be a meeting place of witches near Dadu village, to which they moved in 1982. They named the campus *Kauna* (meaning "love" in Hausa). In 1985, the headquarters was moved twice, first to Jos, and then to an abandoned mining camp at Gana Ropp. In 1989, it was moved back to Jos where it has remained ever since. The leaders grew theologically. For Famonure, who led the organization conceptually, the heart of missions is discipleship, and death in Christ is the key as he outlined in his book *Training to Die*[116] (65). To remain an interdenominational society was not easy when its main engagement became planting new churches. Through the wise advice from one of the organization's friends, the leadership decided in 1983 that it would plant nondenominational "independent self-led churches" (70).

It was perhaps the registration of Calvary Ministries (CAPRO) with the government of Nigeria in 1987[117] that led Lawanson to call the next stage a structuring phase. During this phase (1988 to 1997), CAPRO recruited more volunteers, staff, and missionaries. It pioneered church planting missions in Cote d'Ivoire, Togo, and Benin in West Africa; and Botswana and Malawi in Southern Africa.[118] By the last decade of the twentieth century, CAPRO developed its Vision 2000, a mission plan for the first decade of the twenty-first century. It aimed to deploy one thousand new missionaries to plant self-propagating independent churches among unreached people in Nigeria and West Africa.[119] The phase of expansion (1997 to 2004) also turned out to be a phase of structural changes as CAPRO increasingly became flexible and open. CAPRO's "relational process celebrates process over structure,"[120] says Lawanson.

CAPRO's emergence and development as a missionary society typifies an indigenous missionary agency of the majority world in general and Africa in particular. It was not a well-planned and well-thought-out organization, but one formed spontaneously following a spiritual awakening. It learned its way as it grew and discovered its true self and worth as it evolved. The informal and spontaneous missionary outreaches in many parts of Africa, Asia, and Latin America, which grew into formal organizations with emergent structures, are typical of majority-world missional efforts in Africa. Although CAPRO now understands itself to be a cross-cultural and worldwide missionary agency, it started as a modest evangelistic campaign by a few young spiritual enthusiasts. The story shows a combination of contagious evangelistic missions and a frontier-crossing missionary endeavors.

Latin American Christian Missionary Outreach

An estimated four thousand missionaries from Latin America to the rest of the world at the end of twentieth century[121] is not a huge number compared to what churches in some countries in Asia and Africa have been doing. But in the unique historical backdrop of Latin America, this shows a significant progress. A study done in 1980 shows that "only 7 per cent of the non-western missionary force is sent from the churches of Latin America. Even though one of every four non-Western Christians is Latin American, they sent only one of every fourteen non-Western missionaries."[122] Based on this finding, Guillermo Cook states, "Latin America clearly lagged behind other regions of the Third World both in number of home-grown agencies and missionaries."[123] Among the Catholics, the Fourth Latin American Missionary Conference (COMLA-4) in 1991 lamented, "Even though 42 percent of the world's Catholics are in Latin America and the evangelization of the continent began five hundred years ago, Latin Americans do not even make up two percent of the missionaries in the world."[124]

Since its suppressive "evangelization" in the sixteenth and seventeenth centuries, Christianity in Latin America did not seem to see itself as missionary nor burden itself with the work of evangelizing others. The region has been outside the purview of missionary developments and discussions for much of the nineteenth and twentieth centuries. Although there were Protestant missionaries serving in Latin America mainly to convert Catholics, the Edinburgh 1910 meeting excluded Latin Americans because it was considered to be evangelized and no missionary agency was noted to represent it. At the time, some missionary executives—including Robert Speer of the American Presbyterian Mission—voiced their disagreement at the exclusion of Latin American missions and missionaries. The objection resulted in the calling of the Congress on Christian Work in Latin America, which met in Panama City in 1916. Modeled on the Edinburgh Conference, the congress drew together members of mission boards, missionaries, and Latin American church leaders, as well as various interested

Christians from Europe and North America.[125] The Congress helped to recognize Protestant missions in Latin America and became "a milestone for the Protestant missionary efforts" on the continent.[126]

Protestant missionaries (especially of faith missions from the United States and Europe) increased from the mid-twentieth century as missionary doors were closing in Asia and some parts of Africa. The new missions were heavily influenced by American ideology, including anti-communism.[127] Pentecostalism in some parts of Latin America is as old as the Pentecostal movement itself, even though its early progenitors were mostly Americans from the United States. Despite all these movements, missionary movements by Latin Americans were lagging. Only a few Protestant denominations (including Baptist, Methodist, and Assemblies of God) had sent missionaries to Latin America and beyond.[128] Notable developments in the Latin American church during the twentieth century were mostly those of internal renewal. Liberation theology of both the Catholic and Evangelical Protestant versions aimed at renewing Christian experience and meaning in the region Pentecostalism in Latin America seemed to see itself mostly as bringing spiritual revival to nominal and syncretistic Catholic Christianity. The renewal movements in the twentieth century nonetheless enhanced key figures in the Christian faith and generated important missionary outcomes.

Cross-cultural missionary consciousness among Latin American Protestants and Catholics became heightened in the 1970s and the 1980s. For Catholics, the growing missionary awareness follows a series of the Latin American Missionary Conference (COMLA). Originally inspired by Pope Paul IV's encyclical *Evangelii Nuntiandi* of 1975, COMLA is held every four or five years since 1977 "to foster missionary responsibility of local churches...and to invite them to cooperate...at home and beyond their own frontiers."[129] Protestants also drew inspiration from other continents and worldwide missionary movements. The story of COMIBAM is the story of the growing missionary movement among Protestants in Latin America. Guillermo Cook attributed influences from the World Mission Conference of the Commission on World Mission and Evangelism of the WCC in Mexico City in 1963, the Berlin Congress on World

Evangelization in 1966, as well as the Lausanne Congress of 1974 for the emergence of the missionary movement in Latin America.[130]

Among Latin American countries, Brazil takes the lead in Protestant missions as both the largest sending and receiving nation of missionaries. A report in the late 1990s showed that more than half of cross-cultural missionaries from Latin America came from Brazil.[131] Starting as early as the beginning of the twentieth century, the Brazilian Baptist Convention has been sending missionaries.[132] Even in the new missionary awareness, it was an evangelical movement sparked among the Brazilian students that led the way. Inspired and motivated by the 1974 Lausanne Congress on World Evangelization, the Alianca Biblica Universitariat convened a missionary congress on the campus of the University of Paraná in Curitiba, Brazil, in July 1976, which impacted students in Brazil and other parts of Latin America.[133] The congress showed a combination of sound missiology with a call for in-depth missionary engagement. The "Declaration of Curitiba" expressed its concern at the "lack of missionary vision in Latin America," and declared that "the church that is not missionary is not church." It called "all Christians" to commit "the entirety of their lives" to mission.[134] Most of the leaders of the congress and other attendees became missionaries or mission promoters.[135] The breakthrough in the Latin American missionary movement, however, came through another congress, more accurately a series of congresses, which also function as a networking movement. This is popularly called COMIBAM, an acronym for the Spanish Cooperación Misionero Iberoamericano (Ibero-American Missionary Congress).

COMIBAM and the New Missionary Movement in Latin America

By the sheer numbers it has produced and the intensity of the movement it has generated, COMIBAM could not help being called the missionary factor of Latin American Protestantism today. In 1987 when the first COMIBAM was held, there were an estimated 1,600 workers from some 70 mission agencies in attendance. By 2006 when the third decadal congress was held in Granada, Spain, there were almost 10,000 missionaries sent by approximately 400 mission organizations.[136] COMIBAM

(Cooperación Misionero Iberoamericano) is a missionary network that connects evangelical Christians in Latin America and the Iberian Peninsula (Spain and Portugal). One reason for its strength has been its flexibility. A number of writers have described COMIBAM as a process. It began as a congress, then turned into a movement. So, the name Ibero-American Missionary Congress became Ibero-American Cooperation in Missions (COMIBAM).[137] The congresses, held about every ten years, are rallying points for the cooperative missionary movement and evaluative reflections on the organization's efforts. In the second and third congresses in 1997 and 2006, the leaders at these gatherings engaged in important self-evaluations of the movement.

The first of the series of the Ibero-American Missionary Congress was held in São Paulo, Brazil in November 1987. Attended by 3,100 delegates representing all the Latin American countries and 25 other nations, it was called and organized by CONELA (Confraternity of Evangelicals of Latin America).[138] The congress adopted a meaningful commitment statement: "United by the fervent desire to be light to the nations, we—the participants in COMIBAM 87 . . . invite all of our brothers and sisters in Ibero America to get involved with us in the faithful completion of the mission that He has given us: I have made you a light for the gentiles, that you may bring salvation to the ends of the earth (Acts 13:47)."[139]

Some credited the success of the meeting and the movement it produced to the leadership of the coordinator, Luis Bush.[140] Others saw the "managerial missiology" of the United States dominating the first congress and the early period out of which gradually evolved a sound contextual theology in cooperation with other Latin American evangelical thinkers.[141] Using an appropriate slogan "from mission field to mission force," the congress generated an enthusiasm for mission and turned itself into a movement. From the very beginning, the emphasis was not so much on evangelism within one's culture, but on "cross-cultural evangelism and church planting both across Latin America's thousands of cultural lines as well as to the entire world."[142]

When the second congress (COMIBAM 97) was held in Acapulco, Mexico, in November 1997, the number of missionaries had reached about 4,000, 40 percent of whom served in Latin America, with the rest outside of the region.[143] The success of the first period is due to the "emergence of national movements" to use Luis Bush's words. By this time, each of the Ibero-American nations had established national missionary structures through which mission agencies cooperated and missions promoted. Indeed, Brazil, referred to as "the older brother," continued to lead as it represents about half of the efforts and activities of missions.[144] The second congress was intended to be "an evaluation and projection" of the mission movement. The focus was mainly on the missionary process, such as missionary screening, training, sending, and providing pastoral care and supervision in the field.[145] David Ruiz recounted one theme that has not been featured, namely "social action as missions' work." He said that the theme was not dealt with theoretically but done practically when more than half of the congress delegates went out in the streets of Acapulco helping victims of Hurricane Pauline that had devastated the area a few weeks before the meeting.[146]

Bertil Ekstrom was elected as the new president of COMIBAM International, succeeding Luis Bush at COMIBAM 97. Right from the beginning, Ekstrom outlined the plan to make COMIBAM a "facilitator and a catalyst, working to strengthen existing mission efforts in Latin America and to start new ones."[147] Ekstrom seemed intentional in developing a networking system in order to prevent authoritarian headship by charismatic leaders. Julia Guarneri credited the fluidity of a network structure for the efficiency of COMIBAM International.[148] Overall, "COMIBAM's lean organization in terms of staff," he said, "allows for a more objective opportunity to evaluate its work."[149] Ekstrom was soon succeeded by David Ruiz, who until then was the executive director. In his personal reflection on COMIBAM III, Samuel Escobar credited David Ruiz's "diplomatic and organizational abilities" as the main reason for the significant growth enjoyed by COMIBAM since 1997 and for a successful third congress.[150]

By doing a self-evaluation for two years leading up to the third congress, COMIBAM III, which met in Granada, Spain, in November 2006, combined evaluative study and the effort to chart the future course of the movement. Almost two thousand delegates attended the congress representing twenty-five Ibero-American countries.[151] David Ruiz mentioned three immediate purposes of the congress as follows:[152] First, the congress wants to understand missions from the perspective of the field. The 288 missionaries who attended the congress helped the meeting in this regard. Second, to evaluate the effectiveness of COMIBAM's catalytic role. The evaluative research done before and at the meeting itself showed the need for better training, missiological education, and better care for the missionaries.[153] Third, the congress sought to make fresh proposals for the future. On this, serious dialogue occurred between practicing missionaries and mission executives trying to chart a meaningful future course for missional work in Latin America and beyond. The life of the movement and the effectiveness of those proposed steps were evaluated at the fourth congress meeting from August 22–25, 2017, in Bogotá, Colombia.[154]

The fact that a continent-wide organization generated and led a missionary movement is unique. William Taylor suggests it as a model for others and voiced his regret that such a regional alliance on mission does not exist in other continents and regions.[155] In this regard, some of the unique features of Latin America that made this possible should be noted. For one, the linguistic and cultural make-up of the region is much less diverse than other continents like Asia and Africa. The very use of the term "Latin" indicates the strong bond of its Latin unity through the domination of Spanish and Portuguese languages. Thus, cultural tensions involved in serving from one country to another seemed relatively less in Latin America than in other regions. The relative homogeneity of the region in language and culture helped to unify the missionary movement. Through the wise use of the common language and Iberian identity, COMIBAM has really taken off, seeing extraordinary success in just a few decades. On the other hand, as David Ruiz has clearly testified, the unified missionary movement also provoked and enhanced the unity of the church in the region and built mutual relations among Christians.[156]

CONCLUSION

A Highlight of the Salient Points

To pair "Christianity" and the "world" can prompt different questions to those outside the field of this kind of study. Questions range from the worldwide character of Christianity to concerns that this approach might make Christianity too worldly. One baffling question connected to the project of studying "world Christianity" is: "How can one possibly think about and talk about all the Christians of the world?" Our inquiry is focused on world Christianity as a phenomenon in history, a particular development we discern in Christianity's story; and our attempt is to see its nature and key characters.

Christianity experienced a major remaking worldwide in the second half of the twentieth century. Beginning in the third quarter of the twentieth century, a few keen observers recognized an emerging religious phenomenon in the Christian world, which turned into a movement. Traditional Christian regions of the West—mainly Europe, the "new world" of North America, and Oceania (Australia and New Zealand)—experienced religious decline, and new Christian movements emerged in the non-Western "southern" continents. At the heart of the new Christian movement is a vital and spirited form of Christianity attracting a great number of people, both Christians and non-Christians in the non-West "majority" world. This exuberant Christianity has been influential, reshaping older

177

forms of Christianity in the majority world, complementing their Christian existence, and engendering new life in the spirit.

By the beginning of the twenty-first century, the movement received serious attention. Perhaps in an effort to capture a wider audience, some authors have presented dramatic pictures of the new Christian movement in the global South. The term "global South" has become a prevalent term among missiologists to differentiate the newer Christian communities in the Southern Hemisphere from the older forms of Western Christianity. Due to the ambiguity of the term "global South" that often includes references to the global East and North-East, we use the term "majority world" in this work. Furthermore, the term "majority world" is helpful as it recognizes the reality of demographic trends in those regions where most of the world's population resides.

We began our study by surveying how world Christianity has traditionally been recognized and investigated. World Christianity is in vogue today in the field of the history of Christianity, becoming a sub-discipline of inquiry. What are the salient features of world Christianity and what characterizes it theologically? This is the heart of our investigation in this book. At the most basic level, world Christianity is about demographic changes of Christianity. Not only has Christianity become worldwide by the end of the twentieth century, as pioneering scholars Walbert Bühlmann and Andrew Walls have expressed, but the center of gravity of Christianity has shifted from the northwest part of the globe toward the southern continents. The shift is the result of a dramatic increase of the Christian population in Africa, which was accompanied by Latin America's spiritual renewal and rejuvenation of faith and practice, and an eagerness for Christian witness expressed by Asian Christians. The overview of Christianity we have provided on the southern continents and the islands reveal how the charismatic Christianity of different stripes has powerfully impacted these continents and islands. For more stable Christian communities in the Pacific Islands, this new charismatic Christianity was more upsetting than settling, yet it also invigorated Christian lives in those very places.

World Christianity, we argue, is not only about the *number* of Christians in the world, as much as it is about the changing and diversifying *character* of global Christianity. In fact, the percentage of Christian population has not changed much between the beginning of the twentieth century and the twenty-first century. According to *Atlas of Global Christianity*, 34.8 percent of the world's population were Christians in 1910; and in 2010, the Christian population percentage slightly decreased to 33.2.[1] Studies in world Christianity have emphatically demonstrated the changing character of Christian faith following recent demographic shifts of Christianity in a global context. Along with the rise of Christianity in different parts of the world came a recognition of the dynamic universality of Christian faith itself. The catholicity of the Christian faith finds new meaning in the world Christian movement. Christianity is a shared religion in that people of different cultures and societies can make it their own while being transformed by faith and practice. World Christianity is testifying to this dynamism of the Christian faith. What some scholars call the translatability of Christianity is an essential character of Christianity that makes it adaptable to all cultures while challenging each with its transformative power.

Accompanying the rise of majority-world Christianity are deliberations on the contextualization of the Christian gospel. We identified two lines of discussion, which ideally complement each other. Contextualization of the gospel through meaningful interpretation and communication of the gospel message both constitute part of an essential missional calling. However, a lack of theological vision often hampers the extent of the ongoing discussion of this group. Various forms of contextual theologies that relate Christian faith with the day-to-day realities of indigenous people arise and are on the rise. Driven by both social and political experiences, these theologies came to challenge a dominant Western theology. They called into question traditional theological methods funding older forms of Christianity that ignored the subjectivity and context of theologians attempting to articulate doctrinal and theological themes. From our examination, we have also seen that the sociopolitical stance driving liberative approaches to indigenous theologies of majority world forms of Christian faith often limit the salvific scope of these theologies.

Contextual theologies range from radical social liberation that pleads for far-reaching political and socioeconomic transformation to a theology of inculturation that calls for identification with the culture of the people in their traditions. We have argued that the three regions of Africa, Latin America, and Asia have different emphases in their theology as they respond directly to their sociopolitical realities. While these three areas share many of the same theological themes, Latin America has claimed liberation theology as its own (though not sole) possession. Meanwhile in most regions of Africa, inculturation is a dominant theology. For missional Christianity in Asia, these two forms of contextual theology are accompanied and swayed by a theology of religious plurality. Even so, dominant contextual theologies of the majority world all too often represent elitist voices and concerns, as a holdover from the Enlightenment tradition of modern Western education. The rising charismatic Christianity that represents vibrant forms of popular Christianity, we argue, provides an alternative contextual theology in the form of its indigeneity.

Perhaps the most noteworthy discovery about world Christianity that has come to light is the recognition of two significantly different forms of Christian faith, the older Western Christianity and the newer Christianity of the majority world. Driven by two significantly different spiritual worldviews, there is tension between the two. Perhaps, the tension may be more creative than destructive for the two forms. The older Christianity of the post-Enlightenment West tends to rationalize Christian faith in order to make it meaningful for a secularizing society, while the newer Christianity of the majority (non-Western) world is drawing on forms of Christianity that deal with its on-the-ground realities. While some, especially the educated and sometimes elitist groups in the non-Western world turn to sociopolitical frames/ meanings of Christianity, majority-world Christians look for spiritual meaning and answers for their daily lives—lives imbued with a sense of powers both natural and supernatural. While the Western and majority-world Christians may be described as two streams of Christianity, they can also be seen as one ongoing faith with two distinct worldviews. At one end is the Enlightenment-driven Christianity that functions almost exclusively by filtering reality through human rational faculties (often with a strong distaste for human emotions and experiential religion). At the other end is the charismatic Christianity driven largely by the belief in the experience of the power of the Holy Spirit for life, which is commonly expressed through human affections and emotive experience. The elites and mainline churches of the majority world seem to be caught in between. I suggest that it is most appropriate to locate world Christianity between these two streams of culture-inflected faith, modernist Enlightenment-driven Western Christianity and the spiritually driven charismatic Christianity of the majority world. It has not been an easy existence for many churches in the majority world that find themselves caught between these two sensibilities.

What were called "mission churches" became mainstream churches largely following their mother denominations in the West. The logical expectation, along with secularization theory, was that these mainline mission churches will become secularized like their mother denominations and eventually lose their religious and spiritual strength and vitality. A dry rationalism was predicted as the eventual pathway for them. But the rise of charismatic renewal and Pentecostal movements seems to have challenged this logic. Rationalism does not seem to be predominate in these churches and the hold of the Enlightenment tradition on these Christians is never absolute. The rise of charismatic Christianity has revealed that beliefs in the existence and power of the Holy Spirit over all other spirits together with the possibility of the Holy Spirit's supernatural and miraculous works prevail among the Christians, including mainline churches found in the majority world. Many of the mainstream "mission churches" in the majority world are turning charismatic. Even among those who have not outwardly expressed such characters, belief in the empowering Holy Spirit is widespread. Will such a faith tradition withstand the demystifying onslaught of Western secular rationalism?

The tension between continuity and change marking Western and majority-world Christianity can be seen throughout the history of Christian missions. The Christian missionary enterprise experienced the most dramatic changes in the twentieth century. The core of the change was conceptual. Through a painful crisis, the missionary enterprise reestablished itself theologically and its impact on the re-conception of the global church has been significant. All major Christian confessional bodies seem to be in broad consensus that if Christians have a mission *in* the world, it is participation in God's redemptive and reconciling mission *to* the world. Different confessional traditions may have varying interpretations and emphases, but they increasingly agree that the foundation of all ecclesial-sponsored missional efforts is God's mission (*missio Dei*). The change also involved passing beyond the Western modernist concept of "foreign missions" to the "global mission" of the world church. The "moratorium on missions" demanded by some Christian leaders from the majority world signified their church's struggle for true participation in the Christian missionary enterprise. At the time of this call, it was quite controversial, but in retrospect, many see this as a significant passageway for churches in the non-Western world to lay claim to their missionary role in the *missio Dei*.

Our overview of missions shows that there are both continuities and significant changes between the previous work of modern Western mission efforts and emerging missionary movements in the majority world. By and large, most missionaries from the majority world understood themselves as conservatively following the missionary tradition of the West. Cross-cultural diffusion of the gospel, which served as the dominant understanding of mission in the modern Western missional sensibility, continues to be upheld by most missionary advocates of the majority world. Yet, the practice of diffusional mission itself has changed, and other appropriate forms of mission have been added. Because the larger number of missionary activists come from the periphery of the society and of the church, missions in the majority world are largely a movement from the margin to the center. Compared to the missionaries of the nineteenth and early twentieth centuries, majority-world missionaries are lowly and vulnerable within the complicated and pluralistic societies they serve. An understanding of mission as "witness from everywhere to everywhere" seems to have changed the very nature and means of missionary engagements. Alongside cross-cultural diffusional mission comes a near neighbor form of missionary engagement. This is an attractional model of spontaneous witness and a spiritual movement that is contagious in nature. And it fits well with the prevalent charismatic Christianity of the majority world. The missionary works of house church Christians in China and the charismatically engaged evangelistic missions in Africa characteristically display this form of mission. Yet another striking development is what some call "diaspora missions." Either as a way of ministering to the spiritual needs of migrants or as an outreach by migrants beyond their communities, Christian migrants from the majority world are actively engaging in missions in the West, with former colonizers becoming recipients of the new missionary message.

NOTES

Preface

1. Lalsangkima Pachuau, *Ethnic Identity and Christianity: A Socio-historical and Missiological Study of Christianity in Northeast India with Special Reference to Mizoram* (Frankfurt: Peter Lang, 2002), 111–43.

2. See, for instance, Bengt G. M. Sundkler, *The Bantu Prophets in South Africa*, 2nd ed. (London: Oxford University Press for the International African Institute, 1961); and Lamin Sanneh, *West African Christianity: The Religious Impact* (Maryknoll, NY: Orbis Books 1996), esp. 168–209.

3. Andrew Walls, "The Gospel as Prisoner and Liberator of Culture," in *The Missionary Movement in Christian History: Studies in the Transmission of Faith* (Maryknoll, NY: Orbis Books; Edinburgh: T&T Clark, 1996), 7–9.

4. The term "inculturation" is coined from the more familiar term "enculturation" popular in social and cultural studies by Catholic scholars in the early 1960s. It describes the insertion of the Christian faith in a culture. Inculturation theology, as will be expounded later, refers to the creative and dynamic relationship between the Christian gospel and human culture. See, inter alia, Peter Schineller, *A Handbook on Inculturation* (New York: Paulist Press, 1990).

1. Introduction: World Christianity and Its Studies

1. Roland Robertson, *Globalization: Social Theory and Global Culture* (London: Sage, 1992), 8.

2. *The Cambridge History of Christianity*, ed. Sheridan Gilley and Brian Stanley, vol. 8, *World Christianities, c.1815–c.1914* (Cambridge: Cambridge University Press, 2006).

3. Mary Farrell Bednarowski, "Multiplicity and Ambiguity: Introduction," in *A People's History of Christianity*, vol. 7, *Twentieth-Century Global Christianity*, ed. Mary Farrell Bednarowski (Minneapolis: Fortress Press, 2008), 7:1–11.

4. David B. Barrett, George T. Kurian, and Todd M. Johnson, eds., *World Christian Encyclopedia: A Comparative Survey of Churches and Religions in the Modern World*. 2 vols. (Oxford: Oxford University Press, 2001).

5. Michael Jaffarian, "The Statistical State of the Missionary Enterprise," *Missiology: An International Review* 30, no. 1 (January 2002): 19.

6. Todd Johnson and Kenneth Ross, eds., *Atlas of Global Christianity* (Edinburgh: Edinburgh University Press, 2009), 8.

7. Dale Irvin, "World Christianity: An Introduction," *Journal of World Christianity* 1, no. 1 (2008): 1.

8. Adding to the two christological and ecclesiological constants of Andrew Walls, Stephen Bevans and Roger Schroeder added four more: eschatological, soteriological, anthropological, and the gospel's relation with culture. For details, see Stephen B. Bevans and Roger P. Schroeder, *Constants in Context: A Theology of Mission for Today* (Maryknoll, NY: Orbis Books, 2004), 33–34. The most important unity factor in Christian faith is God's omnipresence in the world.

9. For early use of the term, see M. Thomas Thangaraj, "An Overview: Asian and Oceanic Christianity in an Age of World Christianity," in *Asian and Oceanic Christianities in Conversation: Exploring Theological Identities at Home and in Diaspora*, ed. Heup Young Kim, Fumitaka Matsuoka, and Anri Morimoto (Amsterdam: Rodopi, 2011), 12.

10. Henry P. Van Dusen, *World Christianity: Yesterday, Today, Tomorrow* (New York: Abingdon-Cokesbury Press, 1947), 124.

11. Ibid., 133.

12. Michael Kinnamon, *The Vision of the Ecumenical Movement and How It Has Been Impoverished by Its Friends* (St. Louis: Chalice Press, 2003), 2.

13. Andrew F. Walls, "Origins of Old Northern and New Southern Christianity," in *The Missionary Movement in Christian History: Studies in the Transmission of Faith* (Maryknoll, NY: Orbis Books, 1996), 68. (Originally published in *Bilanz und Plan: Mission an der Schwalle zum dritten Jahrtausend*, ed. Hans Kasdorf and W. Müller [Bad Liebezell: Verlag der Liebezeller Mission], 1988.)

14. Walbert Bühlmann, *The Coming of the Third Church* (Maryknoll, NY: Orbis Books, 1977), ix. (Originally published in German as *Es kommt die dritte Kirche*, 1974.)

15. Walbert Bühlmann, *The Church of the Future: A Model for the Year 2001*, trans. Dame Mary Groves (Maryknoll, NY: Orbis Books; Melbourne, Australia: Dove

Communications; Slough, England: St. Paul Publications, 1986), 5–6. (Originally published in 1981 as *Welt Kirche: Neue Dimensionen—Modell für das Jahr 2001*.). Citations are from the English translation.

16. Ibid.

17. Ibid., 6.

18. Ibid., 4.

19. Ibid., 4.

20. Ibid., 120.

21. Walbert Bühlmann, *With Eyes to See: Church and World in the Third Millennium* (Maryknoll, NY: Orbis Books, 1990), 7.

22. Bühlmann, *The Church of the Future*, 131–51.

23. For further information on Walls's life, characters, and impacts on students and colleagues, see *Understanding World Christianity: The Vision and Work of Andrew F. Walls*, ed. William R. Burrows, Mark R. Gornik, and Janice A. McLean (Maryknoll, NY: Orbis Books, 2011).

24. Quoted in "introduction" to *Understanding World Christianity*, Ibid., 3.

25. Kwame Bediako, *Theology and Identity: The Impact of Culture Upon Christian Thought in the Second Century and in Modern Africa* (Oxford: Regnum Books International, 1999).

26. *World Christian Encyclopedia*, 2nd ed., ed. David B. Barrett, George T. Kurian, and Todd M. Johnson (New York: Oxford University Press, 2001), Excluding the preliminary pages, the two volumes have 1699 pages.

27. Jaffarian, "The Statistical State of the Missionary Enterprise," 22.

28. Gerald H. Anderson, "World Christianity by the Numbers: A Review of the *World Christian Encyclopedia*," 2nd ed., *IBMR* 26, no. 3 (July 2002): 129.

29. Ibid.

30. David B. Barrett, Todd M. Johnson, Christopher R. Guidry, and Peter F. Crossing, *World Christian Trends, AD 30–AD 2200: Interpreting the Annual Christian Megacensus* (Pasadena, CA: William Carey Library, 2001).

31. Todd M. Johnson, Kenneth R. Ross, and Sandra S. K. Lee. *Atlas of Global Christianity 1910–2010* (Edinburgh: Edinburgh University Press, 2009).

32. The original edition was published in 1989 and the second, revised and expanded edition in 2009. The second edition is used here. Lamin Sanneh, *Translating the Message: The Missionary Impact on Culture*, 2nd ed., rev. and exp. (Maryknoll, NY: Orbis Books, 2009).

33. Ibid., 1.

34. Lamin Sanneh, *Summoned from the Margin: Homecoming of an African* (Grand Rapids: William B. Eerdmans, 2012), 217.

35. Sanneh, *Translating the Message*, 72.

36. Lamin Sanneh, *Whose Religion Is Christianity?: The Gospel beyond the West* (Grand Rapids: William B. Eerdmans, 2003), 22.

37. Drawing together critiques from various leaders and thinkers as Jomo Kenyatta, Vincent Donovan, and Lesslie Newbigin, he provided a strong critique against Western domination of Christianity for the birth of world Christianity. See Lamin Sanneh, *Encountering the West: Christianity and the Global Cultural Process* (Maryknoll, NY: Orbis Books, 1993), 152–83.

38. Two other African scholars, Kwame Bebiako and Tite Tiénou, supported Sanneh's point. See Kwame Bediako, "Conclusion: The Emergence of World Christianity and the Remaking of Theology," in *Understanding World Christianity: The Vision and Works of Andrew F. Walls,* ed. William R. Burrows; Mark R. Gornik, and Janice A. McLean (Maryknoll: Orbis Books, 2011), 248; Tite Tiénou, "Christian Theology in an Era of World Christianity," in *Globalizing Theology: Belief and Practice in an Era of World Christianity*, ed. Craig Ott and Harold A. Netland (Grand Rapids: Baker Academic, 2006), 41.

39. There are scores of critiques against Western hegemony and neo-colonization through globalization in the ecumenical circles of the majority world. For critiques against Western domination through globalization by evangelical scholars from the majority world, see, inter alia, René Padilla, "Imperial Globalization and Integral Mission," *The Princeton Seminary Bulletin 27*, no. 1 (2006): 5–22; David S. Lim, "Missional Church in a Globalization Era," in *Asian Churches in Global Mission: Compendium of the 10th AMA Triennial Convention*, ed. Eun Moo Lee and Timothy P. Park (Pasadena, CA: East-West Center for Missions Research and Development, 2012), 89–100.

40. *Disciples of All Nations: Pillars of World Christianity* (Oxford: Oxford University Press, 2008).

41. Ibid., 274–75, 280.

42. Ibid., 282.

43. Philip Jenkins, *The Next Christendom: The Coming of Global Christianity* (Oxford: Oxford University Press, 2002), 12.

44. Philip Jenkins, "After the Next Christendom," *International Bulletin of Missionary Research*, 28, no. 1 (January 2004): 20.

45. Gerald H. Anderson, "Review of *The Next Christendom: The Coming of Global Christianity* by Philip Jenkins," *International Bulletin of Missionary Research* 27, no. 1 (January 2003): 45.

46. In the words of Robert Wuthnow, the book became "the most popular rendition of the new paradigm [of global Christianity]." See Wuthnow, *Boundless Faith: The Global Outreach of American Churches* (Berkeley: University of California Press, 2009), 34.

47. For a brief summary of these reviews, see Wuthnow, *Boundless Faith*, 265n13.

48. *Global Christianity: Contested Claims* (ed. Frans Wijsen and Robert Schreiter [Amsterdam: Rodopi, 2007]) is an assessment of Jenkins's book.

49. Jenkins, *The Next Christendom*, 2.

50. Philip Jenkins, *The New Faces of Christianity: Believing the Bible in the Global South* (Oxford: Oxford University Press, 2006), 5.

51. I understand and acknowledge that the intended readers are Westerners and not the majority-world Christians.

52. See Peter Phan's strong critique of Jenkins's Christendom thesis in "A New Christianity, But What Kind?" *Mission Studies: Journal of the International Association for Mission Studies*, 22, no. 1 (2005): 59–83, especially 60–65.

53. "Christianity in the Non-Western World: A Study in the Serial Nature of Christian Expansion," in *The Cross-Cultural Process in Christian History* (Maryknoll: Orbis Books, 2002), 45.

54. Jenkins, *The Next Christendom*, 107.

55. Two of my articles using my own native Mizo Christianity as a case would clearly show my contrasting perspective on this point. See Pachuau, "Mizo 'Sakhua' in Transition: Change and Continuity from Primal Religion to Christianity," *Missiology: An International Review*, 34, no. 1 (January 2006): 41–57; and Pachuau, "Primal Spirituality as the Substructure of Christian Spirituality: The Case of Mizo Christianity in India," *Journal of African Christian Thought*, 11, no. 2. (December 2008): 9–14.

56. Jenkins, *The Next Christendom*, 73.

57. Ibid., 75.

58. Ibid., 127.

59. Douglas Jacobsen, *The World's Christians: Who They Are, Where They Are, and How They Got There* (Chichester: Wiley-Blackwell, 2001).

60. Sebastian Kim and Kirsteen Kim, *Christianity as a World Religion: An Introduction*, 2nd ed. (London and New York: Bloomsbury Academic, 2016.

61. Timothy C. Tennent, *Theology in the Context of World Christianity: How the Global Church Is Influencing the Way We Think about and Discuss Theology* (Grand Rapids: Zondervan, 2007).

62. Noel Davis and Martin Conway, *World Christianity in the Twentieth Century* (London: SCM Press, 2008).

63. Noel Davis and Martin Conway, *World Christianity in the Twentieth Century: A Reader* (London: SCM Press, 2008).

64. Davis and Conway, *World Christianity in the Twentieth Century*, 17.

65. Ibid., 15.

66. Robert Wuthnow, *Boundless Faith: The Global Outreach of American Churches* (Berkeley: University of California Press, 2009), 33.

67. Jaffarian, "The Statistical State of the Missionary Enterprise," 22. In the same article, Jaffarian also showed that 1.6 billion people of the world (26.9 percent) of the world's population) are "unevangelized" (26).

68. For instance, "Joshua Project," a research initiative on global religious statistics for Christian mission, shows that out of the 16,804 people groups of the world, 7,289 (or 43.4 percent) are "unreached peoples." http://www.joshuaproject.net /great-commission-statistics.php (last accessed October 16, 2013).

69. These are (1) my small ethnic "oriental" Mizo world of Northeast India, which is my primary world of being, (2) my adoptive country of India whose strange Indic culture became my engaging partner of life and thoughts, and (3) my professional world of the free-but-dominating West, which now channels my academic life and professional livelihood. Culturally speaking, the first is most closely associated with Southeast Asia, the second world is the Brahminic cultural world of Indic India, and the third is the Enlightenment-driven secularizing Western world.

2. Modernization, Modern Missions, and World Christianity

1. Samuel P. Huntington, *The Clash of Civilizations and the Remaking of World Order* (New York: Simon & Schuster, 1996), 184.

2. Niall Ferguson, *Civilization: The West and the Rest* (New York: Penguin Press, 2011).

3. Donald Kagan, "A Good Run," review of *Civilization: The West and the Rest*, by Niall Ferguson. *New York Times*, November 25, 2011, Sunday Book Review. http://www.nytimes.com/2011/11/27/books/review/civilization-the-west-and-the -rest-by-niall-ferguson-book-review.html?_r=0, accessed July 21, 2016).

4. See, among others, Bernard Porter, review of *Civilization: The West and the Rest*, by Niall Ferguson. *The Guardian*, March 25, 2011. https://www.theguardian .com/books/2011/mar/25/civilization-west-rest-niall-ferguson-review, accessed July 21, 2016; and Ricardo Duchesne, review of *Civilization: The Six Ways the West Beat the Rest*, by Niall Ferguson (review no. 1225). Review in History, March 2012. http:// www.history.ac.uk/reviews/review/1225, accessed: July 21, 2016.

5. Lesslie Newbigin, *Foolishness to the Greeks: The Gospel and Western Culture* (Grand Rapids: William B. Eerdmans, 1986), 23.

6. John Garraty and Peter Gay, "Society and Politics in the Enlightenment," in *Tributaries of History*, ed. Lawrence Davidson et al. (Dubuque, IA: Kendall/Hunt Publishing Company, 1991), 36.

7. Gertrude Himmelfarb, *The Roads to Modernity: The British, French and American Enlightenments* (London: Vintage Books, 2008), 5.

8. Ibid., 4–8.

9. Ibid., 6.

10. Ibid., 119.

11. Newbigin, *Foolishness to the Greeks*, 23.

12. Lesslie Newbigin, "Can the West Be Converted?" *Princeton Seminary Bulletin* 6, no. 1 (1985): 25–37. Newbigin later expanded this lecture into the book Foolishness to the Greeks.

13. Newbigin, *Foolishness to the Greeks*, 34.

14. Ibid., 37.

15. Ibid.

16. David J. Bosch, *Transforming Mission: Paradigm Shifts in Theology of Mission* (Maryknoll, NY: Orbis Books, 1991), 267–73.

17. Newbigin, *The Foolishness to the Greeks*, 1.

18. Tennent's seven megatrends are: the collapse of Christendom; the rise of postmodernism; the collapse of the "West-Reaches-the-Rest" paradigm; the changing face of global Christianity; the emergence of the fourth branch of Christianity; globalization; and a deeper ecumenism. See Timothy C. Tennent, *Invitation to World Missions: A Trinitarian Missiology for the Twenty-first Century* (Grand Rapids: Kregel Publications, 2010), 15–51.

19. James Scherer, *Gospel, Church, and Kingdom: Comparative Studies in World Mission Theology* (Minneapolis: Augsburg, 1987), 9–50.

20. Andrew F. Walls, "The Protestant Missionary Awakening in Its European Context," in *The Cross-Cultural Process in Christian History* (Maryknoll, NY: Orbis Books, 2002), 196.

21. Stephen Neill, *A History of Christian Missions*, 2nd ed., rev. by Owen Chadwick, *The Penguin History of the Church*, vol. 6 (London: Penguin Books, 1986), 6:73.

22. Ibid.

23. Kenneth Scott Latourette, *A History of the Expansion of Christianity*, vol. 4, *The Great Century: Europe and the United States*; vol. 5, *The Great Century: The Americas, Australia and Africa*; and vol. 6, *The Great Century: North Africa and Asia* (New York: Harper & Brothers Publishers, 1941, 1943, and 1944).

24. Ronald K. Orchard, ed., *Witness in Six Continents: Records of the Meeting of the Commission on World Mission and Evangelism of the World Council of Churches Held in Mexico City*, December 8th to 19th, 1963 (London: Edinburgh House Press, 1964), 175.

25. Carlos Cardoza-Orlandi and Justo González have helpfully identified the modern missionary period into early modern and late modern. See Carlos F. Cardoza-Orlandi and Justo L. González, *To All Nations from All Nations: A History of the Christian Missionary Movement* (Nashville: Abingdon Press, 2013), 133ff., 203ff.

26. Neill, *A History of Christian Missions*, 223.

27. Ibid., 381.

28. Ibid., 380.

29. Andrew F. Walls, "The American Dimension of the Missionary Movement," in *The Missionary Movement in Christian History: Studies in the Transmission of Faith* (Maryknoll, NY: Orbis Books, 1996), 239.

30. See Willem Adolf Visser 't Hooft, "The Genesis of the World Council of Churches," in *A History of the Ecumenical Movement, 1517–1948*, 4th ed., ed. Ruth Rouse and Stephen C. Neill (Geneva: World Council of Churches, 1993), 697–724.

31. William Richey Hogg, *Ecumenical Foundations: A History of the International Missionary Council and Its Nineteenth Century Background* (New York: Harper & Brothers, 1952). See pp. 297–298 on the Church and Mission at Tambaram. The book covers the period up to the end of 1948.

32. Andrew F. Walls, "The Missionary Movement: A Lay Fiefdom?" in *The Cross-Cultural Process in Christian History* (Maryknoll, NY: Orbis Books, 2002), 217.

33. Ibid., 216.

34. Dana L. Robert, *Christian Mission: How Christianity Became a World Religion* (Chichester: Wiley- Blackwell, 2009), 50–51.

35. Ibid., 51–52.

36. Neill, *A History of Christian Missions*, 421.

37. Ibid., 424.

38. David Barrett, George T. Kurian, and Todd M. Johnson, *World Christian Encyclopedia*, vol. 1 (Oxford: Oxford University Press, 2001), 1:4.

39. Neill, *A History of Christian Missions*, 462.

40. "Christians, 1910–2010," in *Atlas of Global Christianity*, ed. Todd M. Johnson and Kenneth Ross (Edinburgh: Edinburgh University Press, 2009), 9.

41. For a study on Mahatma Gandhi and Christianity, see Lalsangkima Pachuau. "A Clash of 'Mass Movements'? Christians Missions and the Gandhian Nationalist Movement in India," *Transformation*, 31, no. 3 (2014): 157-74.

42. Lamin Sanneh, "Christian Missions and the Western Guilt Complex," *The Christian Century*, April 8, 1987, 330–34.

43. Ibid., 330.

44. For the text of "The Universal Declaration of Human Rights," see http://www.un.org/en/universal-declaration-human-rights/, accessed, September 3, 2016.

45. Bishop Anastsios of Androusia's "Mexico City 1963: Old Wine into Fresh Wineskin," *International Review of Mission*, 67 (1978): 357.

46. Orchard, *Witness in Six Continents*, 175, emphasis mine.

47. Growing out of the International Congress on World Evangelization which met in Lausanne, Switzerland in 1974, Lausanne Committee for World Evangelization, popularly called Lausanne Movement, is a collaboration of evangelicals around the world for world evangelization. The second and third congresses were held in Manila (Philippines) and Cape Town (South Africa) in 1989 and 2010 respectively. See https://www.lausanne.org/our-legacy (last accessed April 21, 2018).

48. Scott W. Sunquist, *The Unexpected Christian Century: The Reversal and Transformation of Global Christianity, 1900–2000* (Grand Rapids: Baker Academic, 2015), xvi.

49. Ibid.

3. Christian Movements in the Majority World: Part One: Latin America and Africa

1. Todd Hartch, *The Rebirth of Latin American Christianity* (Oxford: Oxford University Press, 2014), 2, Kindle ed.

2. On this point, see, inter alia, Luis N. Rivera, *A Violent Evangelism: The Political and Religious Conquest of the Americas* (Louisville: Westminster John Knox Press, 1992), 64–79.

3. Timothy J. Steigenga and Edward L. Cleary, "Understanding Conversion in the Americas," *Conversion of a Continent: Contemporary Religious Change in Latin America*, ed. Timothy J. Steigenga and Edward L. Cleary (New Brunswick, NJ: Rutgers University Press, 2007), 3.

4. Hartch, *The Rebirth of Latin American Christianity*, 2.

5. Steigenga and Cleary, "Understanding Conversion in the Americas," 3.

6. According to the *Atlas of Global Christianity*, the population of Latin America in 1910 was 78,269,000 of which 70,675,000 (or 90.3 percent) were Catholics. See *Atlas of Global Christianity*, ed. Todd M. Johnson and Kenneth Ross (Edinburgh: Edinburgh University Press, 2009), 176.

7. John Schwaller, *The History of the Catholic Church in Latin America: From Conquest to Revolution and Beyond* (New York: New York University Press, 2011), 59.

8. In some estimates, the native population of the region was reduced from about 80 to 100 million to 10 to 12 million in the first seventy years or so of the colonization. See Rivera, *A Violent Evangelism*, 170–175; Guillermo Cook, "Introduction: The Changing Face of the Church in Latin America," *New Face of the Church in Latin America: Between Tradition and Change*, ed. Guillermo Cook (Maryknoll, NY: Orbis Books, 1994), xiv.

9. Schwaller, *The History of the Catholic Church in Latin America*, 55–58.

10. See Rivera, *A Violent Evangelism*, 218–29.

11. Ondina E. González and Justo L. González, *Christianity in Latin America: A History* (Cambridge: Cambridge University Press, 2008), 3–5.

12. Hartch, *The Rebirth of Latin American Christianity*, 22.

13. Ibid., 29–30.

14. Schwaller, *The History of the Catholic Church in Latin America*, 189–212.

15. Ibid., 216–217.

16. Ibid., 214–15.

17. Hartch, *The Rebirth of Latin American Christianity*, 59.

18. Ibid., 57–90.

19. González and González, *Christianity in Latin America*, 250.

20. Ibid., 252.

21. Ibid., 251.

22. Guillermo Cook, "The Genesis and Practice of Protestant Base Communities in Latin America," in *New Face of the Church in Latin America: Between Tradition and Change*, ed. Guillermo Cook (Maryknoll, NY: Orbis Books, 1994), 150–55.

23. Hartch, *The Rebirth of Latin American Christianity*, 2.

24. Ernesto Cardenal, *The Gospel in Solentiname*, rev. in one vol. (Maryknoll, NY: Orbis Books, 2010). The book was originally published in English in four volumes (1976, 1978, 1979, and 1982).

25. Hartch, *The Rebirth of Latin American Christianity*, 2.

26. González and González, *Christianity in Latin America*, 242.

27. Gustavo Gutiérrez, *A Theology of Liberation: History, Politics, and Salvation*, rev. ed. with a new introduction, trans. and ed. Sister Caridad Inda and John Eagleson (Maryknoll, NY: Orbis Books, 1988), 58–62.

28. González and González, *Christianity in Latin America*, 245–47.

29. Gutiérrez, "Introduction to the Revised Edition: Expanding the View," in *A Theology of Liberation*, xvii.

30. Gutiérrez, *A Theology of Liberation*, 63.

31. José Míguez Bonino, *Faces of Latin American Protestantism: 1993 Carnahan Lectures*, trans Eugene L. Stockwell (Grand Rapids: Eerdmans, 1997).

32. David Martin, *Tongues of Fire: The Explosion of Protestantism in Latin America* (Oxford: Basil Blackwell, 1990); David Stoll, *Is Latin America Turning Protestant? The Politics of Evangelical Growth* (Berkeley: University of California Press, 1990).

33. See Stephen Offutt, *New Centers of Global Evangelicalism in Latin America and Africa* (New York: Cambridge University Press, 2015), 17–21.

34. Hartch, *The Rebirth of Latin American Christianity*, 92.

35. Pew Research Center, "Religion in Latin America: Widespread Change in a Historically Catholic Region," http://www.pewforum.org/2014/11/13/religion-in -latin-america/, accessed January 23, 2017.

36. Ibid.

37. Hartch, *The Rebirth of Latin American Christianity*, 92.

38. Cecil M. Robeck Jr., *Azusa Street Mission and Revival: The Birth of Pentecostal Movement* (Nashville: Thomas Nelson, 2006), 10.

39. R. Andrew Chesnut, "A Preferential Option for the Spirit: The Catholic Charismatic Renewal in Latin America's New Religious Economy," *Latin American Politics and Society*, 45, no. 1 (April 2003): 62.

40. Ibid., 62–63.

41. Edward L. Cleary, *The Rise of Charismatic Catholicism in Latin America* (Gainesville: University Press of Florida, 2011), 10.

42. Allan Anderson, "Revising Pentecostal History in Global Perspective," in *Asian and Pentecostal: The Charismatic Face of Christianity in Asia*, ed. Allan Anderson and Edmond Tang (Oxford: Regnum Books International, 2005), 166.

43. Dana L. Robert, *Christian Mission: How Christianity Became a World Religion* (Chichester: Wiley-Blackwell, 2009), 62.

44. Cleary, *The Rise of Charismatic Catholicism in Latin America*, 55.

45. Hartch, *The Rebirth of Latin American Christianity*, 92.

46. David Martin, *Tongues of Fire: The Explosion of Protestantism in Latin America* (Oxford: Basil Blackwell, 1990), 1.

47. Allan Anderson, *An Introduction to Pentecostalism: Global Charismatic Christianity* (Cambridge: Cambridge University Press, 2004), 63.

48. Juan Sepúlveda, "The Pentecostl Movement in Latin America," in *New Face of the Church in Latin America*, ed. Guillermo Cook

49. Anderson, *An Introduction to Pentecostalism*, 64.

50. Hartch, *The Rebirth of Latin American Christianity*, 96.

51. Anderson, *An Introduction to Pentecostalism*, 64.

52. Ibid., 67.

53. Ibid., 76–77.

54. Ibid., 69.

55. Hartch, *The Rebirth of Latin American Christianity*, 96–97.

56. *Atlas of Global Christianity*, 176.

57. Timothy J. Steigenga and Edward L. Cleary, "Understanding Conversion in the Americas," 5.

58. Martin Meredith, *The Fate of Africa: From the Hopes of Freedom to the Heart of Despair: A History of Fifty Years of Independence* (New York: Public Affairs, 2005), 5.

59. Ibid.

60. Ibid., 141–328.

61. J. W. Hofmeyr, "Mainline Churches in the Public Space, 1975–2000," in *African Christianity: An African Story*, ed. Ogbu U. Kalu (Trenton, NJ: African World Press, 2007), 315.

62. Meredith, *The Fate of Africa*, 368.

63. Adrian Hastings, *African Christianity* (New York: The Seabury Press, 1976), 13, 2.

64. The number of Christians given as 63,193,000 in 1970 by the encyclopedia is a bit low in comparison to numbers given by other scholars. This may be because the encyclopedia reported "adult" Christians, and others reported "total" Christian population. As mentioned above, Adrian Hastings said 90 million in 1975. David Maxwell approximated the number in 1965 already as 75 million. See David Maxwell, "Post-Colonial Christianity in Africa," in *The Cambridge History of Christianity*, vol. 9, *World Christianities* c.1914–c.2000 (Cambridge: Cambridge University Press, 2006), 401.

65. David B. Barrett, et al. eds. *World Christian Encyclopedia: A Comparative Survey of Churches and Religions in the Modern World*, vol. 1, (Oxford: Oxford University Press, 2001), 12.

66. Lamin Sanneh, *Whose Religion Is Christianity?: The Gospel Beyond the West* (Grand Rapids: William B. Eerdmans, 2003), 15.

67. Ibid.

68. Elizabeth A. Isichei, *A History of Christianity in Africa: From Antiquity to the Present* (Grand Rapids: William B. Eerdmans, 1995), 335.

69. Hofmeyr, "Mainline Churches in the Public Space, 1975–2000," 320.

70. *World Christian Encyclopedia*, vol. 1, 12.

71. "Independent" is used a bit vaguely in the encyclopedia. It is used as an equivalent to "post-denominationalist" and "neo-apostolic" that includes "non-white or black/Third World indigenous, white-led post-denominationalists." See *World Christian Encyclopedia*, vol. 1, 41.

72. This is the total sum of Anglican, Catholic, independent, marginal, orthodox, and protestants in 2000 from *World Christian Encyclopedia*, 12.

73. This is the total sum of Anglican, Catholic, independent, marginal, orthodox, and protestant in 2010 from *Atlas of Global Christianity*, 112.

74. Operation World has a category called "doubly affiliated" under which it estimated as many as 3.46 percent of the population. See Patrick Johnstone and Jason Mandryk, *Operation World: When We Pray God Works*, 21st Century ed. (Cumbria: Paternoster Lifestyle, 2001), 21.

75. Here, I am following the description by J. Kwabena Asamoah-Gyadu's "'Born of Water and the Spirit': Pentecostal/Charismatic Christianity in Africa," *Af-*

rican Christianity: An African Story, ed. Ogbu U. Kalu, (Trenton, NJ: Africa World Press, 2007), 339–357, esp. 340–47.

76. Ibid., 340.

77. See Alan Anderson, *African Reformation: African Initiated Christianity in the 20th Century* (Trenton, NJ: Africa World Press, 2001).

78. Asamoah-Gyadhu, "Born of Water and the Spirit," 341.

79. Allan Anderson, *An Introduction to Pentecostalism: Global Charismatic Christianity* (Cambridge: Cambridge University Press, 2004), 103.

80. Afe Adogame, "Up, Up Jesus! Down, Down Satan! African Religiosity in the former Soviet Bloc—the Embassy of the Blessed Kingdom of God for All Nations," *Exchange*, 37 (2008): 310.

81. Asamoah-Gyadu, "Born of Water and the Spirit," 342.

82. J. Kwabena Asamoah-Gyadu, "African Initiated Christianity in Eastern Europe: Church of the 'Embassy of God' in Ukraine," *International Bulletin of Missionary Research*, 30, no. 2 (April 2006): 73.

83. Clifford J. Levy, "An Evangelical Preacher's Message Catches Fire in Ukraine," *New York Times*, April 22, 2011.

84. J. Kwabena Asamoah-Gyadu, *African Charismatics: Current Development within Independent Indigenous Pentecostalism in Ghana* (Leiden: Brill, 2005).

85. Ludovic Lado, S.J., "African Catholicism in the Face of Pentecostalism," in *African Christianities*, ed. Eloi Messi Metogo, Concilium 2006, no. 4 (London: SCM Press, 2006), 22.

86. Jonathan Kangwa, "Pentecostalisation of Mainline Churches in Africa: The Case of the United Church of Zambia," *The Expository Times*, 127, no. 12 (2016): 537–584. Along the same line, Jesse Zink used "Anglocostalism." See Jesse Zink, "'Anglocostalism' in Nigeria: Neo-Pentecostalism and Obstacles to Anglican Unity," *Journal of Anglican Studies*, 10, no. 2 (2012): 231–50.

87. Cephas N. Omenyo, *Pentecost Outside Pentecostalism: A Study of the Development of Charismatic Renewal in the Mainline Churches in Ghana* (Zoetermeer: Uitgeverji Boekencentrum, 2002), 101–98.

88. Ibid., 111–198; Also see J. Kwabena Asamoah-Gyadu, "'I will put my Breath in You, and You will come to Life': Charismatic Renewal in Ghanaian Mainline Churches and Its Implications for African 'Diasporean' Christianity," in *Christianity*

in Africa and the African Diaspora: The Appropriation of a Scattered Heritage (London: Continuum, 2008), 193–207.

89. Cephas N. Omenyo, *Pentecost Outside Pentecostalism: A Study of the Development of Charismatic Renewal in the Mainline Churches in Ghana* (Zoetermeer: Uitgeverji Boekencentrum, 2002), 104.

90. Jonathan Kangwa, "Pentecostalisation of Mainline Churches in Africa: The Case of the United Church of Zambia," *The Expository Times*, 127, no. 12 (2016): 537–84.

91. Closely associated to exorcism, the ministry of "deliverance" in Pentecostal tradition refers to cleansing or deliverance from the captivity of the evil spirit. It is quite close to salvation as liberation from sin except that the emphasis is on the interaction with spirit.

92. Asamoah-Gyadu, "Born of Water and Spirit," 346.

93. Lado, "African Catholicism in the Face of Pentecostalism," 27.

94. Ibid.

4. Christian Movements in the Majority World: Part Two: Asia and the Pacific Islands

1. See http://unstats.un.org/unsd/methods/m49/m49regin.htm, accessed August 6, 2014.

2. See http://esa.un.org/unpd/wup/CDROM_2009/WPP2009_DEFINITION _OF_MAJOR_AREAS_AND_REGIONS.pdf, accessed August 6, 2014.

3. Sebastian C. H. Kim, "Christianity in Asia, 1910–2010," in *Atlas of Global Christianity*, ed. Todd M. Johnson and Kenneth R. Ross (Edinburgh: Edinburgh University Press, 2009), 134.

4. *Atlas of Global Christianity*, 136.

5. For a brief overview, see Ian Breward, "Christianity in Australia/New Zealand, 1910–2010," in *Atlas of Global Christianity*, 96–197. For an interesting look at "creative accommodation" in Australian Catholic missions, see Laura Rademaker, "Tiwi Christianity: Aboriginal Histories, Catholic Mission and a Surprising Conversion," http://www.abc.net.au/religion/articles/2018/02/07/4800150.htm. Cf. Anglican missions in Australia in Laura Rademaker, *Found in Translation: Many Meanings on a North Australian Mission* (Honolulu: University of Hawai'i Press, 2018).

6. Anthony O'Mahony, "Christianity in Western Asia, 1910–2010," in *Atlas of Global Christianity*, 150–51.

7. Douglas Jacobsen, *The World's Christians: Who They Are, Where They Are, and How They Got There* (West Sussex: Wiley-Blackwell, 2011), 76.

8. Ibid., 150.

9. Edmond Tang, "Christianity in Eastern Asia, 1910–2010," in *Atlas of Global Christianity*, 138.

10. Ibid.

11. Carolyn Bowen Francis and John Masaaki Nakajima, *Christians in Japan* (New York: Friendship Press, 1991), 30.

12. Ibid., 33.

13. Mark R. Mullins, "Japan," in *Christianities in Asia*, ed. Peter C. Phan (Oxford: Wiley-Blackwell, 2011), 198.

14. Ibid., 201.

15. Ibid., 209.

16. For a comprehensive overview of Japanese theology, see Yasuo Furuya, ed., *A History of Japanese Theology* (Grand Rapids: William B. Eerdmans, 1997).

17. Mark Mullins, *Christianity Made in Japan: A Study of Indigenous Movements* (Honolulu: University of Hawai'i Press, 1998).

18. Richard Fox Young, "East Asia," in *The Cambridge History of Christianity*, vol. 9, *World Christianities*, c.1914–c.2000, ed. Hugh McLeod (Cambridge: Cambridge University Press, 2006), 452–54.

19. Ibid., 454.

20. Ying Fuk-tsang, "Mainland China," in *Christianities in Asia*, 162.

21. Tony Lambert, *China's Christian Millions*, rev. (Oxford: Monarch Books, 2006), 16.

22. According to Edmond Tang, "Christianity in Eastern Asia, 1910–2010," in *Atlas of Global Christianity*, 138.

23. Yang Huilan, "The Contextualization of Chinese Christian Theology and Its Main Concerns," in *Christianity and Chinese Culture*, ed. Miikka Ruokanen and Paulos Huang (Grand Rapids; William B. Eerdmans, 2010), 201.

24. Daniel H. Bays, *A New History of Christianity in China*, Blackwell Guides to Global Christianity (Chichester, UK: Wiley-Blackwell, 2011), 121, Kindle ed.

25. The church founded by Nee and Lee has been known by various names: Local Church, Little Flock, Assembly Hall, and Lord's Recovery. See Liu Yi, "Globalization of Chinese Christianity: A Study of Watchman Nee and Witness Lee's Ministry," *Asia Journal of Theology* 30, no. 1 (April 2016): 96–114.

26. "Regulations on Religious Affairs" is reproduced in English and Chinese by the Congressional– Executive Commission on China. See https://www.cecc.gov /resources/legal-provisions/regulations-n-religious-affairs, accessed September 13, 2016.

27. Lauren Homer, an expert in international law who serves nonprofit and religious organizations, said that "the promise of the 2005 regulations is almost completely unrealized" even after five years. See Lauren B. Homer, "Registration of Chinese Protestant House Churches under China's 2005 Regulation on Religious Affairs: Resolving the Implementation Impasse," *Journal of Church and Stat*, 52, no. 1 (2010): 50–73.

28. For an analytical review of the statistics of 2010 represented in the *Blue Book of Religions*, see Roman Malek, "People's Republic of China: Churches and Religions Annual Statistical Overview 2010/2011," in *Religions and Christianity in Today's China*, no. 1 (2011): 32–59, http://www.china-zentrum.de/fileadmin/redaktion /RCTC_2011-1.32-59_Malek_Statistical_Overview.pdf, accessed August 16, 2014.

29. The state-recognized China Internet Information Center published a summary of the Blue Book's statistics as 23.05 million "Christians" (by which it seems to mean Protestants) and 5.70 million Catholics. See http://www.china.org.cn /china/2010-08/12/content_20690649.htm, accessed August 9, 2014.

30. Atlas of Global Christianity, 140.

31. See http://www.globalreligiousfutures.org/countries/china#/?affiliations _religion_id=11&affiliations_year=2010&region_name=All%20 Countries&restrictions_year=2012, accessed August 9, 2014.

32. Ying, "Mainland China," 152.

33. Bays, *A New History of Christianity in China*, 194.

34. Ibid., 190–92.

35. Lian Xi, *Redeemed by Fire: The Rise of Popular Christianity in China* (New Haven and London: Yale University Press, 2010), 230.

36. Wang Man Kong, "The China Factor and Protestant Christianity in Hong Kong: Reflections from Historical Perspectives," *Studies in World Christianity*, 8, no. 1 (2002): 126.

37. Lo Lung-kwong, "Taiwan, Hong Kong, Macau," in *Christianities in Asia*, 188.

38. Ibid., 187.

39. Kenneth Scott Latourette, *A History of the Expansion of Christianity*, vol. 3, Three Centuries of Advance, A.D. 1500–A.D. 1800 (New York: Harper and Brothers, 1939), 359–60.

40. See detailed statistical records of Protestants and Catholics in Lo, "Taiwan, Hong Kong, Macau," 178.

41. James Sha and Andrew Shen, "Republic of China," trans. James. H. Taylor, in *Church in Asia Today: Challenges and Opportunities*, ed. Saphir Athyal (Singapore: Asia Lausanne Committee for World Evangelization, 1996), 135.

42. Ibid., 137.

43. Bong Rin Ro, "The Korean Church: God's Chosen People for Evangelism," in *Korean Church Growth Explosion*, rev. ed., ed. Bong Rin Ro and Marlin L. Nelson (Seoul: Word of Life Press, 1995), 13–15.

44. Quoted from Bong Rin Ro, "The Church in Korea," in *Church in Asia Today: Challenges and Opportunities*, ed. Saphir Athyal (Singapore: Asia Lausanne Committee for World Evangelization, 1996), 49.

45. Byong-suh Kim, "Modernization and the Explosive Growth and Decline of Korean Protestant Religiosity," in *Christianity in Korea*, ed. Robert E. Buswell Jr., and Timothy S. Lee (Honolulu: University of Hawai'i Press, 2006), 310.

46. Donald Baker, "Sibling Rivalry in Twentieth Century Korea: Comparative Growth Rates of Catholic and Protestant Communities," in *Christianity in Korea*, ed. Robert E. Buswell Jr. and Timothy S. Lee, 284.

47. See the various chapters of Bong and Nelson, *Korean Church Growth Explosion*.

48. See Boo-Woong Yoo, *Korean Pentecostalism: Its History and Theology* (Frankfurt: Verlag Peter Lang, 1988); Yŏng-hun Yi, *The Holy Spirit Movement in Korea: Its*

Historical and Theological Development (Oxford: Regnum Press, 2009); and Young-Hoon Lee, "The Korean Holy Spirit Movement in Relation to Pentecostalism," in *Asian and Pentecostal: The Charismatic Face of Christianity in Asia*, ed. Allan Anderson and Edmond Tang, 509–526 (Oxford: Regnum Press, 2005).

49. Bong and Nelson, *Korean Church Growth Explosion*, 289–90.

50. John L. Nevius, a Presbyterian missionary in China devised practical ways by which an indigenous church may be planted that is self-propagating, self-governing, and self-supporting. This came to be called the "Nevius Method."

51. Andrew Eungi Kim, "South Korea," in *Christianities in Asia*, 222–23.

52. Steve Sang-Cheol Moon, Hee-Joo Yoo, and Eun-Mi Kim, "Missions from Korea 2015: Missionaries Unable to Continue Ministry in Their Country of Service," *International Bulletin of Missionary Research*, 39, no. 2 (April 2015): 84.

53. Violet James, "Christianity in South-eastern Asia, 1910–2010," in *Atlas of Global Christianity*, 146.

54. Robbie B. H. Goh, *Christianity in Southeast Asia* (Singapore: Institute of Southeast Asian Studies, 2005), 54.

55. Edmund Kee-Fook Chia, "Malaysia and Singapore," in *Christianities in Asia*, 78.

56. Goh, *Christianity in Southeast Asia*, 5.

57. Census of Population 2010: Statistical Release 1: Demographic Characteristics, Education, Language and Religion (Singapore: Department of Statistics, Ministry of Trade & Industry, Republic of Singapore, 2011), 30, http://www.sing stat.gov.sg/docs/default-source/default-document-library/publications/publications _and_papers/cop2010/census_2010_release1/cop2010sr1.pdf, accessed September 19, 2016.

58. See Department of Statistics Malaysia, "Population Distribution and Basic Demographic Characteristics Report 2010 (Updated: 05/08/2011)," https://www.statistics.gov.my/index.php?r=column/ctheme&menu_id=L0pheU43NWJwRWV SZklWdzQ4TlhUUT09&bul_id=MDMxdHZjWTk1SjFzTzNkRXYzcVZjdz09#, accessed September 19, 2016.

59. Kee-Fook Chia, "Malaysia and Singapore," 90.

60. James, "Christianity in South-eastern Asia, 1910–2010," 147.

61. Goh, *Christianity in Southeast Asia*, 43–44.

62. Ibid., 55.

63. Ibid., 43.

64. John Prior, "Indonesia," in *Christianities in Asia*, 63.

65. Goh, Christianity in Southeast Asia, 59.

66. Prior, 64–66, 71.

67. Paul Pedersen shows that there's no evidence of eating the flesh of the missionaries. See Paul B. Pedersen, *Batak Blood and Protestant Soul: The Development of National Batak Churches in North Sumatra* (Grand Rapids: William B. Eerdmans, 1970), 47–72.

68. Ibid., 73–80.

69. *Encyclopedia Britannica*, s.v. "Pancasila," https://www.britannica.com/topic /Pancasila, accessed September 20, 2016.

70. Indonesia-Investments, "Religion in Indonesia" (drawn from Statistics Indonesia, Population Census, 2010). See http://www.indonesia-investments.com /culture/religion/item69, accessed September 19, 2016.

71. Goh, *Christianity in Southeast Asia*, 61.

72. Susan Russell, "Christianity in the Philippines," http://www.seasite.niu.edu /crossroads/russell/christianity.htm, accessed September 20, 2016.

73. Jack Miller, "Religion in the Philippines," Center for Global Education, Asia Society, http://asiasociety.org/education/religion-philippines, accessed September 20, 2016.

74. Philippine Statistics Authority reported that the total population as of August 1, 2015, is 100.98 million, http://psa.gov.ph/content/highlights-philippin e-population-2015-census-population, accessed September 20, 2016.

75. Government of Timor-Leste, "History," http://timor-leste.gov .tl/?p=29&lang=en, accessed September 20, 2016.

76. http://www.thearda.com/internationalData/countries/Country_71_2.asp, accessed September 21, 2016.

77. Lorenzo C. Bautista, "The Church in the Philippines," in *Church in Asia Today: Challenges and Opportunities*, ed. Saphir Athyal (Singapore: Asia Lausanne Committee for World Evangelization, 1996), 171.

78. José Mario C. Francisco, S.J., "The Philippines," in *Christianities in Asia*, 103.

79. The word of President William McKinley of the United States quoted by Lorenzo Bautista, 173.

80. Francisco, "The Philippines," 115.

81. Bautista, "The Church in the Philippines," 180, 178.

82. "Historical Overview of Pentecostalism in [the] Philippines," Pew Research Center, Religion and Public Life, October 5, 2006, http://www.pewforum .org/2006/10/05/historical-overview-of-pentecostalism-in-philippines/, accessed September 21, 2016.

83. Francisco, "The Philippines," 118.

84. "Highlights of the Philippine Population 2015 Census of Population, https:// psa.gov.ph/content/highlights-philippine-population-2015-census-population, accessed September 21, 2016.

85. 2015 Philippine Statistical Yearbook (Quezon City: Philippine Statistics Authority, October 2015), 1–30, https://psa.gov.ph/sites/default/files/2015%20 PSY%20PDF_0.pdf, accessed September 21, 2016.

86. "Other Religious Affiliation" is not explained in the report. It is possible that this may be what the Association of Religious Data Archives (ARDA) report calls "Ethnoreligionist." The ARDA report shows 2.3 percent to be Ethnoreligionists in 2010. See http://www.thearda.com/internationalData/countries/Country_178_2 .asp, accessed September 21, 2016.

87. Bautista, "The Church in the Philippines," 174, 185.

88. Goh, *Christianity in Southeast Asia*, 68–69.

89. The 2014 Myanmar Population and Housing Census: The Union Report: Religion, Census Report Volume 2-C (Nay Pyi Taw: Department of Population, Ministry of Labour, Immigration and Population, July 2016), 3, 5, http:// myanmar.unfpa.org/sites/asiapacific/files/pub-pdf/UNION_2-C_religion_EN_0 .pdf,accessed September 22, 2016.

90. Samuel Ngun Ling, "Christianity in Burma (Myanmar)," *The Oxford Encyclopedia of South Asian Christianity*, ed. Roger Hedlund et al. (New Delhi: Oxford University Press, 2012), 118.

91. The violent assault and displacement (some would say ethnic cleansing/ genocide) of the Muslim Rohingya people in Myanmar, that began in August 2017, has created an ongoing humanitarian crisis. The Rohingya people migrated from the neighboring Bangladesh and some in Myanmar saw the rapid increase of Rohingya people as a threat to their nation.

92. Pum Za Mang, "Buddhist Nationalism and Burmese Christianity," *Studies in World Christianity* 22, no. 2 (2016): 148–167.

93. Lian H. Sakhong, "Christianity and Chin Identity," in *Exploring Ethnic Diversity in Burma* (Copenhagen: NIAS Press, 2007), 200.

94. La Seng Dingrin, "Conversion to Mission Christianity among the Kachin of Upper Burma, 1877–1972," in *Asia in the Making of Christianity: Conversion, Agency, and Indigeneity, 1600 to the Present*, ed. Richard Fox Young and Jonathan Seitz (Leiden: Brill, 2013), 131–32.

95. Jay Riley Case, "Interpreting Karen Christianity: The American Baptist Reaction to Asian Christianity in the Nineteenth Century," in *The Changing Face of Christianity: Africa, the West, and the World*, ed. Joel A. Carpenter and Lamin Sanneh (New York: Oxford University Press, 2005), 135–57.

96. Ruth Ann Tipton, "Unrealized Expectations: A History of Christian Union Mission and World Gospel Mission's Work among the Nembi and Melpa People of Papua New Guinea" (PhD diss., Asbury Theological Seminary, 2015), 1.

97. Allan K. Davidson, "'The Pacific Is No Longer a Mission Field?': Conversion in the South Pacific in the Twentieth Century," in *Christianity Reborn: The Global Expansion of Evangelicalism in the Twentieth Century*, ed. Donald M. Lewis, Studies in the History of Christian Missions (Grand Rapids: William B. Eerdmans, 2004), 138.

98. Stephen Neill, *A History of Christian Missions*, 2nd ed., The Pelican History of the Church, ed. Owen Chadwick, vol. 6 (London: Penguin Books, 1986), 252.

99. Ibid., 253.

100. Fetuna'i Ben Liua'ana, "Christianity in Melanesia, Micronesia, and Polynesia," in *Atlas of Global Christianity*, ed. Todd M. Johnson and Kenneth R. Ross (Edinburgh: Edinburgh University Press, 2009), 200.

101. Davidson, "The Pacific Is No Longer a Mission Field?" 139.

102. Liua'ana, "Christianity in Melanesia, Micronesia, and Polynesia," 201.

103. Sione Latukefu, foreword to *The Role of Social Change in the Rise and Development of New Religious Groups in the Pacific Islands* by Manfred Ernst (Hamburg: Lit Verlag, 1996), v.

104. Manfred Ernst, *The Role of Social Change in the Rise and Development of New Religious Groups in the Pacific Islands* (Hamburg: Lit Verlag, 1996), 110.

105. For detailed statistics, see ibid., 316–17.

106. Liua'ana, "Christianity in Melanesia, Micronesia, and Polynesia," 201.

107. See "Christianity in Melanesia, 1910–2010," in *Atlas of Global Christianity*, 202.

108. Although the name "Syrian Christian Community" has become popular, historically, they were known as the "St. Thomas Christians of India." See C. P. Mathew and M. M. Thomas, *The Indian Churches of Saint Thomas*, rev. (Delhi: ISPCK, 2005), 1.

109. 2011 Census Data: C-1 Population by Religious Community, Government of India, Ministry of Home Affairs, Office of the Registrar General and Census Commissioner, http://www.censusindia.gov.in/2011census/c-01.html, accessed September 23, 2016.

110. *World Christian Encyclopedia*, vol. 1 (Oxford: Oxford University Press, 2001), 360.

111. *Atlas of Global Christianity*, 144.

112. The Catholic Bishops' Conference of India, *The Catholic Directory of India 2013* (Bangalore: Claretian Publications, 2013), 83.

113. F. Hrangkhuma, "The Church in India," in *Church in Asia Today*, ed. Saphil Athyal, 402.

114. Allan H. Anderson, "Pentecostalism and Charismatic Movements in Asia," in *The Oxford Handbook of Christianity in Asia*, ed. Felix Wilfred (Oxford: Oxford University Press, 2014), 166.

115. Michael Bergunder, *The South Indian Pentecostal Movement in the Twentieth Century* (Grand Rapids: William B. Eerdmans, 2008), 15.

116. For a discussion on this point, see Lalsangkima Pachuau, "A Clash of 'Mass Movements'? Christian Missions and the Gandhian Nationalist Movement in India," *Transformation*, 31, no. 3 (2014): 157–74.

117. Korula Jacob, "The Government of India and the Entry of Missionaries," *International Review of Missions*, 47 (1958): 411–412; "Editorials: The Council and the Government," NCCR 74, no. 12 (December 1954): 519.

118. The inquiry was officially called "The Christian Missionary Activities Inquiry," but it is popularly known as "the Niyogi Committee" in connection with the name of the chairman of the Inquiry Committee, Mr. Bhawani Shankar Niyogi. See *Report of the Christian Missionary Activities Enquiry Committee*, Madhya Pradesh, 1956, Volume 1, Volume 2 Part A, Volume 2 Part B (Nagpur: Government Printing Press, 1956).

119. B. Manohar James, "The Influence of the Niyogi Committee Report of Madhya Pradesh on Hindu Nationalism and Its Resistance to Christian Missions in Independent India" (PhD diss., Asbury Theological Seminary, 2016).

120. M. K. Gandhi, *Christian Missions: Their Place in India*, ed. B. Kumarappa, 2nd ed. (Ahmedabad: Navajivan Publishing House, 1957), 61. This book is a collection of Gandhi's speeches and writings on Christianity. The first edition was published in 1941, during Gandhi's own lifetime.

121. See F. Hrangkhuma, *Christianity in India: Search for Liberation and Identity* (Delhi: ISPCK, 1998).

122. J. Waskom Pickett, *Christian Mass Movements in India: A Study with Recommendations*, 2nd Indian ed. (Lucknow: Lucknow Publishing House, 1969), 159–164, esp. 161.

123. Charles Amjad-Ali, "From Dislocation to Dislocation: The Experience of the Christian Community in Pakistan," *International Review of Modern Sociology*, 41, no. 1 (Spring 2015): 12–16.

124. See Rabia Mehmood, "The Neverending Plight of Christians in Pakistan," Aljazeera, April 7, 2016, http://www.aljazeera.com/indepth/opinion/2016/04/never-ending-plight-christians-pakistan-160406095729110.html, accessed September 26, 2016; "Who Are Pakistan's Christians?" BBC News Asia, March 28, 2016, http://www.bbc.com/news/world-asia-35910331, accessed September 26, 2016.

125. Wajahat S. Khan, "Why It Feels Like a 'Crime' to Be Christians in Pakistan," NBC News: World, March 28, 2016, http://www.nbcnews.com/news/world/why-it-feels-crime-be-christian-pakistan-n179511, accessed September 26, 2016.

126. Bal Krishna Sharma, "A Hindu Kingdom and Conflicting Models in Nepal," in *News of Boundless Riches: Interrogating, Comparing, and Reconstructing Mission in a Global Era*, vol. 1., ed. Max L. Stackhouse and Lalsangkima Pachuau (Delhi: ISPCK, 2007), 174–77.

127. Rishikesh Shaha, *Three Decades and Two Kings (1960–1990)*, (New Delhi: Sterling Publishers, 1990), 82, quoted by Sharma, ibid., 177.

128. Sharma, "A Hindu Kingdom and Conflicting Models in Nepal," 177.

129. Cindy L. Perry, *Nepali around the World: Emphasizing Nepali Christians of the Himalayas* (Kathmandu: Ekta Books, 1997).

130. Sharma, "A Hindu Kingdom and Conflicting Models in Nepal," 189 (see also footnote 38).

131. National Population and Housing Census 2011 (Kathmandu: Central Bureau of Statistics, Government of Nepal, November 2012), 184, http://unstats .un.org/unsd/demographic/sources/census/wphc/Nepal/Nepal-Census-2011-Vol1 .pdf, accessed September 27, 2016.

132. *Atlas of Global Christianity*, 55.

133. Ibid., 144.

134. Jason Mandryk, *Operation World: The Definitive Prayer Guide to Every Nation* (Downers Grove, IL: IVP Books, 2010), 619.

135. Bal Krishna Sharma, "Pentecostalism and Its Impact on Nepalese Christianity," in *News of Boundless Riches: Interrogating, Comparing, and Reconstructing Mission in a Global Era*, vol. 1., ed. Max L. Stackhouse and Lalsangkima Pachuau (Delhi: ISPCK, 2007), 109–23.

136. Jeyaraj Rasiah, "Sri Lanka," in *Christianities in Asia*, ed. Peter C. Phan (Chichester: Wiley-Blackwell, 2011), 53–55.

137. Department of Census and Statistics, Sri Lanka, "Census of Population and Housing," http://www.statistics.gov.lk/PopHouSat/CPH2012Visualization /htdocs/index.php?usecase=indicator&action=Data&indId=10, accessed September 28, 2016.

138. G. P. V. Somratna, "History of Christian Mission in Sri Lanka," in *Missiology for the 21st Century: South Asian Perspective*, ed. Roger E. Hedlund and Paul Joshua Bhakiaraj (Delhi: ISPCK, 2004), 269.

139. Rasiah, "Sri Lanka," 53, 55-56.

5. Contextualization, Contextual Theology, and Global Christianity

1. John Parratt, introduction to *An Introduction to Third World Theologies*, ed. John Parratt (Cambridge: Cambridge University Press, 2004), 9.

2. A former missionary and mission historian Stephen Neill named contextualization the second "worst" term (next to "conscientization") of the "ecumenical barbarism by which the English language has of late been debased." See Stephen Neill, *Salvation Tomorrow: The Originality of Jesus and the World's Religions* (Nashville: Abingdon, 1976), 109n5.

3. Peter Schineller, S.J., *Handbook on Inculturation* (New York: Paulist Press, 1990), 19, mentions an establishment of a fund for "contextualizing the gospel" in 1957 by Rockefeller Foundation. However, no source is mentioned for verification.

4. Shoki Coe, "In Search of Renewal in Theological Education," *Theological Education*, 9, no 4 (Summer 1973): 241.

5. The list is drawn from Alan Neely, Christian Mission: A Case Study Approach (Maryknoll, NY: Orbis Books, 1995), 3–12.

6. Coe, "In Search of Renewal in Theological Education," 240.

7. See, for instance, M. M. Thomas, "India: Toward an Indigenous Theology," in *Asian Voices in Christian Theology*, ed. Gerald H. Anderson (Maryknoll, NY: Orbis Books, 1976), 11–35.

8. Paul L. Lehmann, "On Doing Theology: A Contextual Possibility," in *Prospect for Theology: Essays in Honour of H. H. Farmer*, ed. F. G. Healey, 119–136 (Digswell Place: Nisbet, 1966), quoted by Paul Duane Matheny, *Contextual Theology: The Drama of Our Times* (Eugene, OR: Pickwick Publications, 2011), 65–66.

9. A clear sign of the shift in using "inculturation" among the Protestants was at the World Mission and Evangelism Conference in Salvador da Bahia, Brazil, in 1996. See Called to *One Hope: The Gospel in Diverse Cultures*, ed. Christopher Duraisingh and Ana Langerak (Geneva: WCC Publications, 1998), 54–57.

10. Coe, "In Search of Renewal in Theological Education," 233.

11. Paul G. Hiebert, "Critical Contextualization," *International Bulletin of Missionary Research* (July 1987): 104.

12. Lesslie Newbigin, *The Gospel in a Pluralist Society* (Grand Rapids: William B. Eerdmans, 1989), 142.

13. Robert L. Montgomery, "Can Missiology Incorporate More of the Social Sciences?" *Missiology: An International Review*, 40, no. 3 (July 2012): 281–92.

14. William A. Dyrness, "Evangelical Theology and Culture," in *The Cambridge Companion to Evangelical Theology*, ed. Timothy Larsen and Daniel J. Treier (Cambridge: Cambridge University Press, 2007), 145.

15. Charles Taber, *To Understand the World, to Save the World: The Interface between Missiology and the Social Sciences* (Harrisburg, PA: Trinity Press International, 2000).

16. The movement, also called Lausanne Committee for World Evangelization, grew out of the International Congress on World Evangelization in 1974 held in Lausanne, Switzerland. It had held two other major world congresses: Manila in 1989, and Cape Town 2010. See https://www.lausanne.org/about-the-movement, accessed October 6, 2016.

17. See Covenant 10 "Evangelism and Culture" of the Lausanne Covenant. See John Stott, *The Lausanne Covenant: An Exposition and Commentary* (Minneapolis, MN: World Wide Publications, 1975). The text of the covenant is also available online: https://www.lausanne.org/content/covenant/lausanne-covenant, accessed October 6, 2016.

18. "Lausanne Covenant," https://www.lausanne.org/content/covenant/lausanne-covenant, accessed October 6, 2016.

19. Ibid.

20. The papers and the report are published in two separate books (the same content): *Gospel and Culture*, ed. John Stott and Robert T. Coote (Pasadena, CA: William Carey Library, 1979); and *Down to Earth: Studies in Christianity and Culture*, ed. John Stott and Robert T. Coote (Grand Rapids: William B. Eerdmans, 1980).

21. For an online version, see https://www.lausanne.org/content/lop/lop-2, accessed October 6, 2016.

22. Charles H. Kraft, "The Development of Contextualization Theory in Euro-American Missiology," in *Appropriate Christianity*, ed. Charles H. Kraft (Pasadena, CA: William Carey Library, 2005), 21.

23. Ibid., 24.

24. Robert J. Priest, "Anthropology and Missiology: Reflections on the Relationship," in *Paradigm Shifts in Christian Witness: Insights from Anthropology, Communication, and Spiritual Power* (Maryknoll, NY: Orbis Books, 2008), 28.

25. A. Scott Moreau, *Contextualization in World Missions: Mapping and Assessing Evangelical Models* (Grand Rapids: Kregel Publications, 2012), 36.

26. Darrell L. Whiteman, "Contextualization: The Theory, the Gap, the Challenge," *International Bulletin of Missionary Research*, 21, no. 1 (January 1997): 2 (author's emphasis).

27. Ibid., 4.

28. Charles H. Kraft, "Why Appropriate?" in *Appropriate Christianity* (Pasadena, CA: William Carey Library, 2005), 5.

29. Charles H. Kraft, "Why Isn't Contextualization Implemented?" in *Appropriate Christianity*, 68–69.

30. Paul G. Hiebert, "Critical Contextualization," *International Bulletin of Missionary Research*, 11, no. 3 (July 1987): 109.

31. Ibid.

32. Ibid., 104.

33. Michael Rynkiewich, *Soul, Self, and Society: A Postmodern Anthropology for Mission in a Postcolonial World* (Eugene, OR: Cascade Books, 2011), 41.

34. Matheny, *Contextual Theology*, 17, 18.

35. Melba Padilla Maggay, ed., *The Gospel in Culture: Contextualization Issues through Asian Eyes* (Manila: OMF Literature, Inc. and ISACC, 2013).

36. Shoki Coe, "Contextualization as the Way toward Reform," in *Asian Christian Theology: Emerging Themes*, ed. Douglas J. Elwood (Philadelphia: Westminster Press, 1980), 48–55.

37. Masao Takenaka, "The Basic Thrusts of Christian Conference of Asia in Ecumenical Movement," *Asia Journal of Theology*, 3, no. 1 (1989): 161–73.

38. Kosuke Koyama, "Some Reflections on Contextualization," unpublished (mimeographed), Singapore, 2, quoted by Gerald H. Anderson, introduction to *Asian Voices in Christian Theology*, 5.

39. Elsa Tamez, "Liberation Theologies: Liberation and Theology," *The Cambridge Dictionary of Christianity*, ed. Daniel Patte (Cambridge: Cambridge University Press, 2010), 725.

40. Suh Nam-Dong, "Towards a Theology of Han," in *Minjung Theology: People as the Subjects of History*, rev., ed. *The Commission on Theological Concerns of the Christian Conference of Asia* (Singapore: Christian Conference of Asia; London: Zed Press; Maryknoll, NY: Orbis Books, 1983), 58.

41. Such as reflected in the collection *Feminist Theology: A Reader*, ed. Anne Loades (Louisville: Westminster John Knox Press, 2010).

42. For a discussion on the development of feminist theology ethnically, internationally, and transnationally, see Rosemary Radford Ruether, "Feminist Theology: Where Is It Going?" *International Journal of Public Theology*, 4 (2010): 5–20.

43. See Stephanie Y. Mitchem, *Introducing Womanist Theology* (Maryknoll, NY: Orbis Books, 2002).

44. Matheny, *Contextual Theology*, 27.

45. Gustavo Gutiérrez, *A Theology of Liberation: History, Politics, and Salvation*, rev., trans. and ed. Sister Caridad Inda and John Eagleson (Maryknoll, NY: Orbis Books, 1988), xxv.

46. For a brief discussion of its founding and the first ten years of EATWOT, see Franklyn J. Balasundaram, *EATWOT in Asia: Towards A Relevant Theology* (Bangalore: Asian Trading Corporation, 1993), 38–88.

47. K. C. Abraham, ed., *Third World Theologies: Commonalities and Divergences* (Maryknoll, NY: Orbis Books, 1990), 197.

48. Ibid., 199.

49. Matheny, *Contextual Theology: The Drama of Our Times*.

50. Matheny tends to see contextual theology as a definite and already well-formed theology rather than one being formed. He projected the theology to have been formed in the 1970s. On this, see Matheny, *Contextual Theology*, 39, 71. Not only is this definitive presentation of contextual theology questionable, the existing multiple ways of understanding and approaching contextual theology does not allow a restrictive understanding.

51. Matheny, *Contextual Theology*, 63.

52. Ibid.

53. This is exemplified by the compiled work of Noel Davies and Martin Conway titled *World Christianity in the 20th Century*, SCM Reader (London: SCM Press, 2008).

54. Soong-Chan Rah, *The Next Evangelicalism: Freeing the Church from Western Cultural Captivity* (Downers Grove, IL: InterVarsity Press, 2009).

55. For the declining narrative, see Robert P. Jones, *The End of White Christian America* (New York: Simon & Schuster, 2016).

56. C. René Padilla, *Mission between the Times: Essays on the Kingdom*, rev. and exp. (Cumbria: Langham Monographs, 2010), 103–14.

57. Hwa Yung, *Mangoes or Bananas: The Quest for an Authentic Asian Christian Theology* (Oxford: Regnum Books International, 1997), 61–121.

58. Craig Ott and Harold A. Netland, eds., *Globalizing Theology: Belief and Practice in an Era of World Christianity* (Grand Rapids: Baker Academic, 2006).

59. Donald M. Lewis and Richard V. Pierard, eds., *Global Evangelicalism: Theology, History and Culture in Regional Perspective* (Downers Grove, IL: InterVarsity Press, 2014).

60. Timothy Larsen and Daniel J. Treier, eds., *The Cambridge Companion to Evangelical Theology* (Cambridge: Cambridge University Press, 2007).

61. Jeffrey P. Greenman and Gene L. Green, eds., *Global Theology in Evangelical Perspective* (Downers Grove, IL: InterVarsity Press, 2012).

62. Stephen B. Bevans and Roger P. Schroeder, *Constants in Context: A Theology of Mission for Today* (Maryknoll, NY: Orbis Books, 2004), 34.

63. John Travis [pseud.], "The C1 to C6 Spectrum," in *Perspective on World Christian Movement: A Reader*, 3rd ed., Ralph Winter and Steven C. Hawthorne, eds. (Pasadena, CA: William Carey Library, 1999), 658–59.

64. Ibid., 659.

65. Jonas Adelin Jørgensen, "'Becoming Faithful': Conversion, Syncretism, and the Interreligious Hermeneutical Strategies of the 'Faithful of Jesus' (Īsā Īmāndārs) in Today's Bangladesh," in *Asia in the Making of Christianity: Conversion, Agency, and Indigeneity, 1600s to the Present*, ed. Jonathan A. Seitz and Richard Fox Young (Leiden: Brill, 2013), 269–93.

66. For a recent study of Khristbhaktas, see Vinod John, "Believing Without Belonging?: Religious Believed and Social Belonging of Hindu Devotees of Christ, A Case Study in Varanasi, India," (PhD diss., Asbury Theological Seminary, 2013); Dasan Jeyaraj, *Followers of Christ Outside the Church in Chennai, India: A Socio-Historical Study of a Non-Church Movement* (Hyderabad: Keeans, 2010). For a combination of Īsā Īmāndārs and Khristbhaktas, see Jonas Adelin Jørgensen, *Jesus Imandars and Christ Bhaktas: Two Case Studies of Interreligious Hermeneutics and Identity in Global Christianity* (Frankfurt: Peter Lang, 2008).

67. Stephen B. Bevans, *Models of Contextual Theology*, rev. and exp. ed. (Maryknoll, NY: Orbis Books, 2002), 7.

68. Douglas John Hall, *Thinking the Faith: Christian Theology in a North American Context* (Minneapolis: Augsburg Press, 1989), 21.

69. Robert J. Schreiter, *Constructing Local Theologies* (Maryknoll, NY: Orbis Books, 1985), 24–36.

70. David Bosch, *Transforming Mission: Paradigm Shifts in Theology of Mission* (Maryknoll, NY: Orbis Books, 1991), 421.

71. Ibid., 423–25.

72. Ibid., 454.

73. Dean Flemming, *Contextualization in the New Testament: Patterns for Theology and Mission* (Downers Grove, IL: InterVarsity Press, 2005), 20.

74. Stephen B. Bevans, *Models of Contextual Theology*, rev. and exp. Ed. (Maryknoll, NY: Orbis Books, 2002).

75. Robert J. Schreiter, foreword to *Models of Contextual Theology*, x.

76. Bevans, *Models of Contextual Theology*, 7.

77. Ibid.

78. Ibid., 54.

79. Ibid., 117.

6. Contextual Theologies in the Majority World

1. David Bosch, *Transforming Mission: Paradigm Shifts in Theology of Mission* (Maryknoll, NY: Orbis Books, 1991), 453.

2. John Mbiti, "Christianity and Traditional Religions in Africa," *International Review of Mission*, 59, no. 236 (1970): 432.

3. S. J. Samartha, *One Christ—Many Religions: Toward a Revised Christology* (Bangalore: South Asia Theological Research Institute, 1992), 43.

4. C. K. Yang, *Religion in Chinese Society: A Study of Contemporary Social Functions of Religion and Some of Their Historical Factors* (Prospect Heights, IL: Waveland Press, 1991), 4.

5. Ibid.

6. Tissa Balasuriya, *Planetary Theology* (Maryknoll, NY: Orbis Books, 1984), 79, emphasis mine.

7. John S. Mbiti, *Introduction to African Religion*, 2nd ed. (Oxford: Heinemmann Educational Publishers, 1991), 10.

8. Odina E. González and Justa L. González, *Christianity in Latin America: A History* (Cambridge: Cambridge University Press, 2008), 7.

9. Peter Bakewell, *A History of Latin America: Empires and Sequels 1450–1930* (Oxford: Blackwell Publishing, 1997), 25.

10. Franklyn J. Balasundaram, *EATWOT in Asia: Towards A Relevant Theology* (Bangalore: Asian Trading Corporation, 1993), 111–113; John Parratt, introduction to *An Introduction to Third World Theologies*, ed. John Parratt (Cambridge: Cambridge University Press, 2004),12. On the Bandung Conference itself, see Richard Wright, *The Color Curtain* (New York: World Publishing Co., 1956).

11. United Nations Human Development Programme, Human Development Reports in http://hdr.undp.org/en/2015-report, accessed October 19, 2016.

12. Ibid.

13. Jacob Olupona, foreword to *Religion and Poverty: Pan African Perspectives*, ed. Peter L. Paris (Durham, NC: Duke University Press, 2009), xix.

14. Optimistically, *Make Poverty History* says it "won great steps forward, however there remains work to do and to hold governments to account for their promises." See http://www.makepovertyhistory.org/achievements/, accessed October 21, 2016.

15. John Illife, *The African Poor: A History* (Cambridge: Cambridge University Press, 1987), 2, quoted by Olupona, foreword to Religion and Poverty, xi.

16. Olupona, foreword to *Religion and Poverty*, xix.

17. González and González, *Christianity in Latin America*, 243.

18. Adrian Hastings, *African Christianity* (New York: Seabury Press, 1976), 78.

19. Ogbu U. Kalu, *Power, Poverty and Prayer: The Challenges of Poverty and Pluralism in African Christianity, 1960–1996* (Frankfurt: Peter Lang, 2000), 50.

20. Peter C. Phan, *Being Religious Inter-religiously: Asian Perspectives in Interfaith Dialogue* (Maryknoll, NY: Orbis Books, 2004), 116.

21. Ibid.

22. Robert Bellah, *Beyond Belief: Essays on Religion in a Post-Traditional World* (New York: Harper & Row, 1970), 63.

23. Asha Mukherjee, "Culture, Tradition and Globalisation: Some Philosophical Questions," *Social Alternatives*, 35, no. 1 (2016): 56.

24. "Commonalities, Divergences, and Cross-Fertilization among Third World Theologies: A Document Based on the Seventh International Conference of the Ecumenical Association of Third World Theologians, Oaxtepec, Mexico, December 7–14, 1986," in *Third World Theologies: Commonalities and Divergences*, ed. K. C. Abraham (Maryknoll, NY: Orbis Books, 1990), 199.

25. Ibid., 198.

26. Ibid., 197–98.

27. Roberto Oliveros, "History of the Theology of Liberation," trans. Robert R. Barr, in *Mysterium Liberationis: Fundamental Concepts of Liberation Theology*, ed. Ignacio Ellacuría, S.J., and Jon Sobrino, S.J. (Maryknoll, NY: Orbis Books, 1993), 3.

28. Todd Hartch, *The Rebirth of Latin American Christianity*, Oxford Studies in World Christianity (Oxford: Oxford University Press, 2014), 60, Kindle ed.

29. Ibid., 58.

30. Gustavo Gutiérrez, *A Theology of Liberation: History, Politics, and Salvation*, rev., trans. and ed. Sister Caridad Inda and John Eagleson (Maryknoll, NY: Orbis Books, 1988), 5–9.

31. Ibid., 11.

32. Quoted in Arthur F. McGovern, *Liberation Theology and Its Critics: Toward an Assessment* (Maryknoll, NY: Orbis Books, 1989), 32.

33. Gutiérrez, *A Theology of Liberation*, 9.

34. Gustavo Gutiérrez, "Option for the Poor," in *Mysterium Liberationis*, 235–50.

35. Jon Sobrino, "Systematic Christology: Jesus Christ the Absolute Mediator of the Reign of God," in *Mysterium Liberationis*, 459.

36. Gutiérrez, *A Theology of Liberation*, 174.

37. Leonardo Boff and Clodovis Boff, *Introducing Liberation Theology* (Maryknoll, NY: Orbis Books, 1987), 7.

38. See Leonardo Boff, "Trinity," in *Mysterium Liberationis*, 389–404.

39. See Jon Sobrino, "Systematic Christology: Jesus Christ the Absolute Mediator of the Reign of God," in *Mysterium Liberationis*, 440–51.

40. Ibid., 452–58.

41. See José Comblin, "The Holy Spirit," in *Mysterium Liberationis*, 462–482.

42. Sharon E. Heaney, *Contextual Theology for Latin America: Liberation Themes in Evangelical Perspective* (Milton Keynes: Paternoster, 2008).

43. Ibid., 77–80.

44. Ibid., 83.

45. Ibid., 137.

46. Samuel Escobar, "Evangelization and Man's Search for Freedom, Justice and Fulfillment," in *Let the Earth Hear His Voice*, ed. J. D. Douglas (Minneapolis: World Wide Publications, 1975), 322, quoted by Heaney, Contextual Theology for Latin America, 138.

47. Ibid.

48. As David Kirkpatrick recently argued, the concept has a long history with Padilla. David C. Kirkpatrick, "C. René Padilla and the Origins of Integral Mission in Post-War Latin America," *Journal of Ecclesiastical History*, 67, no. 2 (April 2016): 351–71.

49. See, inter alia, Emmanuel Martey, *African Theology: Inculturation and Liberation* (Maryknoll, NY: Orbis Books, 1993).

50. Mercy Amba Oduyoye, *Beads and Strands: Reflections of an African Woman on Christianity in Africa* (Maryknoll, NY: Orbis Books, 2004).

51. Robert S. Heaney, *From Historical to Critical Post-Colonial Theology: The Contribution of John S. Mbiti and Jesse N. K. Mugambi* (Eugene, OR: Pickwick Publications, 2015), 150.

52. Aylward Shorter, *Toward a Theology of Inculturation* (Maryknoll, NY: Orbis Books, 1988), 11.

53. See the discussion in Aylward Shorter, *African Christian Theology: Adaptation or Incarnation?* (Maryknoll, NY: Orbis Books, 1977), 149–55.

54. Congregation for Divine Worship and the Discipline of the Sacraments, "Instruction: Inculturation and the Roman Liturgy," Fourth Instruction for the Right

Application of the Conciliar Constitution on the Liturgy issued on March 29, 1994, http://www.ewtn.com/library/curia/cdwinclt.htm, accessed October 28, 2016.

55. Peter Schineller, *A Handbook on Inculturation* (New York: Paulist Press, 1990), 6.

56. D. S. Amalorpavadass, *Gospel and Culture: Evangelization and Inculturation* (Bangalore: National Biblical Catechetical and Liturgical Centre, 1985).

57. By Brahminic tradition, we refer to the dominant Hindu tradition led by the priestly Brahmins at the top of the Hindu social and religious hierarchical (caste) system.

58. See D. S. Amalorpavadass, NBCLC Campus, *Milieu of God-experience: An Artistic Synthesis of Spirituality* (Bangalore: National Biblical Catechetical and Liturgical Centre, 1982).

59. Peter C. Phan, *In Our Own Tongues: Perspectives from Asia on Mission and Inculturation* (Maryknoll, NY: Orbis Books, 2003), 88.

60. Ibid., 89.

61. Ogbu U. Kalu, "Introduction: The Shape and Flow of African Church Historiography," in *African Christianity: An African Story*, ed. Ogbu N. Kalu, (Trenton, NJ: Africa World Press, 2007), 3.

62. Kwame Bediako, "John Mbiti's Contribution to African Theology," in *Religious Plurality in Africa: Essays in Honour of John S. Mbiti*, ed. Jacob K. Olupona and Sulayman S. Nyang (Berlin: Mouton De Gruyter, 1993), 375.

63. John S. Mbiti, "Christianity and Traditional Religions in Africa," *International Review of Mission*, 59, no. 236 (1970): 430–40.

64. Ibid., 435.

65. John S. Mbiti, "Christianity and African Culture," *Journal of Theology for Southern Africa*, 20 (September 1977): 26–40.

66. Ibid., 30, author's emphasis.

67. John S. Mbiti, *Introduction to African Religion*, 18–19.

68. Kwame Bediako, *Christianity in Africa: The Renewal of a Non-Western Religion* (Edinburgh: Edinburgh University Press; Maryknoll, NY: Orbis Books, 1995), 97.

69. Ibid., 212.

70. Ibid., 216–30.

71. Laurenti Magesa, *Anatomy of Inculturation: Transforming the Church in Africa* (Maryknoll, NY: Orbis Books, 2004), 7–8.

72. Ibid., 78.

73. Ibid., 80.

74. Ibid., 81.

75. Ibid.

76. Ibid.

77. Ibid., 83.

78. Ibid., 84.

79. Ibid.

80. Ibid., 85.

81. R. S. Sugirtharajah, ed., *Asian Faces of Jesus* (Maryknoll, NY: Orbis Books, 1993).

82. Vinay Samuel and Chris Sugden, eds., *Sharing Jesus in the Two Thirds World* (Bangalore: Partnership in Mission–Asia, 1983).

83. Phan, *In Our Own Tongues*, 10.

84. Although known as the "Chinese Rites Controversy," it also came to involve the work of Roberto de Nobili in India. The controversy lasted for centuries, and the discussion today remains provocative. At the heart of the debate was "whether the ceremonies honoring Confucius and family ancestors" could be tolerated within Christian belief. The Jesuits endorsed the practice of such rites, and the Dominicans and Franciscans opposed them. The Congregation for the Propagation of the Faith (the body that looked after the missionary affairs of the Catholic Church) flip-flopped on the issue in 1645 and 1656. Two Popes in the first half of the eighteenth century banned the rites which were overturned in 1939 by Pope Pius XII and affirmed by the second Vatican Council (1962-65). See "Chinese Rites Controversy," in *Encyclopedia Britannica* (online), https://www.britannica.com/event/Chinese-Rites-Controversy (last accessed April 22, 2018).

85. Daniel Jeyaraj, *Bartholomew Ziegenbalg: The Father of Modern Protestant Mission—An Indian Assessment* (New Delhi: Indian Society for Promoting Christian

Knowledge; Chennai: Gurukul Lutheran Theological College and Research Institute, 2006), 225–28, also see 121–31.

86. Second Vatican Council, Lumen Gentium (Dogmatic Constitution on the Church), no. 16, quoted in Phan, Being Religious Interreligiously, xxii.

87. For the document, see http://www.vatican.va/archive/hist_councils/ii_vatican_council/documents/vat-ii_decl_19651028_nostra-aetate_en.html, accessed Nov. 8, 2016.

88. For further discussion, see Lalsangkima Pachuau, "Missiology in a Pluralistic World: The Place of Mission Study in Theological Education," *International Review of Mission*, 89, no. 355 (October 2000): 550–51.

89. Alan Race, *Christians and Religious Pluralism: Patterns in the Christian Theology of Religions* (Maryknoll, NY: Orbis Books, 1983).

90. Lesslie Newbigin, *The Gospel in a Pluralist Society* (Grand Rapids: William B. Eerdmans, 1989), 182–83.

91. Paul F. Knitter, *Introducing Theologies of Religions* (Maryknoll, NY: Orbis Books, 2002).

92. Timothy C. Tennent, *Invitation to World Missions: A Trinitarian Missiology for the Twenty-first Century* (Grand Rapids: Kregel Publications, 2010), 220–22.

93. Paul F. Knitter, preface to *The Myth of Christian Uniqueness: Toward a Pluralistic Theology of Religions*, ed. John Hick and Paul F. Knitter, Faith Meets Faith Series (Maryknoll, NY: Orbis Books, 1987), viii.

94. Gavin D'Costa, preface to *Christian Uniqueness Reconsidered: The Myth of a Pluralistic Theology of Religions*, ed. Gavin D'Costa, Faith Meets Faith Series (Maryknoll, NY: Orbis Books, 1990), x.

95. Newbigin, *The Gospel in a Pluralist Society*, 155–70.

96. Ibid., 181–82.

97. Lesslie Newbigin, *The Open Secret: An Introduction to the Theology of Mission*, Revised ed. (Grand Rapids, MI: Wm. B. Eerdmans Publishing Company, 1995), 182-83.

98. Vinay Samuel and Chris Sugden, "Dialogue with Other Religions—An Evangelical View," in *Sharing Jesus in the Two Thirds World Evangelical Christologues from the Contexts of Poverty, Powerlessness and Religious Pluralism: The Papers of the First Conference of Evangelical Mission Theologians from the Two Thirds World*, Bang-

kok, Thailand March 22–25, 1982, ed. Vinay Samuel and Chris Sugden (Bangalore: Partnership in Mission-Asia, 1983), 177.

99. Vinoth Ramachandra, *The Recovery of Mission: Beyond the Pluralist Paradigm* (Carlisle: Parternoster, 1996).

100. M. M. Thomas, "A Christ-centered Humanist Approach to Other Religions in the Indian Pluralistic Context," in *Christian Uniqueness Reconsidered*, ed. Gavin D'Costa (1990), 60.

101. M. M. Thomas, *Risking Christ for Christ's Sake: Towards an Ecumenical Theology of Pluralism* (Geneva: WCC Publications, 1987).

102. Harold A. Netland, "Protestant Perspectives: Christian Mission among Other Faiths—the Evangelical Tradition," in *Witnessing to Christ in a Pluralist World: Christian Mission among Other Faiths*, ed. Lalsangkima Pachuau and Knud Jørgensen, Regnum Edinburgh 2010 Series (Oxford: Regnum Books International, 2011), 47.

103. Ibid., 52.

104. Clark Pinnock, *A Wideness in God's Mercy: The Finality of Jesus Christ in a World of Religions* (Grand Rapids: Zondervan, 1992).

105. John Sanders, *No Other Name: An Investigation into the Destiny of the Unevangelized* (Grand Rapids: William B. Eerdmans, 1992).

106. David Martin, *Pentecostalism: The World Their Parish* (Oxford: Blackwell Publishing, 2002); Harvey Cox, *Fire from Heaven: The Rise of Pentecostal Spirituality and the Reshaping of Religion in the Twenty-First Century* (Cambridge, MA: Da Capo Press, 1995); Stephen Offutt, *New Centers of Global Evangelicalism in Latin America and Africa* (New York: Cambridge University Press, 2015).

107. In addition to *The Next Christendom* previously cited, see also *The New Faces of Christianity: Believing the Bible in the Global South* (Oxford: Oxford University Press, 2006).

108. Amos Yong, *The Future of Evangelical Theology* (Downers Grove, IL: InterVarsity Press, 2014), 17–32.

109. Vinson Synan, ed., *Spirit-Empowered Christianity in the 21st Century* (Lake Mary, FL: Charisma House, 2011).

110. David Martin, *Pentecostalism: The World Their Parish* (Oxford: Blackwell Publishing, 2002), xvii. Note, "penumbra" connotes a shroud or shadow, and here charismatic movement is interpreted as existing in the shadow of Pentecostalism.

111. Paul G. Hiebert, "The Flaw of the Excluded Middle," in *Perspectives on the World Christian Movement: A Reader*, ed. Ralph D. Winter and Steve Hawthorne, 3rd ed. (Pasadena, CA: William Carey Library, 1999), 416–18.

112. Hwa Yung, *Mangoes or Bananas?: The Quest for an Authentic Asian Christian Theology* (Oxford: Regnum Books International, 1997), 73.

113. Kwame Bediako, *Jesus and the Gospel in Africa: History and Experience* (Maryknoll, NY: Orbis Books, 2004), 85–86.

114. Cox uses such terms as "primal piety," "primal hope," and "primal spirituality" as characters of the global Pentecostal movement. See Harvey Cox, *Fire from Heaven*.

115. William E. Phipps, *Supernaturalism in Christianity: Its Growth and Cure* (Macon, GA: Mercer University Press, 2008), xvi.

116. Peter Berger, "The Desecularization of the World: A Global Overview," in *The Desecularization of the World: Resurgent Religion and World Politics*, ed. Peter L. Berger (Washington, DC: Ethics and Public Center; Grand Rapids: William B. Eerdmans, 1999), 2.

117. See, inter alia, David Martin, "Evangelical Protestant Upsurge and Its Political Implications," in *The Desecularization of the World*, 37–49.

118. Selva Raj and Corrine G. Dempsey, "Introduction: Between, Behind, and Beyond the Lines," in *Popular Christianity in India: Riting between the Lines*, ed. Selva Raj and Corrine G. Dempsey (Albany: State University of New York Press, 2002), 1.

119. Luis Maldonado, "Popular Religion: Its Dimensions, Levels and Types," in *Popular Religion, Concilium*, ed. Nornert Greinacher and Norbert Mette (Edinburgh: T & T Clark, 1986), 9.

120. On this, see, for instance, Kim Yong-Bock, "Messiah and Minjung: Discerning Messianic Politics over against Political Messianism," in *Minjung Theology: People as the Subjects of History*, rev., ed. The Commission on Theological Concerns of the Christian Conference of Asia (Singapore: Christian Conference of Asia; London: Zed Press; Maryknoll, NY: Orbis Books, 1983), 183–93.

121. Simon Chan, *Grassroots Asian Theology: Thinking the Faith from the Ground Up* (Downers Grove, IL: InterVarsity Press, 2014), 18.

122. Sebastian Kim, "Mission and Integrity of the Church: Reflections on the Christian Response to the Problem of Poverty in Post-War Korea," in *News of Boundless Riches: Interrogating, Comparing, and Reconstructing Mission in a Global Era*, vol. 2, ed. Lalsangkima Pachuau and Max L. Stackhouse (Delhi: ISPCK, 2007), 32–33.

123. Philip Jenkins, *The New Faces of Christianity: Believing the Bible in the Global South* (Oxford: Oxford University Press, 2006), 7.

7. Christian Mission in the New World of Christianity

1. James Scherer, *Gospel, Church and Kingdom: Comparative Studies in World Mission Theology* (Minneapolis: Augsburg, 1987), 23.

2. In considering the renascence of Hinduism in India, Paul Devanandan shows that other Asian religions, especially Islam and Buddhism, were experiencing the same trend at the same time. See Paul D. Devanandan, "The Renascence of Hinduism in India," *The Ecumenical Review*, 11, no. 1 (October 1958): 52–65.

3. Quoted by Gerald H. Anderson, "A Moratorium on Missionaries?" *The Christian Century*, January 16, 1974, 43.

4. *National Christian Council of India, A Consultation on the Role of Missionaries in India Today*, Nagpur, October 24 to 27, 1961 (Nagpur: National Christian Council of India, n.d.), i.

5. Marvin D. Hoff, *The Reformed Church in America: Structures for Mission* (Grand Rapids: William B. Eerdmans, 1985), 167–68.

6. Cited by Allan R. Tippett, "The Suggested Moratorium on Missionary Funds and Personnel: Editorial," *Missiology: An International Review*, 3, no. 1 (July 1973): 275.

7. Robert Reese, "John Gatu and the Moratorium on Missionaries," *Missiology: An International Review*, 42, no. 3 (2014): 248–49.

8. Quoted by Hoff, *The Reformed Church in America*, 168–69.

9. Ibid., 169.

10. I. John Hesselink, "Reflection on the Mission Festival '71 Held at Milwaukee, October 6–9," *Reformed Review*, 25, no. 2 (January 1972): 87.

11. Ibid., 88.

12. Adrian Hastings, *African Christianity* (New York: Seabury Press, 1976), 23.

13. Reese, "John Gatu and the Moratorium on Missionaries," 248–49.

14. Tippett, "The Suggested Moratorium on Missionary Funds and Personnel: Editorial," 276.

15. Anderson, "A Moratorium on Missionaries?" 43–44.

16. Reese, "John Gatu and the Moratorium on Missionaries," 246.

17. *The Missionary Obligation of the Church* (London: Edinburgh House Press, 1952), 2.

18. Jürgen Schuster, "Karl Hartenstein: Mission with a Focus on the End," *Mission Studies*, 11, no. I–37 (2002): 65; Rodger C. Bassham, "Seeking a Deeper Theological Basis for Mission," International Review of Mission 67 (1978): 332.

19. *The Missionary Obligation of the Church*, 3.

20. See, inter alia, "Go Forth in Peace: Orthodox Perspectives on Mission," in *New Directions in Mission and Evangelization 1: Basic Statements, 1974–1991*, ed. James A. Scherer and Stephen B. Bevans (Maryknoll, NY: Orbis Books, 1992), 203–31.

21. Stephen B. Bevan and Roger Schroeder, *Constants in Context: A Theology of Mission for Today* (Maryknoll, NY: Orbis Books, 2004), 286.

22. Ibid.

23. David J. Bosch, *Transforming Mission: Paradigm Shifts in Theology of Mission* (Maryknoll, NY: Orbis Books, 1991), 4.

24. James Scherer, *Gospel, Church, and Kingdom: Comparative Studies in World Mission Theology* (Minneapolis: Augsburg, 1987), 35.

25. Gerald H. Anderson, ed., *The Theology of the Christian Mission* (Nashville: Abingdon Press, 1961).

26. Bosch, *Transforming Mission*, 368–510.

27. This assessment is based on an article in *The New York Times*, quoted by Timothy K. Park, "Korean Christian World Mission: The Missionary Movement of the Korean Church," in *Missions from the Majority World: Progress, Challenges, and Case Studies*, ed. Enoch Wan and Michael Pocock (Pasadena, CA: William Carey Library, 2009), 97.

28. Violet James, "Christianity in South-eastern Asia, 1910–2010," in *Atlas of Global Christianity* (Edinburgh: Edinburgh University Press, 2009), 147.

29. Robbie B. H. Goh, *Christianity in Southeast Asia* (Singapore: Institute of Southeast Asian Studies, 2005), 43–44.

30. As an example, see my discussion of the native converts' contribution in the evangelization of Northeast India in "Church Mission Dynamics in Northeast India," *International Bulletin of Missionary Research*, 27, no. 4 (October 2003): 154–61.

31. Steve Sang-Cheol Moon, *The Korean Missionary Movement: Dynamics and Trends, 1988–2013* (Pasadena, CA: William Carey Library, 2016), xviii.

32. Peter C. Wagner, *Stop the World, I Want to Get On* (Glendale, CA: Gospel Light Publishers, 1974), 110–111, quoted by Larry E. Keyes and Larry D. Pate, "Two-Thirds World Missions: The Next 100 Years," *Missiology: An International Review*, 21, no. 2 (April 1993): 189.

33. See Andrew F. Walls, "The Legacy of Samuel Ajayi Crowther," *International Bulletin of Missionary Research* (January 1992): 15–21. We will deal with Crowther's story in a more detailed manner later.

34. Vanlalchhuanawma, *Mission and Tribal Identity: A Historical Analysis of the Mizo Synod Mission Board [of the Presbyterian Church of Mizoram] from a Tribal Perspective, 1953–1981* (Delhi: ISPCK, 2010), 128–29.

35. Larry E. Keyes and Larry D. Pate, "Two-Thirds World Missions: The Next 100 Years," *Missiology: An International Review*, 21, no. 2 (April 1993): 190.

36. Larry D. Pate, "The Changing Balance in Global Mission," *International Bulletin of Missionary Research*, 15, no. 2 (April 1991): 58, 59.

37. Ibid., 58.

38. Guillermo Cook, "Protestant Mission and Evangelization in Latin America," in *New Face of the Church in Latin America: Between Tradition and Change*, ed. Guillermo Cook, American Society of Missiology Series, no. 18 (Maryknoll, NY: Orbis Books, 1994), 44–48.

39. Alexander Mar Thoma Metropolitan, *The Marthoma Church: Heritage and Mission*, 5th impression (Tiruvalla: Christava Sahitya Samithy, 2010), 66; K. Rajendran, *Which Way Forward Indian Missions?: A Critique of Twenty-Five Years, 1971–1997* (Bangalore: SAIACS Press, 1998), 55.

40. K. H. Ding, "Evangelism as a Chinese Christian Sees It," *Missiology: An International Review*, 11, no. 3 (July 1983): 311.

41. Ibid., 313.

42. Ibid., 314.

43. Yalin Xin, "Inner Dynamics of the Chinese House Church Movement: The Case of the Word of Life Community," *Mission Studies: Journal of the International Association for Mission Studies*, 25 (2008): 166.

44. Ibid., 162.

45. Ibid., 165.

46. See Sung-Deuk Oak, "Presbyterian Mission Methods and Policies in Korea, 1876–1910," in *Korean Church, God's Mission, Global Christianity*, ed. Wonsuk Ma and Kyo Seong Ahn, Regnum Edinburgh Centenary Series, V. 26 (Oxford: Regnum Books International, 2015), 37–44.

47. Timothy K. Park, "The Missionary Movement of the Korean Church: A Model for Non-Western Mission," in *Korean Church, God's Mission, Global Christianity*, 19–20.

48. Ibid., 24. Moon, *The Korean Missionary Movement*, xix.

49. Ibid., xix.

50. Ibid., xx.

51. Ibid.

52. Steve Sang-Cheol Moon, Hee-Joo Yoo, and Eun-Mi Kim, "Missions from Korea 2015: Missionaries Unable to Continue Ministry in Their Country of Service," *International Bulletin of Missionary Research*, 39, no. 2 (April 2015): 84.

53. Park, "The Missionary Movement of the Korean Church," 24.

54. Ibid., 26.

55. Moon, *The Korean Missionary Movement*, 4.

56. Ibid., 4–5.

57. Ibid., 5.

58. Moon et al., "Missions from Korea 2015," 84.

59. Eun Soo Kim, "The Edinburgh Conference and the Korean Church," in *Korean Church, God's Mission, Global Christianity*, 17.

60. Rebecca Y. Kim, *The Spirit Moves West: Korean Missionaries in America* (New York: Oxford University Press, 2015), 45.

61. Ibid., 32–34.

62. Ibid., 79.

63. Ibid., 80.

64. Yun Ki Chung, "The University Bible Fellowship: A Forty-Year Retrospective Evaluation," *Missiology: An International Review*, 31, no. 4 (October 2003): 483–84.

65. https://cultnews.com/category/universitybiblefellowship/, accessed December 24, 2016.

66. Kim, *The Spirit Moves West*, 130.

67. Chung, "The University Bible Fellowship," 482–83.

68. Rob Moll, "'Korean Evangelicals on Steroids': Meet the Band of Intensely Devoted Asian Missionaries Working around the Clock to Re-Christianize America," *Christianity Today*, June 25, 2015, http://www.christianitytoday.com/ct/2015/june -web-only/korean-evangelicals-on-steroids.html, accessed Dec. 29, 2016.

69. Kim, *The Spirit Moves West*, 136.

70. Quoted from *Times of India* by E. Stanley Jones in his open letter to Gandhi. "Reports: Two Open Letters to Mr. M. K. Gandhi, 1. Letter from Rev. E. Stanley Jones," *National Christian Council Review*, 51, no. 5 (May 1931): 271. For further discussion on Gandhi and Christian missionary enterprise in India, see Lalsangkima Pachuau, "A Clash of 'Mass Movements'?: Christian Missions and the Gandhian Nationalist Movement in India," *Transformation*, 31, no. 3 (2014): 157–74.

71. See the letter "No. 6/28/ 52–F I, Government of India, Ministry of Home Affairs," dated May 31, 1955, in *Revolution in Mission—A Study Guide on the Subject: "The Role of Missions in Present Day India,"* A Symposium Intended for Further Study and Discussion, ed. Blaise Levai (Vellore: The Popular Press, 1957), 280. Also see Korula Jacob, "The Government of India and the Entry of Missionaries," *International Review of Missions*, 47 (1958): 411ff.

72. Jeremy Weber, "Incredible Indian Christianity: A Special Report on the World's Most Vibrant Christward Movement," *Christianity Today*, November 10, 2016, http://www.christianitytoday.com/ct/2016/november/incredible-india -christianity-special-report-christwardmov.html, accessed November 10, 2016.

73. Alexander Mar Thoma Metropolitan, *The Marthoma Church*, 66.

74. "Appendix I: The Minutes of the General Meeting Held at the College, Serampore, on the Twenty-fifth Day of December 1905," in *The Founders of the National*

Missionary Society of India, comp. C. E. Abraham (Madras: The National Missionary Society of India, 1947), 28.

75. M. G. Manickam, "Indian Missionary Society, Tirunelveli," in *Emerging Mission: Reporting on a Consultation, Bangalore, India—November 2004*, ed. Mark Oxbrow and Emma Garrow (London: CMS; Bangalore: IEM; Delhi: ISPCK, 2005), 19.

76. The mission was renamed "North-East India General Mission" in 1922. As it expanded and missionaries were sent to Burma, the name was changed again to "Indo-Burma Pioneer Mission" sometime in 1925. Vanlalchhuanawma, *Mission and Tribal Identity: A Historical Analysis of the Mizo Synod Mission Board [of the Presbyterian Church of Mizoram] from a Tribal Perspective, 1953–1981* (Delhi: ISPCK, 2010), 128–29.

77. By 2004, the Synod Mission Board of the Mizoram Presbyterian Church had 606 missionaries and 397 evangelists (local) spread over 334 mission centers. See Zosangliana Colney, "Mizoram Presbyterian Church Synod Mission Department," in *Emerging Mission*, 26.

78. "Synod Mission Board Report," in *Presbyterian Church of India, Mizoram Synod: Synod Inkhawmpui Vawi, 93-na, 2016, Programmes, Agenda, Appendices, and Reports* (Aizawl: Mizoram Presbyterian Church, 2016), 195.

79. See Andrew Lalhmangaiha, "Salvation and Mission: Local-Global Conversations on Mission Theory and Practice with Special Reference to the Mizo Baptists" (PhD diss., Asbury Theological Seminary, 2016), 148. The annual report shows 1,127 missionaries, http://www.mizobaptist.org/bcm-mission-reports-june-2015/, which included missionary spouses and those recognized but not supported financially by the church. When those not financially supported are excluded, the total number is 949.

80. C. Barnabas, "Dynamic Expansion of the Missionary Movements in India," in *Biblical Theology and Missiological Education in Asia: Essays in Honour of Rev. Dr. Brian Wintle*, eds. Siga Arles, Ashish Chrispal and Paul Mohan Raj (Bangalore: Asia Theological Association, Theological Book Trust, Centre for Contemporary Christianity, 2005), 270–71.

81. Samuel T. Kamaleson, "The Friends' Missionary Prayer Band," in *Reading in Third World Missions: A Collection of Essential Documents*, ed. Marlin L. Nelson (Pasadena, CA: William Carey Library, 1976), 128.

82. Jason Dharmaraj, "100 Years of Cross-cultural Mission and Issues for Today," in *Emerging Mission*, 13, 13n2.

83. Theodore Williams, "The Indian Evangelical Mission," in *Reading in Third World Missions: A Collection of Essential Documents*, ed. Marlin L. Nelson (Pasadena, CA: William Carey Library, 1976), 132.

84. http://www.iemoutreach.org/, accessed January 22, 2011.

85. P. T. Abraham, "Pentecostal-Charismatic Outreach," in *Proclaiming Christ: A Handbook of Indigenous Missions in India*, ed. Sam Lazarus (Madras: Church Growth Association of India, 1992), 101.

86. P. Solomon Raj, *The New Wine-Skins: The Story of the Indigenous Missions in Coastal Andhra Pradesh, India* (Delhi: ISPCK; Chennai: Mylapore Institute of Indigenous Studies, 2003), xx.

87. Ibid., 13, 48. Rajendran quotes S. Vasantharaj Albert, *A Portrait of India*, III (Madras: Church Growth Association of India, 1995), 36.

88. Quoted from "India Missions Association: An Introduction," http://www.imaindia.org/aboutus/main.htm, accessed December 27, 2016.

89. Mr. Zohmingthanga, executive secretary of IMA, North India region, email interview with the author, January 13, 2011.

90. Rajendran, *Which Way Forward Indian Missions?* 63.

91. Ibid., 84.

92. http://www.imaindia.org/membermissions/main.htm, accessed December 27, 2016.

93. Todd John and Kenneth Ross, eds., *Atlas of Global Christianity* (Edinburgh: Edinburgh University Press, 2009), 261.

94. Fohle Lygunda li-M, "Understanding and Evaluating the Participation of Francophone Africans in World Mission: Congolese Working in Burundi," *Evangelical Review of Theology*, 39, no. 3 (2015): 255.

95. Ibid., 256.

96. Andrew F. Walls, "The Legacy of Samuel Ajayi Crowther," *International Bulletin of Missionary Research* (January 1992): 18.

97. Ibid., 15–16.

98. Ibid., 17.

99. Ibid., 18.

100. Ibid., 19.

101. Ibid.

102. Ibid., 17.

103. Isaac Oyebamiji, *Travail and Triumph: The Story of Capro* (Jos: Tishbeth Publishers, 2012), 25.

104. Quoted by Oyebamiji, in ibid.

105. Ibid., 25–26.

106. Originally used to abbreviate "Calvary Productions," CAPRO became the official name even after the name Calvary Productions was abandoned by the organization.

107. See "Our Mission" in http://nematoday.org/about/missions.php?gotopage =mission, accessed December 30, 2016.

108. http://nematoday.org/membership/missions.php?gotopage=members, accessed December 27, 2016.

109. Oyebamiji, *Travail and Triumph*, 56–57.

110. Ibid., 56.

111. Ibid., 72.

112. Ibid., 34. Henceforth, page citations from the book *Travail and Triumph* are placed in parentheses.

113. Tesilimi Aderemi (Remi) Lawanson, "Calvary Ministries (CAPRO): A Case Study on a Model of Majority World Initiatives in Christian Mission," in *Missions from the Majority World: Progress, Challenges, and Case Studies*, ed. Enoch Wan and Michael Pocock (Pasadena, CA: William Carey Library, 2009), 342.

114. Ibid., 323, 346, 347.

115. Lawanson, "Calvary Ministries (CAPRO)," 344.

116. Bayo Famonure, *Training to Die: A Manual on Discipleship* (Jos, Nigeria: CAPRO Media Services, 1989), quoted by Oyebamiji, *Travail and Triumph*, 65–66.

117. Oyebamiji, *Travail and Triumph*, 79.

118. Lawanson, "Calvary Ministries (CAPRO)," 347.

119. Oyebamiji, *Travail and Triumph*, 84–85.

120. Lawanson, "Calvary Ministries (CAPRO)," 348.

121. Samuel Escobar, *Changing Tides: Latin America and World Mission Today*, American Society of Missiology Series, no. 31 (Maryknoll, NY: Orbis Books, 2002), 153.

122. Quoted by Guillermo Cook, "Protestant Mission and Evangelization in Latin America," in *New Face of the Church in Latin America: Between Tradition and Change*, ed. Guillermo Cook, American Society of Missiology Series, no. 18 (Maryknoll, NY: Orbis Books, 1994), 50.

123. Ibid.

124. Quoted by Escobar, *Changing Tides*, 160.

125. "Committee on Cooperation in Latin America and Congress on Christian Work in Latin America Records, 1914–1956," Columbia University Libraries, Archival Collections, http://www.columbia.edu/cu/lweb/archival/collections/ldpd_5950860/, accessed January 6, 2017.

126. Escobar, *Changing Tides*, 25.

127. Cook, "Protestant Mission and Evangelization in Latin America," 44–45.

128. Escobar, *Changing Tides*, 153.

129. Ibid., 161.

130. Cook, "Protestant Mission and Evangelization in Latin America," 48.

131. David L. Miller, "COMIBAM '97: Mission-Minded Latinos No Longer Staying Home," *Christianity Today*, December 8, 1997, 71.

132. Escobar, *Changing Tides*, 156.

133. Ibid., 157.

134. Quotations from the "Declaration of Curitiba" are quoted by Escobar, *Changing Tides*, ibid.

135. Ibid., 158.

136. Julia Guarneri, "COMIBAM: Calling Latin Americans to the Global Challenge," in *Missions from the Majority World: Progress, Challenges, and Case Studies*, ed. Enoch Wan and Michael Pocock (Pasadena, CA: William Carey Library, 2009),

237. The exact number of missionaries in 2006 as shown in Appendix B (page 248) is 9,265.

137. Rudolfo "Rudy" Giron, "The Latin-American Missionary Movement: A New Paradigm in Missions," http://www.ad2000.org/celebrate/giron.htm, accessed January 9, 2017.

138. Escobar, *Changing Tides*, 158–59.

139. Quoted by David D. Ruiz M. "COMIBAM as a Process Leading to a Congress," in "Reflections from COMIBAM III, Spain," *Connections: The Journal of the WEA Mission Commission*, 6, no. 1 (April–May 2007): 9.

140. Guarneri, "COMIBAM," 234.

141. Escobar, *Changing Tides*, 159.

142. Escobar, *Changing Tides*, 159.

143. Luis Bush, "COMIBAM 97: An Assessment of the Latin American Missions Movement," http://www.ad2000.org/re71216.htm, accessed January 8, 2017.

144. Ibid.

145. David D. Ruiz M., "COMIBAM as a Process Leading to a Congress," in "Reflections from COMIBAM III, Spain," *Connections: The Journal of the WEA Mission Commission*, 6, no. 1 (April–May, 2007): 10.

146. Ibid.

147. Quoted by David Ruiz, ibid.

148. Guarneri, "COMIBAM," 236, 238.

149. Ibid., 241.

150. Samuel Escobar, "COMIBAM III: A Personal Perspective," in "Reflections from COMIBAM III, Spain," *Connections: The Journal of the WEA Mission Commission*, 6, no. 1 (April–May 2007): 26.

151. Jesus Londoño, "General Report of the III Ibero-American Missions Congress," in "Reflections from COMIBAM III, Spain," *Connections: The Journal of the WEA Mission Commission*, 6, no. 1 (April–May, 2007): 11.

152. Ruiz M., "COMIBAM as a Process Leading to a Congress," 10.

153. Londoño, "General Report of the III Iberoamerican Missions Congress," 12.

154. http://www.comibam.org/es/iv-congreso-misionero-iberoamericano/, accessed January 9, 2017.

155. William Taylor, "Editorial: From the Heart and Mind of the Editor," in "Reflections from COMIBAM III, Spain," *Connections: The Journal of the WEA Mission Commission*, 6, no. 1 (April–May 2007): 4.

156. Ruiz M. "COMIBAM as a Viable Regional Movement," 5–6.

Conclusion: A Highlight of the Salient Points

1. *Atlas of Global Christianity*, ed. Todd M. Johnson and Kenneth R. Ross (Edinburgh: Edinburgh University Press, 2009), 9.

INDEX OF NAMES

237

INDEX OF SUBJECTS